CRICKET-STUMPS
AND
STICKLEBACKS

ABOUT THE AUTHOR

Born at Coatham, North Yorkshire, in 1921, the author lived most of his childhood on the Durham side of the River Tees. He first attended school in the village of Hartburn, moved on to Billingham Intermediate School when his father settled into employment in ICI's new chemical factory in Billingham and, gaining a scholarship, completed secondary education at Stockton-on-Tees (Boys') Secondary School. Awarded a County Scholarship in 1940 and a Bursary at Dalton Hall, Manchester, he read Modern Languages at Owen's University. Faced with the prospect of call-up after his first year of study, he joined the University Air Squadron as a cadet in October 1941. He gained his 'wings' as a sergeant-pilot in South Africa in November 1943, and served as a flying-instructor at No.11 E.F.T.S. (Scone, Perthshire, Scotland).

The appeal of the Scottish countryside influenced him in making his career as a teacher in Scotland. He completed a wartime degree course in September 1946, spent a year in the Lycée Champollion (Grenoble, France) as an English 'assistant', and qualified as a teacher on the auspicious date of April 1st 1948 in Morgan Academy, Dundee. A keen supporter of the Dundee-Orleans Fellowship during his 18 years at Morgan, he was awarded the Bronze Medallion of Joan of Arc by the city of Orleans for services rendered.

On St Valentine's Day, 1966, he sailed to Lerwick to take up the post of Head of Modern Languages in the Anderson Educational Institute, Shetland. After 3½ years he returned to the mainland to Forfar Academy, from where he retired in 1981.

In 1950 he married a Scots 'lassie'. They have three daughters. A victim of polio in 1956, his interests now are: corresponding with friends world-wide, writing, 'Scrabbling' and gardening.

CRICKET-STUMPS
and
STICKLEBACKS

A Childhood on Teesside

by

Don Smith

Illustrated by Frank McDiarmid

BRIDGE
PUBLICATIONS

PENISTONE · ENGLAND

Bridge Publications
2 Bridge Street, Penistone
Sheffield S30 6AJ

British Library Cataloguing in Publication Data

Smith, Donald B. (Donald Barlow) 1921-
   Cricket-stumps and Sticklebacks: a
   childhood on Teesside.
   1. Cleveland. Social life, 1901- –
   Biographies
   I. Title 942.8'5082'0924

   ISBN 0-947934-24-3
   ISBN 0-947934-23-5 (pbk)

Photoset 10½ on 12pt Times Roman by Bridge Publications
Printed and Bound in Great Britain by
Whitstable Litho Printers Ltd., Whitstable, Kent

This book is dedicated to our grand-children in Canada, great-nieces and great-nephews throughout the world, to all the old pals of school-days, whether mentioned here or not, and to their succeeding generations.

Contents

PART II: WIDER HORIZONS

Foreword

I remember one of my colleagues on the Staff of Stockton Secondary School (one who figures in these pages) pointing out to me that if teachers are said to be 'in loco parentis' to children, then the children are 'in loco filiorum' to their teachers. So that a teacher in a career of about forty years acquires one or two thousand part-sons or part-daughters. The fraction is obviously too small to count for very much in most cases, but in the cases of those with whom we come in contact after they have grown up, a teacher does get from his former pupils some of the pleasure and satisfaction which he gets from his own children. This applies specially when the individuals concerned have both followed the same profession and so have links beyond those of having spent some years at the same school.

For me, therefore, Don Smith is a member of a select band — as far as I know, the senior member — of those who, despite or because of the ministrations of my colleagues and myself, went from school to University, took a degree in French and spent their careers imparting to others the pleasures and terrors of that language and those people.

As this implies, I am somewhat prejudiced in his favour. My high expectations were not at all disappointed when I read these memoirs of his school-days. He has indeed produced a very lively and interesting book. School-days remain in some ways what they always were for succeeding generations. Yet in many details they have changed enormously in this country over the last fifty years. So the interest of this book is not only personal but also historical, and it should take its place among memoirs of life in England in the 'Thirties.

To me this book is fascinating both historically and personally. I knew many of the people Don mentions, and remember many of the scenes described — though I have completely forgotten some in which I was involved!

I recommend the book to all as a 'good read'.

GORDON RATTENBURY

1st July 1989   Hartburn

Acknowledgements

To Harry Jamieson and his daughter of Kirriemuir, who gave me a couple of years to produce a book or they would know the reason why!

To my old Dalton Hall room-mate, Geoff Hill, who put me on to *Years of Grace*, written by his cousin, Phyllis Crossland, the ingredients of whose book made me think I ought to have a dab at tackling something of a similar nature from a boy's point of view;

To Jen, Roy and family, Betty, Lena and Charles, for hospitality and encouragement during this period of writing;

To Ro (exiled across the Tamar!), his wife Olive and daughter Denise, for hospitality and information about ICI locos (names and numbers, as he remembers them);

To Bill 'Pluff' Jelley, for information and interest in the project;

To his brother, George 'Judd' Jelley (the 'baby' of the gang) and his wife Doreen, for hospitality, information and happy hours of reminiscing;

To my teachers, for their counsel and guidance in my school-days;

To Les Still, former class-mate and retired Chief Librarian of Cleveland, for his advice;

To Teesside library staffs, for help in my research: The Group Librarian at Billingham Branch; Mrs J.E. Chesney and Miss Anita Brown of Stockton Reference Library; Mr J.S. Mallam of Darlington Branch; and the Staff of Middlesbrough Reference Library;

To Education officials of the Education Department, Cleveland; R.J. Ball, Personnel Officer of Stockton Borough Council; and Mr A.H. Stokoe, Headmaster of Billingham South Primary School (formerly Billingham Intermediate School);

To Mr J. Sugden, of the Cleveland County Council's Surveying and Engineering Department, for transport information;

To Monikie Village School, for reprographic facilities;

To 'our Eric', my kid brother, for his critical reading of the MS, corrections and information;

To Frank McDiarmid, for providing the illustrations;

To Gordon Rattenbury, who found, in a busy domestic life, time to write such a generous foreword;

And, last of all, to my wife, who with a shrewd blow of the hammer hits the nail right on the head in her remark, made with feeling, 'I wish *I* had a wife!!!'

Part I

CHILDHOOD

All our
Discontent
About What We
Want Springs
from the Want of
Thankfulness
For What We
Have.

CHAPTER ONE

Thankfulness

IT HUNG at the front door — for the best part of forty years, I reckon — a plain bit of board, maybe ten inches long and eight inches wide. There was a spot of colour about it, an edging of painted flowers. But the message that it bore was burnt into the wood. Aye, and burnt into our memories, wherever we are — Joyce and her husband Jim in Australia, Eric and his wife Stella still on Teesside, and me sitting at half past six on this bright June morning in my 'den' at Craigton, Monikie, some ten miles northeast of Dundee, two hundred and odd miles from 'home'. I should not be surprised if even Judith and Lyn, Joyce's daughters, remember it well; because they looked in on their Gran, our Mam, in their childhood and early teens.

It was a motto. At least, I think that is what they called it. How it came to be there I can no longer recall. It must have been a gift to Mam and Dad presented by Mr D.F. Smith, a local philanthropist whose links with our family will be related further on in this tale.

To print the words on a typewriter is to do the message an injustice. Those words deserve the more artistic style of the hand that burnt them into the wood.

Did we, as bairns, really understand what the motto meant? Discontent did raise its head momentarily from time to time; but, more often than not, that was an expression of our unwillingness to do the odd chore about the house when the sun was calling us outside to play with the other bairns.

If, on other occasions, we showed we envied other kids, and said in front of our parents, 'I wish I could have ... like Bill!', we soon learnt how Dad would cope with the hint of dissatisfaction.

'Come here!' he would say. We had to follow as he opened the kitchen door and led the way into the vestibule. Then he would point up to the motto and ask, 'What does it say on there?' Dutifully, even dolefully, we read the words that spelt doom to our longings. Dad's laugh meant we were never likely to win. We learnt that, in a way, he 'was having us on'; because, though we never had pocket-money, we never lacked things that really mattered, even toys. They could be instructional, just as a nature film had an educational value that he respected.

It was only natural that we jibbed at having to stay indoors, because there was plenty of fun in New Road, or up in the 'Rec' (the Recreation Ground, to give it its full title).

If we crossed the road and went over the field down to the beck, its waters offered other attractions. We could go down the road to the 'Gully' and its row of gnarled trees, whose branches spread over the lane and the footpath, tempting lads and lasses alike to perform 'Tarzan-like' feats above the heads of those poor earthbound mortals who plodded up the lane or staggered down it on their way home from the pub, blissfully unaware of us.

Thankfulness, too, is to a child just another word. I suppose it was only later in life, on looking back over those childhood days and the trials and tribulations of more recent adulthood, that the real meaning struck home. There is no doubt that we had plenty to be thankful for. That is what this story is about.

CHAPTER TWO

Legends and Infant Memories

11 NEW ROAD, BILLINGHAM, and the motto, however, are not the beginning of the story. I am the eldest, born on the 21st September 1921 at 92 High Street, Coatham, Redcar, North Yorkshire.

Like most families, we have our legends. The injured fingers of Dad's left hand, with a finger-nail and a joint missing, were a daily reminder of one. What episode this related to, whether at sea or on land, I cannot tell. The accident could easily have occurred on the epic voyage from Archangel when his ship, carrying a cargo of Russian timber, foundered off the North Cape of Norway. If it had not been for that cargo I should not be sitting here writing this!

Whether he had clung to a plank of floating wood, or whether his ship had kept above water with its holds and deck laden with timber, I do not know. That was Dad's first voyage – and he was only thirteen years of age!

Later, ashore, he had been indentured to become a fitter and turner. He had ultimately gone seafaring as an engineer, on board some of the 'Pool' boats of the Ropner Line of Stockton.

In 1919 he married Mam, née Edith Barlow. I understand that when she knew she was expecting, she had delivered to Dad the ultimatum, 'Alf, you'll have to make your mind up! You'll have to choose between the sea and me!' I have a fancy that Alf knew which side his bread was buttered on. He came ashore.

As I had been born in Yorkshire, and though I spent only the first few months of my life there, all through my childhood and youth I clung to my birthright, tenuous as it must seem to a one-hundred-per-cent 'Tyke'. The first qualification one must have, if one aspires to play for the county cricket team, is that Yorkshire is one's birth-place.

And, pre-World War Two, what a team they had! Year in, year out, it headed the County Championship table, with a roll-call of some of the greatest names in the game – Herbert Sutcliffe (opening bat for the County and England), Big Bill Bowes, Hedley Verity, Maurice Leyland and Len Hutton, all capped for England over many seasons in Test teams.

Yet I never actually went to a cricket-ground to watch those heroes play. Instead, their exploits were followed religiously in the daily reports of *The Northern Echo* or on the wireless. For most of us, the cost of the journey and admission to the ground would have been well beyond our means. We made up for that absence by happily adopting those favourite names when we took out the bats and played our own version of the game in the 'Rec'.

When only months old, I was taken from Coatham to live in Hartburn, a little village on the main Darlington road and a couple of miles out from Stockton High Street. Before we left Hartburn, some six or seven years later, a by-pass had been built. The long-distance buses no longer came into the village. Only the Corporation buses of No. 3 service, bound for the terminus at the west end of the village, disturbed the peace of that quiet spot.

Memories of the village over the next five years fall into two categories – vivid personal recollections and the legends which pre-date my memories. Legends about us bairns were, to our elders, memories of recent events which cropped up so often in family conversation that the shadowy happenings concerning us were imprinted on our minds to become something that we now recall as personal to ourselves and as close as memory.

The first of these legends is of an early Christmas-box, bought for me by fond parents. It was a rocking-horse, fortunately a small one. Mam and Dad had sat me on it and, no doubt with encouraging words, got me to set the horse rocking. The next minute I had tumbled over its head to land on mine, biting my lip in the process. I blared my eyes out! They probably hoped that I would try again, but not me! A few minutes later they found me in a corner, happily playing with a bit of stick and an old biscuit-tin, oblivious of the hurt of moments before. 'Well, that's that!' said Dad. 'Back to the shop it goes!' And, there and then, he wrapped it up!

In later childhood I was to meet up with another rocking-horse, belonging to my cousin Ray, who moved in a different stratum of society from us as his dad, Uncle Charlie, was a school-teacher. Ray's horse was a sturdy animal, a proud steed, beautifully carved in wood, with muscular legs, snorting nostrils and mouth agape with the bit between its teeth. Luckily it was held in check by a wooden frame, which allowed it to slide back and forth but by means of some cunning device changed the sliding movement into rocking. I have a notion that it stood some seven or eight hands high, as tall as my kid brother at the age of four.

A second horsey legend involving me concerned a pony that pulled a cart for Dad and his brother, Uncle Jack. This was in the early 'twenties, when both of them were unemployed. They tried to make a living hawking tripe about the neighbourhood, so the pony and cart were needed. The success or failure of this venture is not recorded, since all the members of that generation have now passed away.

Blackie the pony turned me off the equine race. I had been given a tit-bit to feed to him. Being only a 'titchy' I had had to reach up to his muzzle, and he bit me. Today I watch diminutive lasses in full riding-gear presenting lumps of sugar, on the palm of the hand, to barrel-like Shetlands and pure-bred Arabs, without the slightest flinch!

Note that by 'the equine race' I mean real live horses. There was another breed that we held in awe, for far different reasons. They were all a-glitter, gold-caparisoned martial steeds, their circle limited, their gallop restrained as they whirled round to the wheezy piping music of the fairground organ.

Little nippers like us had to wait until the grown-ups made up their minds to hoist us aboard, up front where we held on like grim death to the pole. Then off we went, majestically prancing, safe in the arms of Dad or Uncle, enthralled by the music, the glitter and lights, enthusiastically waving to Mam and aunties, looking ahead each round to be sure they were still there to see what skilful riders we were. This was at the 'Hirings' on Stockton Town Moor, when farmers and farm-labourers met to contract for work. My ears registered 'Iron Rings'! Please do not laugh − quoits was a popular game in the country in those days!

In another legend I was a babe-in-arms, travelling on the train to Thornaby. Mam was seated opposite a couple of nuns, who were so taken by the little chap smiling at them that one pronounced a blessing on him! As I look back over my life, especially from my late teens on, I feel that the blessing has followed me. Someone is keeping a Fatherly eye on me, guiding my path through life. I am not ashamed to admit that events have not been pure coincidence. On the day of my retirement, in September 1981, I conveyed the gist of that sentiment to my colleagues of Forfar Academy (the last school I taught in) so many miles from 'home'.

Another legend, about Dad, had its origin in our first home in Hartburn, in a house rented from Mrs Bain. It was situated up a lane at the end of a short terrace. The front door was recessed into the gable-end.

Like many a young husband and father, Dad had taken an interest in wireless, an expensive and worthless hobby as Mam must have considered it. I had the same failing, because a month or so before I was married I launched into the purchase of a sailing-sharpie and a Seagull outboard-engine. Our Canadian son-in-law is a great one for being tempted into buying intricate and expensive tools for D.I.Y. tasks about the house. Young house-wives today might find themselves saddled with a man given to playing with a computer and video-games, or attempting to drown out the screams of wilful off-spring with the latest high-powered addition to his hi-fi equipment.

Dad was certainly 'with it'. Crystals, headphones, cat's-whiskers − and later, valves, amplifiers, coils and condensers, along with bits of wire and terminals − began to clutter up the place. I heard talk of superhets, twin-valve sets and five-valve marvels. The room was littered with strange diagrams, in which blobs were linked by straight lines or cryptic zig-zags. Numbers and letters referred to circles representing valve-seatings which would hold those eerie lamps that glowed dark-red inside.

One particular evening, Dad was sitting in the corner of the living-room, by the door to the passage. His ears were slackly cupped by the head-set, as his fingers tickled the cat's-whisker, the term used for that delicate operation of trying to make a contact on the magic crystal. Success would bring the ethereal voices of the wireless broadcasters all the way from Droitwich.

Suddenly, an excited cry! 'Edie, here! Come and listen to this, Edie!' Carefully, Dad handed the ear-phones over to Mam. Right enough, he had made contact, almost like a medium at a seance. What a thrill! What intimacy with the speakers! Intimacy is the right word, but nothing to do with the new-fangled wireless!

Remember where Dad was sitting? What he could hear were the sweet nothings on the other side of the door where, in the recess at the gable, a courting couple billed and cooed!

So much for legends. There are memories of substance too, scenes in my mind's eye as clear now as on the day they happened. I have written earlier of a Christmas-box. Three Christmases later, for me, THE gift, which was a source of wonder and delight, came in its cage − a metal wheel, spinning on its axis, a whirl of rainbow colours.

Dad and Uncle Jack pored over the instruction sheet. Their first pulls on the string set the gyroscope in motion with a faint whirring. I shouted with delight as they balanced it, as if by magic, on the tips of their fingers, on the edge of the table, on the blade of a knife. Then disaster! According to the instructions, if this wonder-toy was set on a length of string stretched taut between two chairs, it would gyrate its colourful way along.

With bated breath we all watched enthralled when, CRASH! − down to the floor it fell. The finely-balanced wheel lay askew its axis. Tears followed. Promises that the soldering-iron would set all to rights brought hope. Wasn't Dad a dab hand with the solder from all that faffing about with wireless-sets? The thought just strikes me now as I write, that it had been a hopeless cause. Despite their skill they could not restore the critical balance, which was the secret element that had given movement to what was now a mere handful of useless metal!

Another Christmas in our Hartburn cottage home was memorable because the proceedings were graced by the presence of that benefactor, D.F. Smith, whose name-sake I am. The 'F' (for Fothergill), though, was not added to my name. D.F. meant much to Dad and Jack. As a token of gratitude for help in the past, Dad had registered my birth as 'Donald Smith'. Mam was a Baptist and therefore did not believe in infant baptism. Dad was a member of the Church of England, but in deference to Mam's wishes he had none of us baptized.

This Christmas D.F. had brought a special present, one any laddie would have been thrilled to own. It came in a biggish box, a train-set with rails, coaches and a little Bing locomotive, bright in its dark-red livery, with a key to wind it up. It was not much bigger than my podgy mitt, but what a treasure − and power, too! The little rails were solid pressed-out lengths of curves and straights, the sleepers painted across in brown at regular intervals, each section moulded on miniature embankments painted green to look like grass. Children and men-folk all played, down on our knees in that snug room with blazing Yule-tide fire, below the paper decorations strung across the ceiling. That is the only room I remember there.

In my early months D.F. gave me a silver christening cup and a gold half-sovereign, both of which I still have.

Possibly from that same Christmas, there comes to my mind's nose (why should the eyes always have it?) a strange, pungent, phosphoric smell. It is linked to a book − just a little book telling the story of 'Sunny Jim', the character from 'Post Toasties', a breakfast cereal I loved. Or was it, now, a book that had some connection with Colman's Mustard? Why should a child get such a present in his stocking? Was the book an advertising gimmick, put out to promote those well-known household names?

I have no recollection of my kid brother's arrival on the scene. I was just two when he was born, on Hallowe'en, 1923. His imminent appearance might have been the reason for our move to the other end of the terrace, to a bigger house.

At the end of the back lane a gate in a high fence opened into a vastness of tall grass and fruit-trees, with a barn inside this orchard-garden. One warm summer's day, as I played outside the barn trying to make colours into paint by crushing red and yellow chalks and then mixing the dust with water, an apprentice lad working about the place thought he would play a joke on me. He had picked a hen up by its legs. Suddenly I found a squawking Rhode Island Red flung through the air at me, its enraged wings beating against my face. Another phobia had come to haunt me!

To this day I have a horror of entering any room where owners of budgies or similar cage-birds are wont to let their little charges stretch their joyful wings. The flutter of those tiny pinions above my unprotected head sends shivers down my spine.

My country-born wife and our daughters can pick up tiny sparrows, thrushes or blackies that have bumped their heads against broad expanses of window-pane, stunning themselves for the moment. I can only look on sympathetically. I marvel at the sight on T.V. of falconers, holding their tame hawks not even at arm's length. They seem unconcerned at those sharp, curved bills, beneath hypnotic eye, that are far too close for my liking.

A legendary figure, unconnected with our family but known to many of the village-folk, was Marley Christon. I never saw him, though he came about our village. He worked too early in the morning at his unsavoury task. Yet, thanks to his labours, his market-garden produced some of the tastiest vegetables you could imagine. For did he not empty the ash-pits or earth-closets, and incorporate their nutrients in the rich soil of his garden? We were not to know the sanitary improvement of a flush-toilet in our own home until we made the next and final move of our childhood, out of the village into a garden-township, closer to Dad's work.

From 'Orchard House' (it did not bear that name) I must have gone piggy-back with Dad, whilst Mam carried baby brother, over the fields to 'Tatie Hall' (Potato Hall, marked on the O.S. map). On the way we passed the post-office-cum-general-store. We had gone to watch Stephenson's 'Rocket' chuff past, celebrating the centenary of the opening of the Stockton to Darlington Railway in 1825. I have a vague recollection of a trail of folk wending their way homeward over the field-paths from the railway-line; but any parade of locomotives or coaches is just a blank in my memory. Perhaps we had arrived too late and had missed the show!

The freedom of infancy was drawing to a close. A last memory from those carefree days is of the birth of a baby sister, Joyce. It was a time of some anxiety and tension. Mam had been taken to hospital in the ambulance, a Ford 'Tin-Lizzy'. Etched clearly on my mind is its distinctive radiator and its black, heavily-spoked wheels, probably rubber-shod, but not pneumatic!

CHAPTER THREE

Early Schooldays in Hartburn

UNCLE CHARLIE was a teacher. Whether this fact had any influence on my decision to be one too, I cannot really say. Other lads might have wanted to be engine-drivers, sea-captains, eminent cricketers or footballers. I wanted to be nothing else but a teacher, right from the first day I stepped over the worn stone threshold of Hartburn Village School.

Uncle served the profession for many more years than the normal forty, since he had begun as a pupil-teacher in his early teens. This was a common practice. He received instruction from his teacher, then under that master's jurisdiction he instructed his fellow-pupils. In Stockton Boys' Secondary School I sat alongside lads whose fathers, as well as themselves, and even a grandfather, had been taught by my uncle in Tilery, a district of Stockton.

I experienced no trauma in going to school for the first time. My baby sister, Joyce, was to make up for that later, when it came to my turn to shepherd her to school.

I have a faint recollection of going through the main door of the village school into the cloakroom, where we hung our coats on black-enamelled pegs. On cold, wet days, when heavy coats were hanging there, the place had a special warm, sweaty smell about it. From the cloakroom we passed into the infants' room, which had a fireplace in the corner opposite the doorway.

Mrs Rudman was my first teacher; a stoutish lady with dark, greying hair. She kept us in our places. I remember getting my knuckles rapped with a wooden ruler; but, all in all, I enjoyed school.

It is strange the odd memories that float back again, even as I write. 'An Apple for the Teacher' was to be a 'hit' later. However, already in the mid-twenties, young impressionable pupils were bringing 'gifts' to their mentors. I distinctly recall Leslie Fitzgerald presenting a bunch of flowers to Mrs Rudman. Well she knew that his folk were not likely to have grown them in their garden, if ever they cultivated one. Leslie swore blind that the bouquet had come from home. Eventually the truth emerged, that his generous act was only possible thanks to unsuspecting neighbours from whose gardens he had plucked the blooms on his way to school. Beautiful, they were, too; B-E-A-U-T-I-F-U-L was one of the first 'big' words that Mrs Rudman taught us to spell, through the phrase: 'Boxed Eggs Are Useful; Tea Is Fairly Usefu-L!'

Mention of this episode reminds me of the Hartburn school garden. It was fenced off from the school yard. We each had our strip where we sowed seeds; but the harvest is now a mystery. Here, I had my first school photograph taken. I distinctly remember Michaelmas daisies that stood as tall as myself. Now, from experience, I realize that their flowering dates the photo. It would be October, 1926.

The school itself was perched on a slight grassy knoll. In front of the building grew a tall shady tree. Fairfield Back Lane passed on the west. Just below, to the east, stood a terrace of substantial red-brick houses. The whole block behind them was isolated inside a high brick wall, with a path running round the outside.

Our usual approach to the school from the village was up Fairfield Back Lane from the Darlington Road. This stretch was bordered on one side by beech and other deciduous trees, growing in the grounds of a private house which later became a reception centre for ICI. On the other side a fence enclosed Marley Christon's market-garden. In Autumn it was a delight to shuffle our feet through the depths of red, orange, brown and yellow leaves, raising an earthy, mushroomy kind of smell that I can still sense. To trudge through similar leafy depths today takes me back, back, back into childhood.

Like the red-brick terraced houses, the school was roofed with slate. Slates! That word, with its bluey-grey associations, 'screeches' back at me as I see a podgy fist grasping a slender spill of grey − the slate-pencil which we used in our first attempts to write. Each boy and girl had a slate, enframed in wood. Close at hand we kept a damp rag to erase the trial letters. A dab of spit and a jersey-sleeve was just as effective! I do not think I turned a hair when the pencil squeaked its way along the slate. But, oh! The shivers run down my spine when novice teachers cause their chalk to screech as a hard bit in the white stick claws at the blackboard.

Now that I come to think of it, it was in a writing lesson that I had my knuckles rapped! From slates we had progressed on to exercise-books, ruled with those horizontal tramlines that little 'a', 'c' and 'e' fitted into, or the roundness of little 'b', 'd', 'g' or 'q'. The wider space above the tramline took the loops of 'b', 'h', 'l' and 'k', and a good half of the capital letters, whilst the space below the bottom tram-line took the tail-loops of 'f', 'g', 'j' and 'y' and so on.

Despite individual coaching in the graphic art, my letters were not fitting neatly into their spaces, hence the rap! If only Mrs Rudman could see my writing now, her ruler would be going like a bee's wing over the rheumaticky joints!

Mam must have been proud of her first-born and his progress through school, because for years she kept samples of my early work. Mrs Rudman gave us a farmyard project. We drew the farmyard creatures in crayon of the appropriate colour. My chicks

would not have surprised a mother ostrich, such were their dispro-
portions! On the other hand, in his early teens 'our kid' (my
brother Eric) could draw Walt Disney's animal characters as
skilfully as the master himself.

Practical classes gave us the opportunity of gaining skill with
our hands. Once we were given a canvas grid and skeins of
coloured raffia. I chose red, black and yellow. We were to make a
handbag, which fond mams lined, no doubt with cloth, to smooth
the itchy contact of the raffia. Mam kept sewing materials in hers.
For years the bag lay about the Billingham cupboards, possibly till
the day she died. It could not have been the clumsy workmanship
that preserved it. In those days, materials were meant to last!

The little school was a two-teacher establishment. I must have
made progress in my initial learning, because I was promoted,
before my time, to Miss Stevenson's class. As the headmistress
she was in charge of the older girls and boys who, at the age of
eleven or twelve, would sit the Scholarship exams. If successful,
they would move on to the Secondary School.

I was to be away from Hartburn long before those critical days.
In that little country school I learnt a lot and quickly, so that when
I did move to a bigger school, at Billingham, I was a jump ahead
of my contemporaries.

History was not a favourite subject of mine. Except for dates
like 1066, which I associate more readily with those funsters
Sellars and Yeatman and their *1066 and All That* than with the
Battle of Hastings and William the Conqueror, or 1314, the Battle
of Bannockburn, dates of world events leave me cold. So, I
suppose I ought to consult an almanac for an event that is etched
deep in memory, the eclipse of the sun, total or partial, which
took place in 1927, according to the records.

I see myself on top of the wall separating our garden and Molly
Johnston's, huddled in an overcoat of Dad's. Just minutes before,
I had been plucked from a cosy bed, at some unearthly hour like
four o'clock on a Spring or Summer's morning, and told to look in
a certain direction. I now imagine it ought to have been easterly,
but I am sure I was looking more to the south! The grown-ups had
given me a piece of brownish glass, photographic plate, to protect

my eyes. They talked in excited tones as I gazed in vain to watch the phenomenon. The whole exercise was lost on me.

Back in the house, now wide-awake, all I wanted to do was to get dressed properly, have my breakfast and get off to school. All my schooldays (except as a teacher!), I had a dread of being late. Punishment for lateness was either summary (the cane) or delayed (detention after classes). This was in other schools, not in Hartburn.

'But, Mam, it's time to go to school!' I had finished my breakfast and was ready to be off. 'No, Donald! It's only half past seven!' To a five- or six-year-old, what do the mysteries of the hands of a clock and the figures on the dial mean? For me, the intervals between getting dressed, breakfasting and leaving for school were set. Breakfast was over, so it was time to leave. I had to go. In the end they let me. Off I went.

There was nobody else going my way; nothing extraordinary about that. Usually we straggled to school from all directions. There was no sign of life in the playground. Perhaps I was just the first. But the school door was firmly locked. After a while the strange silence became too much for me. Back home I went, bawling my eyes out, thinking the end of the world had come! Once the proper time came round, Mam had to make a special trip to school to reassure me.

In the 'fifties, as a teacher in Morgan Academy, Dundee, I went up onto the school roof one lunch-time to see a partial eclipse of the sun over the city. It was one of the eeriest experiences of my life as the sharp outlines of buildings and factory chimneys blurred and the bright green of the leafy trees and the grass on the Law gradually turned dim and dull on that sunny day. Even the watchers were subdued. Then I understood the awe-inspiring nature of celestial events which had governed the actions of our early ancestors, the Picts and Druids, with their stone circles that still hold such mysteries.

'Put your hands up if your parents get a daily newspaper!' Very few went up in answer to Mrs Rudman's order. Even a penny a day for a paper was more than many a family budget could stretch to in those days. The local daily was *The Northern Echo*, printed in Darlington. Amongst its features was a children's page. Youthful readers could become members of the 'Nig-nogs', a club which sported a metal badge, worn to let members recognize each other. Once, in a 'Nig-nog' competition, I won a simple box-camera; but I could not afford the cost of the 120-size eight-exposure spools of film.

Twenty years later on, and more than two hundred miles from 'home', I was introduced to a Yorkshire lass from Bradford, the wife of a colleague in Morgan Academy. We discovered that we shared a common bond, membership of the 'Nig-nogs'! The emblem on the club badge was two 'Nig-nogs', cheeky-looking elf-like creatures, having no connection with the unfortunate term and its connotations of today.

Another paper, the 'Gazette' (its full title was 'The North-eastern Daily Gazette'), an evening issue, had an 'Andy Capp' type of strip character, known as 'Miffy'. Since this nickname related to the surname 'Smith', I was branded with 'Miffy', one of the many nicknames I have had to bear over the years.

'Miff' was the affectionate by-name Mam was given by a dear next-door neighbour, Doris Dewhirst, known to us as 'Doo'. (A few days ago I had a letter from 'Doo', now into her early eighties, which explains how the nicknames came about. I quote: 'Your Mum had planted some tulips. They were in flower. Sheila, ['Doo's' baby daughter] was on the front. She couldn't talk much. She was pulling the heads off them and your mother rapped on the window to her. I arrived in time to hear her saying, "I only melled [smelled], Miff!" − hence the Miff. She couldn't say Smith. And Joy [our Joyce] couldn't say Dewhirst. It was "Doo". Isn't it funny? And I'm still "Doo" to Joy's children and grand-children!'

CHAPTER FOUR

The Village

IF AN ENGLISHMAN were asked what features he would broadly expect to find in an English village, he would probably list the following: a common, or village green with a duck-pond; the church; a church school or village-hall; a pub or two (depending on the drouthiness of the male population); the Squire's home; a store with a post-office; and cottages or houses with colourful summer gardens. Trees like beech, oak, ash (and perhaps even a spreading chestnut-tree) would be prominent.

How far, then, did Hartburn measure up to this standard? I say Hartburn, but it is marked as East Hartburn on the maps. Yet nowhere in the vicinity have I found a West Hartburn! (You can well imagine the disappointment of our Scottish-born daughters when, in Glen Clova, Angus, they saw the name of a farm, Wester Eggie, and vainly sought, on the other side of the glen, its mouth-watering twin, Easter Eggie. All their visions of a 'Hansel-and-Gretel' house, built of oval-shaped chocolate blocks, cemented together with delicious fondant cream, must have just melted away.)

In Hartburn the unkempt tussocky patch of grass, hardly big enough for the few hens on it to scrat, was a poor substitute for a proper green. Instead of a pond there was at least a well where once, using my school-cap, I scooped up a cool draught. Not many years after, the well was boarded over, as its waters were not so healthful as folk thought!

The church was not some century-revered goal of the faithful, but I was too young to know. It might have passed as a church-hall. However, it did have a little bell-tower, from which came a mere tinkling on Sundays.

Ah, but as if to make up for this short-coming there were two pubs, one at each end of the village, the Stockton Arms nearer Stockton and The Masham at the Darlington end.

Manor Farm, Bessie Johnson's home, impressed me as a child. Down its ornate octagonal chimneys, skilfully masoned in red brick which had weathered away to a warm brown over many a year, you could well believe Father Christmas lowered himself safely, in due season, without any qualms. Nevertheless, you did not doubt that he went down the others in the village, but with a squeeze!

The store and post-office was mid-way along the village. Its chief attraction had been, on one occasion, its tempting sugar-coated bonbons.

I do not recall the prettiness of cottage-gardens, so well appreciated by Leslie Fitzgerald, bouquet-maker to teacher! The memory for me is of our front garden and its path, edged with box (buxus sempervirens), which led down to the main street. Whenever I walk in formal gardens where that same trim edging keeps borders in place, its scent transports me back to Hartburn. Trees, they could not help but be impressive to a little five- or six-year-old. Slim dark poplars stood sentry-go, branches 'presenting arms' to all who passed along the street.

I suppose that in most villages the main street is the main road, leading to the outside world. Again, Hartburn did not conform. The A66 Stockton to Darlington road passed on the northern flank. Where the main street turned off from the main road, at the Stockton end, stood the garage of Wilks and Abel. They had gained the franchise for some make of vehicle, no doubt a feather in their cap in those early days of motor transport. They must have won for themselves a degree of notoriety unknowingly or, as good businessmen, knowingly astute, for one of their displays bore the announcement, 'Wilks & Abel are Sole Agents'. Whenever older people came out with that remark, it was met with roars of laughter. I was quite a bit older before I understood the joke. By that time, however, we were daringly telescoping similar phrases that were going the rounds of street and playground gatherings. We would enjoin our pals to repeat quickly after us, 'I chased a bug around a tree; I'll have his blood, he knows I will!'

The western end of the village was a vague area for a youngster barely three feet tall, as whatever houses there were stood far enough back behind laurel hedges and tall palings to be unseen. One or two were impressive private residences, the sort that have become stylish hotels or equally private nursing homes today.

At that same end of the village, just at the bend where the street headed towards the main road again, a farm lane led off to the left. Up the main street, along the lane and back, was just a canny stroll on a Sunday when Mam and Dad walked us out together.

Two features on this walk stand out in memory: one, a charming nook in a grassy field, an inviting picnic-spot; the other, a sinister pool in Hartburn Beck, close enough to where we walked to make me hold Dad's hand the tighter. Little need to warn me against its dangers and to stay at home. I was unlikely to stray far in any case, unlike cousin Ray. He was found one day wandering across the Victoria Bridge over the Tees to Thornaby. There he was, not old enough to go to school, three miles away from home at the other end of the town, happily trundling his favourite toy cart along behind him.

I have not mentioned the school in the community, because it was not in the village proper. Instead it stood, an outpost of culture, on the lane leading to Fairfield.

CHAPTER FIVE

Village Games and Other Treats

OVER THE LANE from Mrs Bain's house was the tall gable-end of Mrs Holligon's, the upper half of which, towards the chimney-head, was a glistening black. It might have been that smoke was to blame; but I fancy there was a glossiness about it because of pitch, applied to waterproof the wall. This was a marvellous spot for many an exciting game of 'Queenie, Queenie, who's got the Ball?'

In this game, the person who was 'IT', or 'ON' as we said, faced the wall and threw a ball, which rebounded against it back amongst the group of players. Someone caught the ball, then either held on to it or passed it on to another player. We all stood with our hands behind our backs, so as not to give the game away. 'ON' had to guess who was holding the ball. Failure to do so meant that 'ON' stayed 'ON'! A successful guess put the holder of the ball in 'ON's place.

Another ball-game, with more excitement and vigour about it, was 'Callie-out-Name'. A player threw the ball against the gable, calling out another player's name. The named player had to catch the ball cleanly. If he or she did so, the ball was thrown up again and a name called out. Often this was the previous caller's name, as that person was at a disadvantage being still close to the wall. It meant that one had to dash back into the lane for a catch.

If the callee failed to catch the ball, everybody scattered as far as possible within the confined space of the lane. Then 'Butter-fingers' tried to hit somebody with the ball. The person so hit was 'ON'. If nobody was hit, 'Butter-fingers' stayed 'ON'.

Girls *and* boys joined in this game. Boys were often more adept at catching and throwing; but girls had their wits about them, sometimes using their skirts skilfully to net a ball and transfer it to a throwing-hand! George and Maisie Holligon, Bessie and perhaps Molly Johnson, I recall, were participants in these games. I have often wondered what the senior Holligons thought as the ball, a discard from tennis or a 'spongy' from 'Woolies', thudded against the gable-end!

Many a time the girls must have gone home bearing blue marks on tender skin, bruised by the uninhibited throwing of the boys. Later, as we grew older, stronger and more accurate with our aim, we paid little or no attention to sisters or girl-pals, nor even to aunts who joined in the annual seaside holiday games of rounders. 'Hey, our Donald, don't throw that ball so hard!' 'Our Eric, that's not fair! That doesn't half hurt!'

If the complaint came from a sister or another girl, it only encouraged us the more! But, when the elders complained, we eased up, because it would have spoilt the balance of the sides if any of them dropped out.

In our version of rounders there was nothing 'cissy' like getting the ball to the corner-base to run an opponent out. We aimed to hit the runner en route between corners, and no nonsense!

In 1924 (his thirty years' service gold watch proves it) Dad, along with a host of other workmen, found a job in the Chemical Factory at Billingham, about five miles away. Now he needed transport to get to and from work. He bought a little Levis motorbike. Round about five o'clock, tea time, I would wait at the foot of the lane for Dad to appear. Then I was hoisted astride the petrol tank, in front of Dad, and with arms at full stretch would try to grasp the rubber handle-grips as if I were going to steer the machine. At nothing more than a crawl I rode in triumph to the house.

A greater thrill came one Sunday when, unexpectedly, Uncle Charlie, Auntie May and Raymond arrived in their little Austin 7. This Sunday was particular, because it was our first trip in a motor-car. The menfolk were given leave to go for a run. Auntie May, Mam and Joyce stayed at home.

Off we set. Dad sat beside Uncle Charlie at the front; Ray, Eric and I had ample room in the back. It was one of those halcyon days of the summers of yesteryear. We were in an open-tourer, as there was no need for the hood, heading south via Eaglescliffe, Yarm and Thirsk. A fair old whiff of Yarm Tannery assailed our nostrils in the passing. Some remark was also made about Yarm Treacle Docks, which made Dad and Uncle Charlie laugh, but left us out of the joke. It is still a mystery to me, unless there was some mention of the stevedores unloading the sticky cargo into sacks!

On that same run I saw my first windmill water-pump, on a farm. It was a metal contraption, like a miniature Eiffel Tower, with whirling blades and a weathervane to keep it into wind.

The 'hit' of the day was, 'When the Red, Red, Robin goes a-bob, bob, bobbin' along!' We certainly gave it big licks for mile after mile on the way to East Keswick, which turned out to be our destination. There, Dad's sister Mabel and her husband Sam Baker had the unexpected 'privilege' of entertaining us.

If we had gone on to Roundhay, Leeds, we should have met up with Jen, who was a cut above our lot as her husband, Uncle Oswald Wolstenholme, was a businessman in the Wines and Spirits trade. I can only remember them visiting us once in Billingham. By the way our parents spoke it sounded as if the visit was a kind of patronizing 'slumming', since the lifestyle of both parties was so different.

Nevertheless, when in the 1940s as a student at Manchester University I broke my journey home on the bike to stay overnight at Aunt Jen's, I was right royally welcomed and entertained, enjoying the company of my cousins, Don and Derek. Don was already, at nineteen, an Honours graduate of Leeds University, with a Degree in French. Derek was an enthusiastic drummer, owning a full battery of equipment which he handled expertly. My wife, who has never met Aunt Jen, would recognize her instantly, for she modelled knitwear patterns for Paton and Baldwin wools which my wife is familiar with through her own knitting.

It was unlikely that we should remember the return journey from East Keswick, as it was made in the dark. In any case, we probably dozed off in the back of the car after a while. At all events, we were greeted with relief by the womenfolk on their seeing us returning all in one piece, as they had not expected us to be away so long.

Today, when I see the last examples of these tiny box-like veterans at Vintage Car Rallies, I salute them for their Herculean performances, which we can all vouch for. Uncle Charlie would be at the wheel, with Auntie May beside him, holding Joyce on her knees. Mam sat in the back with the three of us lads, as our 'Wonder Horse' carried us not only along relatively flat roads to places like Seaton Carew or Redcar, but even up over the moors beyond Guisborough, via Birk Brow. This was a long, long pull with a one-in-six gradient and a couple of hair-raising bends. Within four or five miles we met a similar gradient on Jolly Sailor's Bank, named after the pub standing by the roadside.

Up on the moor-top, Uncle Charlie would pull into some handy hollow. The front seat was removed, because a little spirit stove was stored there on which the kettle sat to boil merrily. This would call us to tea when its little whistle blew under the head of steam coming from the spout.

When the picnic was over, Uncle would invariably fetch out his easel and prepare to transfer to paper some characteristic scene of Cleveland – a landscape, or lone moorland house of yellow sandstone with red-tiled roof. These water-colours made most acceptable gifts to the Barlows and Smiths. When Uncle died it was felt that his paintings should be returned to Ray for safe keeping as family heirlooms.

One of the delights of Hartburn was truly Epicurean. The special treat was home-made meat pies. Oh, the mouth-watering aroma of those steak-pies! We took a jug along to Mrs Turner's in Harper Terrace to collect the gravy, which was kept separate. Everything was piping hot. When it was all dished up with a filling accompaniment of potatoes, carrots and turnip, all mashed together in the big black pot before the pies were served, I would not have swapped places with King George himself at a State Banquet!

Another mouth-watering delight was sugar bonbons. However, the circumstances by which I came to savour these titbits might have hid a sinister danger. All I can remember is that I came home from school clutching an enormous bag of the sweets. Mam was completely flabbergasted. 'Our Donald, where did you get those sweets?' In all innocence all I could say was, 'Bertie Barratt gave me a half-crown.' (12½p)

Researching a street directory of those days, I discovered that Mr Barratt was a contractor who had bought a fairly secluded house in the village, at the back of our lane. The Barratts moved in different circles from the rest of us. Bertie was much older than I was, probably in his late teens. I was only a bairn living close to their house. The half-crown had been merely a gesture of generosity; but I was warned, in no uncertain terms, never to take money like that again! Mind, if ever I am in a sweet-shop where I spot a tempting jar of those same bonbons, I am quite likely to invest in a quarter. The toffee flavour and the texture are still there, but I take good care to suck them delicately and not chew. I have too many fillings now that might loosen!

A half-crown! We might have been lucky to get such a sum from a fond relative on our birthdays, but we were not allowed to keep such a fortune. Surely, the Yorkshire Penny Bank would know how to look after such sums! I think that that institution had sent agents round to the local schools, and I had been persuaded to go and ask Mam to open an account for me. We literally invested pennies, usually sixpence at a time (2½p). Now halfpence no longer enter into banking calculations.

I still hold an account with that bank, but it has a new name which glosses over its humble origins. It is the Yorkshire Bank Limited! Account No. 60878 of the High Street, Stockton, Branch stands at 69p! I do note, however, that in advice relating to accounts it states that deposits of any sum from one penny upwards may be paid into a customer's account. I observe, with a smile, that at the foot of the only page where there is an entry (dated 1973!), the client is advised, 'You may find a cheque-book useful — ask the cashier about it!'

CHAPTER SIX

Kith and Kin

GOING TO GRANDMA'S was part of the regular pattern of our early childhood. Sixty years ago, families lived in close communities. Often the 'extended' family lived in the same street, Grandpa and Grandma being two or three doors away from the eldest married son. Daughters and their husbands would set up house across the way; and perhaps even the unmarried sister of a grandparent, a favourite great-aunt, had her own little place in the street or in a neighbouring one.

Whilst the family in a country area would not be so localized as in a street in town, it would still be cocooned within the bounds of a village. Even if a family was scattered through a township, its members would be no further than walking-distance apart. The journey from our Billingham home to Gran's house at No. 35 Bedford Street, in the Newtown district of Stockton-on-Tees, could only have been half a mile longer than the traipse from Hartburn; but the legs that toddled from Hartburn were not so sturdy as the older ones that strode out the miles from Billingham.

However, our family was not quite so typical. It might have had something to do with our genes from both sides. Dad's lot were separated as far apart as Australia, and Gran's were poles apart on mainland Britain.

I feel there is something of a cachet in being able to claim Shetland blood in our veins. Whether great-grandfather Robert Smith was a real Viking or not matters little. At any rate he had something of the Viking 'salt' in his blood, for had he not sailed from the Islands to meet up with a 'Geordie' lass in North or South Shields? He had taken her back to that wind-swept, sea-lashed land of peat-bog, rock and heather − but it had been too much for her. He was the one who had had to leave his close ties behind and settle further south.

Grandfather Alfred Smith had married Mary Williams, a Welsh woman from Mold. He was a master joiner and the first Labour councillor in Stockton. By today's ratings he would have been 'as red as they come!' His death in 1906 had been hastened by a fall from a roof where he was working. He is buried in Oxbridge Cemetery.

Having found Grandpa's death certificate, just a year or two before Dad died, we traced the plot of ground allotted to his remains. He could only have been in his forties when he passed away. Whether his premature death had anything to do with it or not, Grandma Smith died too at an early age − of a broken heart, or so it was said.

Hanging in a prominent place in the Billingham house was a large framed picture of Grandpa. He had a sternish look, accentuated by a waxed moustache and a stiff, starched collar. He had the angular, prominent, Smith nose. The Barlow nose is stubbier and rounded. That is more like mine!

On the early death of their parents, the seven children (five girls and two boys) found themselves orphaned. Eva, Jen, Mabel and Ethel (affectionately known as 'Kek') were in their late to early teens. Dad was nine and Jack was seven. Baby sister Lily was a year or two younger.

As the girls grew up, they married. Eva went off from Stockton in the early 'twenties with Ernie Pidd, to make a new life in Australia, where he worked with the railways. The other girls settled in Leeds and the West Riding. Jack was to marry a Stockton girl, Mary Britten, always known to us as 'Auntie Polly'. They lived out their lives on Teesside, probably no more than eight or ten miles from where they had grown up.

There was also a Smith cousin, Joe, and his wife Evelyn. Joe was a skilled craftsman, making intricate mechanical toys. I enjoyed the rare visits to his home, when he would set running a steam engine that he had built himself. I can see again the eerie purplish flame of the meths that burned in a little tray to heat the water in the boiler, can smell the sweetish acrid spirit, and hear the impatient hiss of the steam waiting for the movement of the lever which would allow it to set the pistons thrusting.

There was a 'saltiness' in the veins on Mam's side, too. Grandma was a Temple but her grandfather, my great-great on the distaff side, was a Bell who had been a ship-owner on the Tyne. One may presume that he had done his share of voyaging like my Shetlander.

Another who was a seafarer was Gran's brother-in-law William. He was a bluff stoutish chap, with a very red complexion that pointed more to heart trouble than to exposure to salt spray and gale-force winds. He walked with the rolling gait of a sailor. We heard grown-ups calling him, 'Puffin' Billy', which gives some idea of the way he went about. He probably earned the title as he laboured up Brown Jug Bank to his house in the Mount Pleasant area of the town. The Brown Jug pub stood halfway up the hill.

Gran also had a sister, Laura, who once visited us − a lady in a blue uniform with a white collar. She was 'in service' as a child-nurse or 'nanny'. The stiffness of her garb gave an impression of an unbending attitude towards her small charges, which might have been far from the truth. I trust that I am not misjudging her.

The only other time that she intruded in family matters was one, alas, that she was not aware of. Dad was called to her funeral in Peebles, a town I now know to be just over the Scottish border.

Only recently cousin Ray sent me a letter written by that same lady, our great-aunt Laura, dated during a Christmas period of the First World War. It was addressed to her niece, also called Laura, who was working 'in service' too in Scotland. On the back of the page is a recipe for a 'Granny Loaf'. Interested readers may want to try it out. Knowing how well Auntie Laura could bake, I am sure that great-aunt Laura was passing on a highly-recommendable treat.

In her long lifetime, Auntie Laura found herself working in households from Cambuslang in the Glasgow area down to Kent, then back up to the Midlands from where she returned to Kent before retiring to Stockton (a move she always regretted, as she had grown accustomed to the warmth of the southern climate and

This is a very nice Raisin or (Granny loaf.)

2 lb Flour.
2 Table spoons of Sugar
3 oz Butter.
½ lb Currants
¾ lb Large Rasins (mix with)
1 oz Yeast. (Milk) & I bake it in two
loaves. about 1½ hours. mix the same as
for Tea cakes. don't forget salt to taste
Our people like it immensely this way
but you could add peel & nutmeg a spice if
desired

Mrs Adam sent one to Haldane with
a Xmas cake. & they were charmed
with it - & specially wanted to know
if Temple made it -

had left behind most of her friends of long acquaintance who belonged to the Folkestone district.)

We heard her telling of her epic journeys in the 1914-18 days when, as a single lady, she rode home to Stockton on her bicycle to visit Gran, ensuring the safety of the ten-shilling notes she carried on her person by tucking them down the leg of her knickers! Over a period of years these hard-earned notes bought the Bedford Street house for her mother!

Gran's only son, George, worked for a while on Teesside before he took the road south too, to London where he married Auntie Lily. They had three sons: Derek, Donald (known now as 'Don of the South' to distinguish him from me, 'Don of the North') and Desmond, who sadly died in his early teens. On just one or two occasions the whole family sallied north on visits 'home'. Standing beside these cousins, Ray, Eric and I felt like Lilliputians dwarfed by Gullivers! They were all about six feet tall!

May and Mam remained on Teesside, close to Grandma, who was widowed when Grandpa James Barlow died in 1926. May married Charlie Counter, her childhood sweetheart. Cousin Ray was their only child.

So, it was in this circle of Gran, the Counters, Uncle Jack and Auntie Polly, along with their friends and ours, that our Teesside life was lived. The Leeds folk, for all that they lived only sixty-odd miles away from us, might just as well have lived in Australia, next door to the Pidds! It was too expensive to take our family to Leeds.

CHAPTER SEVEN

Going to Grandma's

HARTBURN was not the only place we knew. Through fairly frequent visits to Grandpa and Grandma Barlow we became familiar with the Newtown district of Stockton. They lived in No. 35 Bedford Street. Only two or three houses away from Gran's, at the bottom of the street, flowed the Lustrum Beck. On the other side of it, beyond the tree-lined bank, was the high fence of Newtown School, where we watched the scholars play at playtime. Cousin Ray was a pupil there. He lived about three-quarters of a mile away from the school in Gray's Road, Grange Estate, an area of substantial houses, where trees lined the streets, and hedges of privet and laurel protected the residents from the prying eyes of passers-by.

Mam would walk us over to Bedford Street quite often, pushing baby Joyce in a push-chair which could be most easily described as a deck-chair on wheels — except for the fact that the canvas seat was made of firmer material and set higher up. However, it belonged to the same family of devilish contraptions which lie in wait to trap curious little fingers.

Eric and I either tagged along behind Mam or darted about in front, wanting to kick stones but being sternly warned not to, 'because you've got on your best shoes, and they cost money!'

We always had to get dressed for those occasions. That meant putting on our best blue serge suits of stiff material that tended to scuff our knees on the soft part of the lower thigh in wet weather, making a sore red mark there.

'Getting dressed' was never my idea of visiting. You could not play. You had to sit still or move with the utmost caution, so that trousers did not get torn or sleeves caught on a branch or fence or whatever. That abhorrence of dress persists with me to this day. One well-moulded suit would do me.

I always enjoyed the story Dad told of the old Yorkshire farmer who had gone on a visit to London in his old farming togs. On being taken to task for this untidy way of meeting with the folk of the City, he retorted, 'Well, tha sees, it's like this. Nawbody knaws me down thee-ar, but ivverybody knaws me oop 'ere.' That could be my sartorial epitaph!

It was quite a tidy walk from Hartburn to Newtown. We went out of the village, down the hill, crossed Hartburn Beck, shouted for an 'echo' under the railway bridge, then toiled up the winding hill to Ropner Park.

The bridge chiefly served to carry the long trains of heavily laden coal trucks that came down from the Durham coalfield. They clanked through Stockton, Thornaby and Middlesbrough to Cargo Fleet, South Bank, Grangetown and Dormanstown. In the ironworks there the coking coal was used in smelting when iron ore was made into steel.

It was no accident that a steel industry had established itself there. In the early days the ingredients for producing iron were all to hand: the ore and limestone in the Cleveland Hills just south of the river, and the coal from the Durham coalfield just to the north. In the 'thirties there were still signs of the aerial rope-ways and the tipping buckets that carried the ore down from the mines near Eston. Railways were laid into the wastes of the North Yorkshire Moors, to places like Rosedale, for the same purpose. It was an impressive sight at night when the covers were lifted off the blast-furnaces. The glow against the clouds of the night sky could be seen for miles.

The river, too, had a part to play in the steel story. Shipyards lined its banks from Stockton almost to the sea. With a river to cross, the bridge builders had every reason for advancing their skills. The name of Dorman Long became known throughout the world. Who built the Tyne Bridge, and the Sydney Harbour Bridge which is modelled on it? And how about the Zambesi River Bridge in Africa and, more recently, the Forth Road

Bridge? Now the company, with a new title Redpath Dorman Long, has staked a claim in the development of North Sea oil with the rigs built at Methil in Scotland.

Once we were safely inside the gates of Ropner Park, away from the main road, we had more freedom of action. The park lake was an awesome spot of dark water, overhung with willow and dark trees. The little ducks were all right whether afloat, doing their ducking act, or waddling ashore after the bits of stale bread that we remembered to take in a brown paper bag for them and the swans.

These majestic birds were an entirely different proposition. We felt fairly safe while they stayed in the water; but even then we had to watch out when offering a chunk of bread, because those long, supple necks could reach much further than we thought. However, when with ungainly gait they emerged on to the footpath, big white graceless creatures ambling two or three together towards us, standing as tall as our infant selves, there was a scurry to get behind the safety of Mam's skirts and the push-chair!

There was a boat on the lake; probably it had been used by one of the park-keepers in his aquatic patrols. My recollection of it is of a vessel lying waterlogged, year in year out, at the edge of the lake.

On the way to the Oxbridge exit out of the park we passed by an aviary of multi-coloured birds − parrots and the like. There may have been a monkey-house; but whether there was or not, this corner was another attraction.

The park was a popular spot in the summer. Bands played in the bandstand. The borders were a blaze of colour with wonderful floral displays. Stockton Flower Show was held there on the spacious greens.

From the park we went along a short street with dark park trees overhanging dark houses. Then we were into Oxbridge Lane. At the corner of one of the streets off the Lane stood the school that Dad and Uncle Jack had attended as boys.

Across from Oxbridge School, we took a street that led on to the Town Moor. Either this or its continuation bore the unforgettable name of Light Pipe Hall Road!

On the Moor we passed by what might have been a derelict ironworks, a scrap-yard or works on its last legs. I saw a crane rotating on its base, steam hissing from the cab by the winch, with a fussy little piston driving the winding-drum. Everything was brown with rust.

The last stretch of the Moor path ran parallel with the main railway line southbound; then it was absorbed into another street that came out at the Newtown Co-op. Bedford Street was opposite the Co-op block of shops − confectioner's, grocer's and butcher's.

Just a short way into Bedford Street, on the left, was a post-office and, over on the right, Bert's barber-shop, a large corner site. In the 'chair' we went through that early trauma of our first hair-cut! Bert must have known all us bairns through the custom of Uncle Charlie and Grandpa, and Dad on the odd occasion; so there were few tears when we felt the cold steel of the scissors shearing away at our locks. As we awaited our turn we listened to incomprehensible chat about horses and dogs, odds-on favourites and the number of shirts that seemed to be leaving many of Bert's clients bare-backed! From Bert's it was downhill the rest of the way, almost to the foot of the street.

I suppose it was a typical English town street. T.V.'s 'Coronation Street' is now the classic example. The roadway was made up of stone blocks that had a sort of glaze to their whitish surface. Where little traffic passed, the odd blade or two of grass managed to seed and take root, no doubt nurtured by the horse-manure deposited there by those faithful haulers of coal-carts, milk-carts, muck-carts and cabs.

Parallel to the street, at the back of the houses, was the back lane which the various tradesmen (like the bin-men who removed household refuse) used. A child must have felt engulfed, in this red-brick canyon with no access to the houses that it separated. Let into the walls were the doors, with their snecks too high for toddlers to reach, so that, of course, once inside the confines of the back-garden, little children were safe from roaming.

In Grandpa's garden a path ran from the lane door up to the backyard, a concreted area where on a fine day the possing-tub would be out. Grandma with her possing-stick would be possing the clothes in the sudsy water, in the weekly ritual of doing the family washing.

The possing-stick was no stick! It was a stout piece of rounded wood, about 3 feet 6 inches high, with a wooden rod passing through the top to make a handle − for both hands were needed. The stem would be as thick as a man's forearm, with the bottom nine or ten inches slightly wider, and split from the base to five or six inches up so that air could get into the soapy water and improve the cleansing action.

Though she lived well into the post-war years of electric washing machines, Grandma never had the pleasure of using one; but Aunty May, especially, must have blessed the day they were invented, when she faced the daily washing of soiled bedlinen over the last years of Grandma's bed-ridden existence.

Between the neighbour's high wall and the garden-path,

Grandpa had a small hen-run and an aviary. He was a great bird-lover. He kept a button-like object that was a whistle. When he placed it in the front of his mouth he could suck or blow through it and imitate bird-calls. It was no use pestering to get a shot of it. Grown-ups did not want to be rushing to doctors or hospital with a bairn choking on the metal disc!

In a glass case he kept a stuffed jay, a multi-coloured testimonial to the art of the taxidermist. At the break-up of Grandma's home, Mam inherited this perky article of blue, grey, white and brown feathers. Perched up on the top of a corner cupboard in the Billingham house, he kept a sharp but glassy eye on Eric and me, lying in our double bed!

Michaelmas daisies I remember from my early days at Hartburn School. 'Nasturtiums' came into my vocabulary and 'diet-sheet', thanks to Grandpa. He grew their fiery red, orange and yellow hoods in the border of his garden path, and offered me a taste of a leaf and seed! The peppery tang almost burnt the tip of my tongue off! That would be one of his jokes! Yet they still remain a favourite flower of mine for their brightness, abundance and ease of cultivation — not forgetting the hosts of wrinkled seeds that cost nothing and hold the promise of more brilliance in a coming year! If I were to introduce bairns to growing things, one of the most satisfying pleasures in life, I would give them a packet of nasturtium seeds.

Bedford Street was not a place where we went to play outside in the garden. It was big enough for us, as tots, to let off a bit of steam when the grown-ups wanted a bit of peace and quiet, or time to discuss important family matters out of reach of our flapping ears! We could hear too much, especially if older folk outside egged us on to repeat a swear-word. Back indoors, in front of our own folk, this never seemed to earn the praise we expected for such cleverness!

The inside of the house was gloomy, thanks to tall poplars shading the rear of the building and an aspidistra blocking out the morning light from the front room window.

But the atmosphere was far from gloomy. There was usually a bright fire blazing in the hearth. This had to be so, as the water for family use was heated in a side-boiler. Grandpa was a tailor to trade. It was in front of this fire that he heated his many and various irons. Different sizes of little flat-irons were held to the heat in a kind of rack. (Grandpa would have heartily approved of the action of an old friend, Dr Bill Chaloner, whose best man I was. Just an hour or so before the wedding, coming up the Oldham Road, Bill suddenly leapt off the bus and darted into an old second-hand shop, to emerge triumphantly brandishing a pair of flat-irons. 'What on earth do you want those old-fashioned things for, Bill?' Ever cautious and with none too much confidence in modern technology, Bill replied in his gravelly tones, 'It's just in case the gas-iron or the electric one breaks down!'

What a man! And he was Reader in Economic History at Owen's, Manchester!)

The 'daddy' of all Grandpa's irons was the 'goose' − a heavy, long, narrow rectangular block of shiny metal which he used for pressing material for suits. He would hold this, hot and threatening, in front of me. It scared me stiff, so any nonsense I might have been contemplating was nipped in the bud.

Not that we planned mischief in the presence of these elders, for Grandma had a touch of Victorian authority about her, and the straight-backed appearance of the old queen, Queen Mary. In any case, the slogan of those days, rigorously upheld, was, 'little children should be seen, but not heard!' So, perhaps, the brandishing of the 'goose' was one of Grandpa's little jokes! He did not live long enough for us to know him well and discover whether he had just been kidding us on.

One of the scariest things in Grandma's was a huge picture in the living-room. Its size allowed the proportions of the subjects to appear lifelike to us. The scene is a village schoolroom. Through the open door a fox, closely pursued by the hounds, has sought refuge. Huntsmen and horses can be seen outside. Inside, all is turmoil, bairns shrieking and cowering in terror, clinging to each other. The school-dame, wearing a mob-cap, waves her hands in a gesture of helplessness. A slate lies shattered on the floor. The gaping jaws of the slavering hounds gave us the 'willies'.

We have the picture hanging in one of our rooms. To this day I still wonder what was the fate of the fox. The signature on the print is 'Arthur J. Elsley', and the date 1898.

The 'willies' were soon dispelled when the pack of playing-cards came out. From a very tender age we were initiated into the mysteries of 'Beggar-my-Neighbour', 'Snap', 'Simple Patience', 'Clock Patience' and 'Pairs'. Gran, Mam and aunties were all keen tutors, as they enjoyed the games themselves. Gran maintained that 'Beggar-my-Neighbour' was as good a way as any to get the cards shuffled for some more important game.

Any number can play. The important cards are the aces and face-cards, and the cracker of all these is the 'Jack' (or 'Knave'). He only needs one 'rubbish' card to bring him and his spoils back to his owner. An Ace, King or Queen needs four, three or two 'rubbish' cards respectively, to ensure safety and winnings. If your 'Jack' disappears under one of the other three 'Jacks' it often spells disaster. It is not so easy to win him back. Then misery is written all over your face. You are almost certainly going to say 'Ta-ta!' to your master-card, and possibly to a whole heap of winnings.

Once a player runs out of cards, that person is out of the game, a mere onlooker now. In such a case, with many a sullen look, we watched as somebody else went on to win. At that age we did not like losing. We had to be chivvied out of our grumpiness with the promise of another game or a change to something else.

In that sense our spinster-aunt Laura, Mam's older sister, never grew up. To her dying day she liked winning, and though as a grown man I can sportingly lose to another player, whenever I played against her I was just as determined as she was to win. And the more she crowed, the harder I became! I had no sympathy for her in defeat. She would make every excuse. She could never accept that most of the games we played depended more on chance than skill. But let us give credit where credit is due. She really was a dab hand at dominoes and cards. In her advancing years (she lived to be almost ninety) nothing delighted her more than to insinuate herself into a game of dominoes (such as threes and fives) among the old boys of the Old Folks' Club and beat them!

Not so long ago I was playing cards with my eldest grandson in Alberta. Ryan, at 7, was just at the age to enjoy card games. Many a time he beat me hands down, but as I played I could see another laddie of much the same age, playing with a grand-parent, just as determined and giving way to expressions of disgust if the game was lost. How can I grow old with that living mirror of my own childhood sitting opposite me, engrossed in his kings and aces?

Mam's simple remark, 'I've got some shopping to do at New-town Stores, and then we'll go on and see Grandma', opened up the prospect of an abundance of pleasures. The walk was an adventure. There was the chance of Mam splashing out on a bag of those little round biscuits, no bigger than a jacket-button, topped with pink, yellow, blue or white star-shaped sugar-icing.

The great delight, however, was dinner at Grandma's, in the working-class North, at midday. Invariably it meant a walk along by the beck to the shops in Durham Road. There was no fear you would lose your way; the appetizing smell of frying would keep you on course. 'A tuppenny fish and a pennorth, four times', or words to that effect, was the password to that bundle of delight. Beyond the counter, fish sizzled in batter and chips bubbled in cauldrons of oil. Stacks of 'The Gazette' or 'The Northern Echo' were to hand to wrap the glowing gold. 'That will be a shilling, Mrs Barlow. Thank you!' said Mr Jones, the fish-and-chip-shop man.

That was not the end of the treat though. Next door the baker charmed Grandma in with his display of cream-buns. With a bag of these, one for each of us, the feast was ready. The fish and chips were only an appetizer! But the cream-buns ...! First we would turn them upside-down to eat, or rather nibble at, the plain bread base. The top with its delicate brown skin came next, till just enough was left to give us a hold before we lingered, slow-tongued, over the cream. I am still tempted to tackle any cream-bun in the same way today; but the cream does not taste the same, nor the doughy bun. A cup of tea washed down the last of the crumbs.

Years later, in Dundee, I met old Mr Jones. His son-in-law, Mr Mann, had been sent up from Stockton to open up the Dundee branch of Timpson's shoe-shop. His daughter was looking after him in her new home. I taught his grand-daughter in Morgan Academy.

CHAPTER EIGHT

The Final Flitting*

A BURNING BALL OF FIRE hangs in the autumn sky to the west, burnishing a path of red and gold light across the surface of the water. Stark, dead branches of an old ash tree reach imploringly to the heavens, clear and cold with a hint of winter. The tree, a rotten, hollow trunk, stands by the expanse of flooded fields. Beyond the tree, etched against the evening sky, the saw-toothed silhouette of the roofs of houses and a church-steeple marks the merging of Norton and Stockton-on-Tees.

Further away, to the south and east, rises the rim of the Cleveland Hills. On a clear day, having good eyesight, one can just make out the notch of Scarth Nick, the pass towards the western edge of the rim of the hills, which links the village of Osmotherly to Swainby lying below in the plain.

The wind-eroded pinnacles of the Wain-stones are clearer as the eye moves east. Further east, yet closer as the hills curve above Great Ayton, the obelisk erected to the memory of Captain James Cook barely emerges above the moorland top. The folk of the village are justifiably proud of their famous son.

Roseberry Topping lends a touch of Ancient Egypt to the scene, a pyramid owing its form in part to Nature and in part to Man, who has tunnelled into its heart to extract the ironstone which brought work and wealth to Teesside.

That was the picture that a boy gazed on long years ago through

---

*The many Scots and their offspring still in Billingham do not need this word explained. For others, it is a 'guid Scots' word, more homely-sounding, for 'moving house'.

the kitchen window of his new home at No. 11 New Road, in the developing township of Billingham. The words are the words of the man, trying to paint the vividness of the scene which will live in his memory till the day he dies.

Billingham had been a village with a green surrounded by cottages and houses. St Cuthbert's Church and its Saxon tower, over a thousand years old, dominated that scene. The saint's bones had once found a temporary resting-place there. Quite a number of St Cuthbert's can be found near the north-east coast of Durham and Northumberland. Sites where the saintly cortège rested were revered and on them, later, churches were built.

Just yards from the lych-gate entry to the churchyard, and

without any consideration for the church and its site, the monstrosity of the Tower Building had been piled up. That act of vandalism has since been expunged. A demolition squad flattened it!

In the middle of The Green was the church school. Beside it stood Fletcher's, the shop of the local provision merchants whose proud boast was plain for all to see. Painted in large white letters on the gable-end of the store, three 'B's proudly stuck out their chests to proclaim, 'Billingham's Best Bacon'!

The A19, the main road from Sunderland, came down from the north via Station Road. It cut through The Green between the church and Fletcher's. Bolted to a wall near the Sunderland bus-stop an AA plaque read, 'London − 240 miles' (an easy number to remember, as 240 pennies made £1 in those days). The Smith's Arms and the Black Horse naturally plied their trade in the vicinity, being at the focal point of the community. Another pub, the Red Lion, stood just round the corner from The Green.

Mill Lane, heading south-east, was a branch road off the A19. It had led to a mill of some sort, either wind- or, more likely, water-powered.

Between Billingham Church and Norton Church lay the fields known as 'Billingham Bottoms'. By the field-track that led to Norton, the ruins of another Old Mill bore sad witness to the earlier presence of a water-mill. A big wheel which was rusting and, steadily choking with reed, a mill-stream that had once channelled the much-needed water, were the only signs that remained of it.

But all this rusticity was to be swamped under a flood of bricks and pantiles as the new Billingham, a giant domestic and industrial complex, remorselessly expanded.

However, to the west and south, the low-lying Bottoms barred any architectural invasion short of the industrial. New Road and Imperial Road owed their existence to the fact that the mound on which the village had been originally founded had extended its flanks just far enough south to allow space for our houses to be built above the flood-level of the Bottoms. And so the vista described at the beginning of this chapter lay open to be enjoyed.

CHAPTER NINE

The Central Stage and Wings

AS BAIRNS, we just accepted the fact that New Road was as it was. We were too busy playing in it and on it to analyse all the features that provided us with such a variety of opportunity for our ploys.

At the Billingham Bank end the road ran through a cutting, the scene of many hours of imaginative play. Then came a lane that we called 'The Gully', a mere cart-track. On the old maps it is named as Old Road, but Old Road to us was the built-up line of houses at the head of the lane. In earlier days this track would have given a more direct access from the centre of the village to beck-side fields than the new system of roads did. The Gully marked the western boundary of our housing area.

The first dozen or so of these houses in New Road were built on a slope, which allowed an open view across the field to The Beck and beyond. Behind them, and continuing along the backs to No. 19, stretched Mr Barker's market-garden. From the back of No. 19 the 'Rec' widened out into an extensive playing field behind the rest of the houses on our side of New Road, with Mill Lane as its eastern limit.

Above the market-garden, the bedrooms of the houses on the edge of the Newcastle Electric Supply Company's estate looked out over our roof-tops. These houses were built chiefly for the company's employees who, to us ordinary working-folk, were a superior race of mortals (as electricians were a superior caste of journeymen in factories!) Some owned their own cars, garaging them in their own wooden garages at the top of The Gully.

This Nesco estate comprised Old Road and South, West, Middle and East Avenues. There was no North Avenue, because that was the A19. Fronting on to the main road, Nesco had a sports pavilion, behind which a bowling green and tennis courts were laid out. At the bottom of East Avenue they had their own cricket-ground, which at one time had been part of the 'Rec'. Altogether, they were a posh lot!

The new Billingham that extended at first north to the L.N.E. railway line and later beyond it, growing out to the hamlet of Cowpen (pronounced 'coo-pen') Bewley, was a northern Welwyn Garden City, then a new concept in town-planning. Our avenues, roads, streets and crescents were relatively spacious and tree-lined. Each house had its gardens, back and front. Indoors the basic layout downstairs was a scullery, a living-room (more commonly called a 'kitchen', presumably because there was an oven built into the side of the fire-place) and a sitting-room on the other side of the entrance-vestibule. This was at the foot of the stairs, which went straight up from the front door. Upstairs we had a bathroom with a proper bath and hot-water tank, two bedrooms and a small back bedroom (still big enough for the parental double-bed).

The 'closets' ('netties', the Geordies called them) were flushing water-closets, a novelty to many of us coming in from the country. They were enclosed in the main fabric of the house; so there was no longer any need to 'go down the yard' as the old Stockton euphemism went for 'going to the lav'. Even so, speech patterns die hard. To the question, 'Where's Dad?' there was nothing cryptic about the reply, 'He's down the yard.' In all probability the enquirer could easily have been standing outside the closet door, blocking Dad's view of the garden as he squinted through the door he kept slightly ajar whilst he enjoyed both pleasures! Though he smoked in the house, he would sit for long enough over an after-tea fag. Cross-legged, we would utter the desperate cry, 'Hurry up, Dad! I can't wait any more!'

Although enclosed in the main fabric, the lavatory was only entered from outside, five or six steps along the back wall. 'Going to the lav' in winter was a perishing experience. In bitter cold weather, folk were involved in the extra expense of keeping a small paraffin heater burning to save the pipes from freezing! This was counterbalanced in summer, when the door was often kept open a little as the occupant 'on the lav' surveyed the flowers and growing vegetables, yet was ready to push the door to at the sound of approaching footsteps.

Houses inside the terraced block had the coal-house indoors! It could only have been a man who planned this nonsense. Coal-men had to bring dirty sacks and boots into clean back-kitchens.

Our coal-house was more accessible in the gable-end, sand-wiched between the inside walls of the 'lav' and the sitting-room. If we were in that room when the coal-man was delivering, we could hear the rumble of the chunks of coal being emptied out of the sacks. By listening for the separate rumbles we could make a tally of the sacks delivered! This was quite important, as a less than scrupulous coal-man, working from his cart parked out of sight at the road-side below eye level, could keep back the odd bag from an unsuspecting housewife ordering her coal in 5 cwt., 10 cwt. or ton lots of best Shilbottle! On more than one occasion Mam had altercation with coal-men on this point! The same men had to be strong, for delivering coal often meant a climb up a flight of anything between five and twenty-five steps, with another twenty or thirty yards to take them to the coal-house! The sloping site was to blame for this.

When it came to the naming of the new streets of houses 'over the station' there was little difficulty for us in identifying the folk that lived in them. Pentland, Grampian, Cheviot Avenues were a give-away! Many were Maryhill Glaswegians, who had left their distant homes and clans-folk for work. We called the area 'Scotch Town', or 'The African Village!' Why this epithet? I can only hazard that the wag who thought it up had visited the Newcastle Exhibition of 1931, where a real African Village was part of the attractions!

A recent letter I received from Bill Jelley, a childhood pal, puts a new slant on the story. I quote: 'Billingham was transformed from a village to a mighty chemical complex. All the Scots set up their clans over the station, and most of the Wallsend men [*Bill's folk were from this Tyneside town*] lived this side. I.C.I. was a saviour. It gave men work and respectability, and also did the locals a powerful good. Stockton particularly was revived. Well, undoubtedly, I.C.I. were very good employers and treat their workers fair and just, and I'm speaking from experience.'

Of course, there were apocryphal stories to back up the 'African Village' appellation. Residents were said to keep coals in the bath, or pigeons in the bathroom. (There was an open fire-place in both of the main bedrooms, usually lit when folk were ill in bed.) Some even went so far as to say one party kept a pony up there!

There was also the story of the housewife confronted with the new facilities who put the washing into the bowl, pulled the chain and, dumbfounded, watched the lot disappear before her very eyes! Now, as I write, I realize we were the 'innocent country-bumpkins' to believe such tales. For the ex-Glasgow citizens must have been more familiar with what was to us a modern marvel, even if they had had to share the toilet in their tenements.

Other sections of the new town, north-easterly and east of The Green, had streets with a more familiar ring about their names – Teesdale, Weardale, Ullswater, Windermere, Rydal and Stokesley. Especially intriguing were the local names preserved in streets – Belasis Lane, Chilton and Tibbersley Avenues – as they all recalled former farms, taken over by ICI for the establishment of their new factory. Scientists whose work had led to the development of the chemical industry elsewhere were honoured in street names like Brunner, Mond and Roscoe.

Most of these latter streets were well enough known to us, as they were either just across Mill Lane or close to our school. The heart of our world was circumscribed by New Road, Mill Lane, The Green, Chapel Lane and the bypass, which led back to the bottom of New Road. The Beck and the fields adjacent to New Road and the bypass gave us a bonus freedom area.

CHAPTER TEN

By Bus to School

NEITHER TOPOGRAPHY NOR GEOGRAPHY was the first concern of my parents. With the move to Billingham, schooling was the major question. I had already started at Hartburn and Eric would not be long in following. In Billingham a new school was just being built which ultimately would have a combined roll of 2,000 pupils (infants, primary and senior), all accommodated in one extensive building. The children were the offspring of parents who had been attracted by offers of work in Billingham with ICI, and the lure of a brand-new house. The 'School-on-The-Green', or the Church School as we knew it, was full. There was talk of places at Port Clarence, four or five miles to the east. If I was going to have to travel, the obvious solution was to keep me at Hartburn.

Hartburn it was. I should have to take the bus from the 'Top of the Bank'. As far as I was concerned, this meant leaving the house at eight o'clock for the 8.20. Any other seven-year-old could have reached the stop in less than ten minutes, just walking; but I had to have plenty of time so as not to be late and miss the bus. The trauma of the episode of the Eclipse of the Sun had left its mark! At the stop in front of the Nesco pavilion I joined a short queue of grown-ups going off to their work in Stockton or beyond.

It has taken nearly fifty years for the wheel to turn full circle. Private enterprise was the fashion in those days. So we had different bus companies serving the route into Stockton, like the 'United', 'Triumph', 'Bloomers' and the Stockton Corporation. I aimed to catch the 'United'. The others, following within the next ten minutes, were a comforting safeguard if I missed my bus or it was already full. It had come from West Hartlepool, and there was a good mile of route, with stops, from the north to the south end of Billingham.

The 'United' was a through-bus from West Hartlepool to Darlington, so I had no problem of changing buses in the town. ('Down the town', 'in the town' and 'from the town' were all expressions relating to Stockton. We never referred to Billingham in those terms.)

If I did have to change from one 'United' to another, or from a 'Triumph', it was most convenient as both companies used adjacent stances in front of the Vane Arms Hotel in Stockton High Street. The least handy was the 'Corporation', which stopped short of the Vane Arms, at the Town Hall, leaving a bairn to negotiate a few hundred yards of busy crowds of morning office and shop workers.

Fear of missing the bus was one thing. Fear of getting on the wrong one was another! Luckily the buses of each company had their own livery. 'United' buses were red. 'Triumphs' were yellow and later changed to a brown. 'Corporation' buses were a deeper chocolate brown. I kept an anxious eye on the stretch of road in front of the 'Sally' (the Salutation Hotel) since the bus came past it from the stop on The Green. The 'Triumph' also came the same way. The 'Corporation' came direct from the east, from its terminus at Port Clarence at the Durham end of the Transporter Bridge. This bus was easier to see, as the road to Port Clarence ran straight towards the top of Mill Lane from the Bank, along South View.

It was two miles from the centre of town to Hartburn School. The bus dropped me off at the stop by the Fairfield Back Lane cross-roads, so that I only had about four or five hundred yards to walk up the lane. Crossing the road was the most dangerous part of the journey, but nothing like the perilous move in today's traffic. The return journey gave me no problems, as there was no road to cross. Gradually I came to recognize drivers, conductresses and inspectors, as they worked on a regular rota. They knew me, since I was the only child travelling from Hartburn to Billingham.

Whether it had been something that I had eaten in my packed lunch, or whether I was sickening for some childish ailment, one day on the way home in the bus I had a 'dose of the trots', a touch of diarrhoea! I must have smelt a 'fruity' travelling-companion! I came home to Mam, waddling in at the back-door, to greet her with the news in a woebegone voice, 'Mam, I've filled my pants!'

Another memory of those days on the buses was the occasion of the autumn floods of 1927, when our bus sloshed to a halt, midway across Billingham Bottoms. (The A19 crossed this swampy stretch on three humpy bridges, where separate arms of The Beck flowed. It was always exciting to rush for the back seat of the bus, for the fun of bouncing up as it went over the 'switch-back'.)

This time the atmosphere was altogether more sinister for a youngster. The autumn sky was grey with rain and darkening every minute. Grey muddy water swirled about the exit-steps. Would the bus be swept away? We knew the water was deep, as to have reached the top of the bank side the water must have risen a good six feet above the normal level of its flow. Now it was a good three feet above that. I did not know it then, but it was quite likely that the extra flush of water from further up the county had met with the rising tide from the river, which had its normal 'high point of tide' just three fields across from our house! In the end, much to my relief, another bus came and towed us to safety.

As I was now away from home all day, Mam packed me some sandwiches in a little brown attaché case of pressed cardboard. My favourites were slices of home-made bread spread with butter and mashed banana, softened with sugar to make it spread more easily. On other occasions a raw egg went into the case, carefully cushioned against breakage and wrapped, with the injunction, 'Be careful and see you don't get it broken!'

Perhaps there were half-a-dozen of us who stayed for lunch. Some came in from the Darlington direction from Elton or Long Newton. Mrs Rudman herself had to stay, as her home was in a totally different direction at Eaglescliffe. When eggs were on the menu Mrs Rudman set a little pot on the schoolroom fire and gently placed the eggs together in it. They were to stay until they were hard-boiled. That would avoid any messiness.

One lunch-time, when the eggs were being boiled, Mrs Rudman decided to try out our knowledge of 'times-tables' by asking us the question, 'If it takes three minutes to boil one egg, how long does it take to boil three eggs?' We were all familiar with the chorus, 'One three is three, two threes are six,' and so on up to twelve times. (It never struck me then that twelve times was an important stage. Of course! It helped in understanding 'pennies and shillings' and 'feet and inches'!) Proudly I answered, 'Nine minutes, Miss.' What a clown I felt when she retorted, with a laugh at my expense, 'No! It only takes three minutes. You put them all in the pot at the same time!' In school life there were to be more catch questions like that, which had nothing to do with classroom logic but a lot to do with everyday practicality!

After lunch we probably had an hour to fill in before afternoon school. There was ample space in the playground, but we were also free to roam just outside the school. The terrace of houses just opposite, and the wall and lane that ran right round them, gave us a chance in the summer-time for a rare game of 'Catchy-kiss!' Round the block we chased the girls, who ran screeching in that 'Stop-it-I-like-it' kind of way!

My family tease me yet about my amorous pursuit of a rosy-cheeked sturdy beauty with long auburn hair who was called Virginia Clark, daughter of the Rector of Elton. I caught her and gave her a solid kiss. A memory lingers of warm lips and a pleasant warm body-odour on a warm summer's day, for we had been running as fast as our little seven-year-old legs could go! I enjoyed the experience, but whether she did or not I cannot say. It did not lead to surreptitious glances in class, the passing of notes, or even the carrying of her books to the bus after school. This was just an innocent childhood game.

With the new school year, in August 1928, Eric joined me at Hartburn, a fact confirmed by a copy of a letter written to me in 1931 by Mrs Rudman. Eric caused no problems to add to my responsibilities.

From the Infants' class I was promoted a year ahead of my contemporaries. From Miss Stevenson, the senior composite class demanded expertise and alertness, and she had to work out each day's programme carefully to keep the various groups working. Bright youngsters, who were able to finish their allotted tasks in quick time, had the chance of picking up advanced knowledge by listening in to the teacher working with an older group. Such teaching, and the grounding which I had in Hartburn, stood me in good stead when at last the new school at Billingham opened its doors to us. We boys and girls were a motley crowd of Teessiders, Geordies, Tykes and Glaswegians, with the odd Cockney thrown in for good measure. A new phase in our lives was about to begin.

CHAPTER ELEVEN

Billingham Intermediate School

BILLINGHAM INTERMEDIATE SCHOOL was a show-piece of the late 'twenties. Its site, size and architectural features set it apart. One such outstanding feature was readily noticeable by people entering the main gates or passing along the main road in front. It was the school football pitch, sandwiched between two 'squares', each big enough to take a game of cricket or rounders. This grassed area ran the full length of the complex. Corresponding almost in area to the grass were the asphalted playgrounds, smooth surfaces which allowed for netball, outdoor gymnastics and the games devised by our enthusiastic teachers in P.T. classes.

The building itself incorporated three schools with a total population of 2,000 scholars, girls and boys from five to fourteen years of age. Fourteen was the leaving age in non-secondary education.

The school faced south. The middle section housed the infants in side-by-side classrooms, with an assembly hall protruding in the middle. The infants had their own headmistress, Miss Twyneham. At the east end was the Primary quadrangular block, with its counterpart at the west end for the Senior School. If in the mid-thirties we had been able to hover above the school in an auto-gyro, the forerunner of today's helicopters, the school would have looked like a letter 'E' lying on its side.

The wings had classrooms built round three sides of a quad-rangle, which had a lawn in the centre. The walk-way round the lawn, leading to the classrooms, was covered by a glazed veranda. The fourth side of the quadrangle was completed by the assembly-hall-cum-gym, which had French windows opening into the quad. This disposition of rooms allowed open-air assemblies to be held for morning prayers in fine weather. The hall was big enough to take all the classes when it was wet. Cloakrooms were next to the entrance doors from the playgrounds. On the upstairs floor there were art-and-craft rooms and, in the Senior School, a science lab. Toilets and bike-sheds were on the north side of the school, out of sight.

Came opening-day! Mothers with beginners and older boys up to the age of ten, milled around, bewildered. (The girls were in their own yard on the other side of the wing, mixed in with the infants.) Brothers hung together, islands of temporary security in a heaving sea of humanity. Foreign sound-waves crashed about our ears as Geordies lilted away to each other in incomprehensible shouts, whilst Scotties rallied each other uttering equally incomprehensible clan-cries!

As nine o'clock approached, teachers appeared at the head of the steps leading to the cloakrooms. Whistles blew. Voices of authority told us to line up in age-groups. Little by little, order was created out of the chaos. Then they marched us in.

There was a clean smell of newness about the place. Even the ink and the big blue registers where our names were entered had a special smell. And those names! Amongst the 'Browns', 'Jones', 'Smiths' and 'Greens', there now were entered, 'MacGregors', 'MacAndrews', 'McKays', 'MacDonalds' an' a'! Later, as we were appointed class-monitors, we had the job on Friday afternoons, when our own work was done, of checking the totals of 'presents' marked with 'X' and 'absences' marked with 'O', and taking the abstract of these critical details along to the school office.

It was not very long before the school began bursting at the seams as the town grew with the influx of new job-seekers and their youngsters. So gaps were cut in the eastern fence and large hutments were erected outside the paling. Their wooden walls were painted black and the trims − sills and door-jambs − were attractively done out in red. I had a spell in one of these class-rooms. I soon settled into my new environment. Since each group had its own classroom, we easily found our way about.

CHAPTER TWELVE

Personalities at Billingham Intermediate School

MY FIRST TEACHER was Miss Ward, a tall Garbo-like blonde without any hang-ups about 'wanting to be alone'! It was in her room that I got the 'stick' for the one and only time in my school career. A proper 'good boy' was I!

It was during a lesson in long division. Neil McAndrew and I sat side by side. We both had the same answer, and we both had it wrong! One of us had 'copied', a heinous crime! With Miss Ward there was no nonsense about 'owning up'. We both got one stroke across the palm with the cane. And that was that!

She was also hot stuff on English, encouraging us to use 'big' words in our compositions. My recollection is certainly of a 'big' word – 'gigantic' – used in describing the superstructure of some big ship, possibly the *Mauretania*! And how neat then was my big round style of handwriting! That was long before university courses forced me into an illegible note-taking scrawl!

We were to meet Miss Ward's brother, Horace, in the Senior School. He also taught English. Plump, where she was sylphlike, with a fleshy, porky, face, he was fond of cracking jokes, even 'naughty' ones. There was a craze current for a question-and-answer type of joke. It went, 'Knock! Knock!' – 'Who's there?' – 'Percy!' – 'Percy who?' – 'Percy Vere!'

Horace had us convulsed with his 'Knock! Knock!' for, in answer to our 'Who's there?', came the reply, 'Peter.' 'Peter Who?' we all bellowed. 'Peter Knight!' and then a pause ... 'before you go to bed!!!' We were completely knocked off balance at such an enormity, but not for long. We just howled with laughter!

Of course, everything that happened or was told at school was duly reported back at home to mams and dads. No doubt some mams and dads were properly shocked at this titbit. Mam and Dad feigned disapproval, but I should like to bet that that one was a new addition to their own private repertoire, for Dad to pass on to his workmates.

Our pals, too, provided us with novel jingles and jokes. Eric may have risked reciting a Scottish dialogue, learnt perhaps from the younger Mills, his class-mate. It went, 'Who farted?' − 'Wee Anna.' − 'Do it again, Ann!' − 'Ah canna!' − 'God bless yer wee bum!'

My male mentor in the Junior School was Mr F.W. 'Bill' (or 'Pop') Lister, a sharp-featured, bespectacled, bright-eyed, enthusiastic teacher from somewhere up-County − possibly from Spennymoor or Chester-le-Street. In later years he became a local celebrity as the author of a couple of novels, *These Four Shall Die* (based on the Roman Occupation of Northern Britain) and *Shadow over Spennylam* (which portrayed life on the dole in the 'thirties in our part of the country). The unemployed in the mines and shipyards of the North-east were only too familiar with this picture.

In the excitement and enthusiasm of teaching his subject, Bill was likely to foam at the mouth. Pupils in the front row were almost in need of an umbrella as he spat out his words in his zeal! He spoke with a nasal sound which must have grated and, at the same time, penetrated to effect! The last report I had of him, quite a few years ago now, was of his appointment as Chaplain to the Dutch University of Leyden!

Another of our heroes in the Junior School was Mr Dixon, not to be confused with the Mr Dixon of the Church School on The Green! He was of much slighter build, yet a sportsman − our Saturday morning arch-enemy, as he ran the rival football team! Our Mr Dixon was a big burly fellow, who just oozed strength. Despite his bulk and weight, he moved about the classroom like a cat, almost soundlessly, so we had to be on our guard not to be trying any under-desk mischief. You did not want him hauling you out in front of the class for the cane! He played as a full-back for Bishop Auckland, a team that was noted for its giant-killing propensities, especially at home when drawn to play against professional sides in FA Cup matches!

Two incidents connected with the time I was in his class stand out in my mind. For parents in any age, keeping children in footwear is a major problem. Not only do they grow quickly out of their shoes, but boys especially hasten on the process by kicking any kickable movable object.

Somehow, somewhere, Dad had heard of the long-wearing characteristics of clogs. These were not Dutch-style clogs, as romantically depicted in the scene of 'The Boy Who Plugged the Hole in the Dyke'. No! These were the work-a-day clogs of the mill workers in Lancashire and the West Riding. Stiff leather uppers were attached to wooden, iron-rimmed soles with pointed toes. What humiliation to be at the end of the line as we filed back into the classroom! Left, clump, right, clump, clump! clump! clump! clump!! We went on our way to our desks amid the gawping silence of our peers. There was no relief. We just had to grin and bear the mortification. It soon wore off though. Only then did we realize the double bonus of our footwear — the warmth those wooden soles afforded and the sheer delight of sliding on winter playgrounds, thanks to the iron rims. Today, the bonus still exists, but much more stylishly and healthily, to judge by what Mr Scholl says!

The other incident was extramural. Jean Smiddy was a 'smasher', and in my class. This time, she *was* a girl to be gazed at surreptitiously, whose company was to be sought on the way home — but, for me, at a distance. I was not bold enough!

Opposite the new police station the roadmen were re-aligning the kerbing of a junction. The long kerbstones lay higgledy-pig-gledy in a heap. Here was a test of balance, a typically boyish ploy! I would cross the heap walking on the upturned edges of the blocks. I reached them as Jean walked with a pal on the other side of the road. I began to show off. Looking for approval I took a false step, slipped suddenly and banged the side of my head against a kerbstone. I felt a trickle of something wet down my cheek. I had nicked a piece out of my left ear. The scar is still there.

Many a night, on my way home from school, I wandered by her house in Rydal Avenue, mooning about her gate. It was all to no avail! During the War she married a Canadian!

'Pa' Wilkinson was our music teacher. Short, smartly dressed, he was an artistic type with a full head of neatly-groomed wavy hair which was showing signs of grey. One day he had the whole lot of us in his room. 'Come here!' he called to Tom Hornby, a slip of a Geordie with a piping falsetto voice. 'Get up on the table and sing them your song!' Tom needed no second bidding. Up he climbed, and straight away launched into one of the most amusing-sounding songs I had ever heard − 'We went to Blaydon Races, 'Twas on the ninth of June, 1862 on a summer's afternoon ...' Strange Geordie phrases, like 'gannin' to Blaydon Races ...' and 'We went back ower-hyem', stuck in my mind.

Many years later I was to buy a record of the 'Geordie National Anthem', sung by the Five Smith Brothers. To its lilt I have set verses of my own concoction telling of family doings or personal events, as when I had to undergo a course of ultra-violet treatment for a skin complaint.

In the 'Skins' department of Ninewells Hospital, Dundee, I had to step inside a cupboard of ultra-violet-ray tubes, clad in nothing more than a pair of dark goggles! Earlier, I had taken two tablets that reacted with the violet light. This is called 'Photo-chemo-therapy'! So ...

> Photo-chemo-therapy, it is an awfu' name.
> They put you in an oven, your hormones for to tame.
> Nursie turns the switches on; she does it with some flair.
> Twenty minutes − overdone, fifteen − medium rare!

Eric must have moved up from the Infants into the Junior School before I left it. Even though there was only an age difference of two years, younger brothers at that stage were 'small fry'. In any case, they had their own pals and played their own games together in the yard.

I loved school. Learning came relatively easily to me. In later years I felt sorry that I had been held up as a model of academic achievement to my kid brother. 'You're not like Donald!' Of course he was not! He had his own qualities which came to light later on.

Later, as a teacher myself, I was often in a similar position of having younger members of a family following their elders. I tried to avoid any reference to or comparison with elders, though I kept a mental note of them. It was often useful to be forewarned!

Joyce was quite another problem. She was five years younger, so she came to start in the infants' while I was in the senior school. In the beginning she did not take at all to coming to school! Many a time, in the first weeks, someone would shout, 'Hey, Don! Joyce has run away back home!' Off I had to go and fetch her. There were quite a few times when I had to drag her, howling, past the whole senior school lined up to go into assembly!

Like Eric, she too suffered comparison with big brother; but, for Joyce, most of it was like water off a duck's back. She had a strong, open personality. A lover of sports, she was a popular player in team-games for girls such as netball, which she eventually played at county level.

The day came when my class was moved up to the senior school, where we were to prepare for the 'Scholarship' exams. The main difference in the school programme was that we had specialist teachers for subjects, as we were later to have in the 'Sec'. A question on everybody's lips was, 'Who've you got for … ?' I had Miss Humphreys for English, Dudley Chapman for Maths, Mr Davison for Art, and Mr Hurt for Geography. At that stage, however, Maths and English were the main subjects, as they formed the basis of the three papers of the 'Scholarship' − Composition, English Grammar and Arithmetic.

Inside the classrooms sat fifty pupils, boys and girls in five double rows of desks and chairs. (One of the last drills of the day was to put the chairs on top of the desks to make the cleaners' work easier.)

The row nearest the door usually held the top pupils in the class. From this 'élite' in the eleven-year-old group the Staff would expect to see the future Scholarship winners. Competitors were entered from the schools in Stockton Borough and the surrounding urban districts. For a total population of 100,000 there were about seventy-five places in the 'Sec' and a similar number at the 'Grammar'.

The unsuccessful in the competition stayed on in their schools till the age of fourteen, when they tried to find employment of one sort or another. Many began their working life in menial jobs, but by dint of hard slogging at night-school, after a day's work in the factory, they made the grade.

A typical example, who had a good start by being apprenticed in ICI, was an old class-mate of mine, Bobby Bell. He had been in the same top row in class. Some twelve years after our Billingham Intermediate days, we were walking together up New Road. I had completed my studies at Manchester University. 'Congrats on your degree,' said Bobby. 'Look, Bob,' I replied. 'If there is anybody going to take hats off to anyone, I'm taking mine off to you! I was at University, where I had nothing else to do but get stuck into my studies; but you − you put in a full eight-hour day at the factory, and then went three or four nights a week to the Constantine (the Technical College in Middlesbrough) to end up with a B.Sc. Engineering! You're the one that deserves the congratulations!'

Even years later, when I was teaching in Lerwick in the Shetlands, I heard news of another old classmate. Fred 'Dickie' Walker had climbed 'well up the BP ladder', according to my informant Mr Manson (a colleague of Dickie's and a Shetlander).

Ron Davy of No. 24 New Road did not make it to the 'Sec', but went to the 'Grammar' instead. He ultimately gained qualifications as a chartered accountant. Today I am sure he could buy me up − lock, stock, and barrel.

In the senior school we began to take an interest in the private lives of our teachers. Rumours were rife that 'Mr So-and-so' was keen on Miss 'X'. We would probably see them always together holding the finishing-tape at the school sports, or they just happened to be paired off as house-master and house-mistress. Probably there was truth in the rumours. The Staff had quite a number of young unattached members, of both sexes, who might have known each other during training college days. Few had accents that showed they were from further afield than County Durham. We were quite disappointed when two favourite teachers did not make a match of it. The one married someone outside of the school circle. The other remained single throughout my school-days, as far as I know.

What must have been a unique incident in the annals of the school happened one day in a senior classroom. Over a period of time the younger lads were being bullied at playtime by a right Glasgow 'keelie', a real tough nut. Our teacher had the answer. He sent for the offender. Then he picked out four or five of the biggest lads in our class. Ben Gamble was one of them, a lad who could 'look after himself'. 'Right,' said the master. 'Sort him out!'

The boys piled in, fists flailing from all sides. For a moment the centre of the floor was a swirling mass of bodies, the bully in the middle. Perhaps like bullies in general he was a coward. Or, maybe, he felt that he was 'on a hiding to nothing'. If he had defended himself successfully the teacher might have administered his own punishment afterwards. Instead he called a halt, gave him a stern warning about future bullying, and dismissed him. There was no more trouble in the yard!

It had not been a question of any anti-Scottish feeling. Many of our best pals were Scots. George Mills was one. We were sure of a right warm Glasgow welcome from his mam, anytime that we called in at his home in Roscoe Road.

One of our greatest heroes on the football field, playing with the school team at an inside-forward position, was Ned Kelly, a fiery, red-headed Scot. The bully was just an odd man out. Is there a lesson today for muggers in the way that the punishment was meted out to fit the crime?

For senior school boys, a man who struck dread in every heart was Mr Carling. He was the deputy-head, a disciplinarian who ruled with a rod of iron. When he was on the prowl round the veranda, silence descended on turbulent, teacher-less classes like the stillness cowering round a field mouse that senses the hawk hovering overhead. During his turn of duty for line-supervision in the playground, we dared not flinch a muscle, turn a head or lose our dressing in the line. A peremptory bark, and we were heading for his room and the cane! Yet I fancy that Joyce told me the girls could twist him round their little fingers!

The man who was in charge of this whole complex was of a stature which measured up to the responsibilities. Mr Warwick had 'presence'. His leonine head was topped with a wispy thatch of white. When he dropped in on a class, or spoke from the assembly rostrum, his wide mouth stretched to the full extent of its elasticity as he clearly enunciated his words, accompanied by broad sweeps of the arms. Clear diction was his password through school. The Durham lilt, that played the tune to his words, held me spellbound.

He had a large nose. The weight of it and of his broad head may have accounted for his gait! He always seemed to be tilted forward, like a runner in a long distance race who leans into the start to get the best advantage. His feet moved rapidly beneath, as if trying to catch up with his head so that he would not fall on his face. Quite an unmistakable gait!

Some years later, after the death of his wife, he married Miss Twyneham, the head of the Infants' School. On retirement they left the North Country and settled on the South Coast. He died in his nineties.

Throughout the period of my schooling in Billingham I was privileged to have such a fine band of teachers. I kept in touch, bringing to them at the end of each term the reports of my progress at the 'Sec'. Even after my school-days were over I maintained the link. In the early months of 1944, when home on indefinite leave from the RAF, I offered to give a hand in teaching, back in the old school!

With so many teachers called up on war service, staffs were below strength. Winter usually played havoc with attendances, in any case. So it was that one afternoon, in the senior school assembly hall, I had to keep control not of one but of four classes, about two hundred youngsters. My service-life came to the rescue. I 'shot them a horrible line' about my recent flying experiences as a trainee pilot in South Africa! It has just struck me to wonder if any of those pupils remember the occasion. What was their reaction, their opinion?

My leave lasted long enough for me to help out quite a few times. I even assisted in French classes for Mrs Dodds. I had embarked on studies to lead towards language teaching after the war. In some small way, I suppose, I was able to repay something of the debt I owed to my teachers for their guidance and encouragement some ten years earlier.

CHAPTER THIRTEEN

Playground Games

SCHOOL was not just classwork. Playtime breaks came mid-morning, at dinner-time and mid-afternoon, when out came the marbles, the fag-cards or blocks of wood. The blocks took the place of tennis-balls or 'spongeys' for football, because there was a risk a ball might fly high and break a window.

Though girls were not quite so boisterous as the boys, they were nevertheless just as energetic, skipping-ropes being well to the fore. They did not play at kicking games, but showed amazing dexterity and nimbleness in catching games – throwing a ball into the air, pirouetting beneath, and even allowing it to bounce under their skirts before catching it safely. Such a move might be 'sevensers', the hardest in a progressive series of catching, spinning and bouncing manœuvres which began with the easiest and most straightforward at 'onesers'. Having our own sisters, and often joining in this type of game particularly, to hear, 'I'm on twosers, what are you on?' could indicate that the questioner had either just begun the game or was making an awful hash of it without making any progress!

Endless games of 'tee-mac-and-ally-oh', probably better known as 'relevo' elsewhere, had us chasing and dodging about the yard most of the year round. The ritual of choosing sides for this game devolved upon the fastest runners or most popular captains (who knew the best players). Ben Gamble and Dickie Walker were quickly picked. Little 'titchies' were not despised. They could quite easily hide in a crowded playground, to dart out suddenly and unexpectedly and 'relieve' their side's prisoners, held captive in the 'den'. 'Titch' Blakey might have been just such an asset.

Sides were often maintained throughout the playtime breaks, not only for a day, but even for a week. This game was so popular that I have seen myself dash home for dinner (a good mile from school), gulp the meal down, then rush back to school again to take it up where we had left off!

'Mount-a-kitty', an energetic game, came to be banned as dangerous. One team made a line of 'backs'; the other side jumped astride them, trying to make the 'backs' collapse as the chant went up, 'Mont-a-kitty! Mont-a-kitty, one, two, three' (repeated three times), 'all off, all off, all off me!' The danger was to the 'backs', since the 'jumpers' tried to land as many of their men as possible on the weakest 'back', in order to keep the right to jump.

Autumn and the falling leaves found us lads scouting around in the village and countryside for signs of 'conkers', or 'cheggies' as we called the fruit of the horse-chestnut. We did not have the patience to wait for them to fall to the ground, but had to be throwing sticks and stones up at the laden branches, much to the annoyance of private house-owners who had the misfortune of harbouring chestnut trees at the road-side edges of their gardens.

Once we had arrived home with our loot, we set about the process of hardening the 'conkers'. There were two or three tried recipes. Some lads baked them in the oven to harden them. Others soaked them in vinegar. Whatever methods used could be of little avail when we were faced by an unscrupulous challenger.

The great thing in a contest was to get the call of 'Fuggy (first) Swipe' in before an opponent did. We might be holding a 'thirty-sixer', a battle-scarred remnant of what had been a shiny, polished chestnut, carefully pierced and strung on a cord. It had thirty-six scalps to its credit. Along came the unscrupulous one, often a bigger fellow. He would succeed in winning the call. Proudly we would hold our champion forth; then – swipe! down would swing the opponent's nut, unerringly striking and shattering our valiant campaigner. It was a nut all right, a three-quarter inch hexagon of steel, tied to a piece of string, craftily hidden behind the cheat's back.

In winter, to slide on the smooth schoolyards was bliss, as they had a slight slope towards the school building. Teachers entering the school, along by the school walls at the end of the slope, were none too happy at the prospect of measuring their lengths on what fast became a sheet of ice! It did not take long, on a frosty morning, for half a dozen boys to make a slide twenty or thirty yards long, with a surface like polished glass!

The fun was fast and furious as we each took our turn and made a run for it, swishing along either upright or down in a 'dolly', on our hunkers, jumping clear at the end to avoid being swept off our feet by the next slider going flat out. Our breath steamed in the raw morning air. Well wrapped up in long scarves, bonnets covering our ears, we were 'roasting' with the exercise.

It must have cost parents a fortune in boot-leather, though some of our dads did their own cobbling at home. One answer was to tack hobnails or 'segs' onto the soles.

In summer-time, parents were pestered to buy us sand-shoes –

simple black or brown plimsolls or stouter thonged sandals with crêpe soles. This was to make us fleeter of foot for the summer games of chasing and dodging, and for the school sports or other athletic events, whether organized at Sunday School picnics or by ICI departments.

Demanding less energy was the collecting of 'fag-cards'. Each pack of ten or twenty cigarettes, put out by W.D. & H.O. Wills under such brand names as 'Gold Flake', 'Capstan' or 'Players', contained a picture-card, with a legend on the back relating to the picture. 'Willie Woodbines', manufactured by the same firm, only had five 'cigs' in a pack, so they did not offer the 'card' bonus!

The oblong cards, one and a half by two and a half inches, came out in series to form sets of fifty cards. Wild Flowers, Butterflies, Wonders of the World, Inventors, Inventions, Famous Sportsmen, Cricketers, Footballers (and other personalities), were portrayed in natural colours. There was a fund of knowledge to be acquired from reading the reverse sides.

We used to save the cards up and swap our 'doubles' for the ones we needed to complete the sets. In our pockets we carried a slip of paper with the 'wanted' numbers pencilled on it. Grown-ups who smoked would be pestered at home. In the street complete strangers, puffing at fags as they walked along, would be accosted by laddies with, 'Got any fag-cards, Mister, please?' Bolder collectors hung about tobacconists' shops. I understand that today such sets of cards, in pristine condition, are changing hands amongst collectors for a small fortune!

With cards that were 'doubles', or from out-dated sets, we played a number of games involving a fair degree of skill. A card was set up against a wall, for players to topple from a line four or five paces back. The winner picked up all the unsuccessfully-thrown cards lying by the wall.

In another game, the object was to pitch a card to fall across an opponent's card. Again the winner picked up all the cards thrown.

Pitching a card the furthest had its devotees. For success, good stiff cards were a must. One also had to have the knack of flicking the cards, held between index and middle fingers. Some of that knack came back to me as a teacher when I returned exercise-

books to their owners, flicking books accurately the length and breadth of the room. Heads ducked to avoid a scalping!

Marbles began to appear in the springtime. The smooth surface of the schoolyard was an ideal marble-pitch. A circle about a foot in diameter was drawn. Inside the ring we put our stakes, or 'dakes' as we called them. These were small clay marbles − blue, brown, red and green. For a few coppers we could buy a bagful. If we were in winning form we could take home another bagful of our opponents' marbles, to be gloated over as we counted them!

We played from a base-line, three or four paces away from the circle. In turn we aimed to knock the marbles out of the ring with our 'boss' marble, which might be a steel ball-bearing, up to three-quarters of an inch in diameter. But mostly we played with 'glassies' − self-coloured green ones that had once been stoppers in an old-fashioned type of lemonade-bottle. Other glass alleys had a whorl of coloured stripes through the centre core. A 'blood alley' was a pure red one and a rarity; hence the term applied to a person who was a 'top-notcher': 'he or she is a right blood alley!'

A player continued his play until he failed to knock any more marbles out of the ring. An expert might clear the lot at one go, before anybody else had had a chance! If your alley knocked marbles out, but did not clear the ring itself, then it was 'fat'. You had to replace the marbles and await a fresh turn.

The big ball bearings were not always the most effective. They often went 'fat', though they had probably scattered the marbles all over the yard! The other limiting factor in their use was the method of pitching. We were not allowed to bowl the alley open-handed. It had to be flicked by the thumb joint, with the index finger holding the thumb like a trigger. The sheer weight of the big 'steelies' made this a difficult flick.

An opponent also had another trick up his sleeve with his call, 'Three fingers flat!' The player now had to flick his alley in the usual way, but holding the remaining three fingers of his hand to the ground. Try it, and you will see how effective was the shout! The counter-cry, 'No fingers!' had to be shouted first.

There were youngsters who had little interest in vigorous play. In pairs and groups, they spent their time swapping things – cards, birds' eggs, foreign stamps and so on.

A secretive few sought the concealment of the lavs to have a crafty puff at a fag. Official retribution, when culprits were discovered, followed swiftly and summarily. One addict of a tender age, Puncheon by name, was warned in the Junior School that he would never grow up if he did not stop smoking! It would be interesting to meet up with him now, fifty years later, to see whether the warning had fulfilled the teacher's prophecy.

An event in our own young lives put me off smoking for ever. Dad had left a full-size 'Capstan' on the fender, in front of the fire. I could have been only six or seven at the time. Eric was with me. We egged each other on to emulate Dad! A good draw filled our lungs. In next to no time my head was spinning. I was feeling sick and turning green! Eric was in similar plight. If the fender had not been in place we should both have fallen into the fire!

Eric was not fully deterred. Like the other lads he picked up 'dumpers' from the gutter, extracted the unsmoked tobacco and rolled his own! Ro and Tom Arnott had a favourite 'weed' –

cinnamon leaves, tightly rolled, that gave off a whiff of exotic perfume!

This was all a sign of 'growing up'. Only too soon, for many, the playground would be nothing but a happy memory as they tried to come to terms with the outside world.

CHAPTER FOURTEEN

School Sports

WITH OUR OWN sports field on the premises, organized games were a prominent part of school life. 'Pop' Lister ran a junior football team and made me captain. Oh, yes! I was the captain, and so were the other ten! We all shouted for the ball. The goalie did not. It came his way more often than he liked!

We did not have the refinement of World Cup teams, playing pat-ball between backs and goalie to waste time. There was a lot of honest endeavour, joyous shouts of victory, or the gloom and despair of defeat. At half-time, gathered round 'Pop', we would listen as, frothing at the mouth, he articulated and gestured the strategy for the second half.

However, when the Senior School 1st XI was playing at home, school football really came alive. The well-established Stockton schools were in for a shock the moment our lads made an appearance in the local league. Bousfield, Oxbridge and Tilery had all ruled the roost in turn, over the years. They had some big strapping players, brought up in some tough quarters of the town, so were not likely to be 'easy meat'. Still, they had never had such a source of talent to draw on as we had − Glaswegians, who imbibed football with their mother's milk; Geordies, inspired by one of the best teams in the First Division, 'The Magpies'; plus the talented local lad to fill in the gaps. Our teachers, quite a few of whom were no mean sportsmen themselves, naturally wanted to create a good impression with their virtuosi.

Eric Garbutt, our goalie, must have been an inspiration to the team. The seemingly impossible saves he pulled off made it look as if he had magnetic fingers. Newcastle United were to sign him up some years later. Billy Williams was a wizard on the left wing, jinking round opponents and crossing the ball skilfully with his left foot. Unfortunately, he became a bit big-headed. Ned Kelly darted his fiery way through the centre. Geordie Myers and Geordie Hawksby were great forwards too.

Mrs Hawksby was a keen and vociferous supporter of the lads, and of her own son in particular, when they were playing at home and at Cup matches wherever they played. She is the only mam I remember to show such interest in the game, come rain or shine.

When we started reaching the Final of the Furness Cup, sponsored by the shipbuilding firm at Haverton Hill, excitement reached fever-pitch. This was an evening match on the firm's sports ground, as keenly supported by the fans as a senior local derby match. Some bonny football was seen. 'Professional fouls' would have made as much sense to us as Greek! The words were not in our vocabulary.

Only once did Dad take me to a professional match – Middlesbrough versus Newcastle, at Ayresome Park on Boxing Day 1931 or 1932. At one point, as tempers had become increasingly frayed, Geordie Camsell (the 'Boro' centre-forward) came to blows with United's centre-half, a big Welshman called Griffiths. That did it for me! On our way out from the Park I turned to Dad and said, 'Well, if that's what football is all about, that's the last professional match I'll go and see. I'd sooner watch the lads at school!'

It was a good fifteen years later that I saw another professional game, one Sunday in the Breton capital of Rennes. Even then it was not really so much for the game as for the chance to open my ears to a new line of vocabulary. French, like British supporters, have their own comments to make about the parentage of players or referee! I certainly did extend my vocabulary in the language I was to teach for over thirty years.

In any case, as far as sport went I was not a spectator. I was much happier being out there on the pitch, having a go myself at rugby, soccer, cricket or hockey.

The junior school offered us a chance to play cricket in the summer, but at that level we were just as well off in the 'Rec'.

However, at school there was one novel advantage — we had pads to protect us, an experience that rarely came our way in the 'Rec'.

School sports, however, had a greater impact. The 'House' system was very much in vogue. We all belonged to one of the four 'houses', named after castles in the county. Lambton's colour was blue, Lumley's yellow, Ravensworth's red, and Hylton's green. We wore these colours as shoulder-bands in the events. The relay batons were painted the same.

On the great day, mams and dads were there to cheer us on as we did our bit. It was a colourful throng on a sunny day. Mams and daughters wore summer frocks. Dads were in their shirt-sleeves.

There were plenty of heats at the various distances, to give those of us who fancied ourselves as runners ample scope to prove ourselves. There was great rivalry. We all wished we had the girls' captain, 'Dandy' Foster, in our 'house'. That blonde 'goddess', the girls' champion (especially in the high jump), was in 'Lumley'. We were in 'Lambton'!

The final event of the day, bringing the excitement to a climax, was the Senior Boys' Relay. Often the result here could completely change the destination of the 'House' Cup. One runner, whose performance was crucial, was 'Lolly' Green, the school 220-yards champion. In inter-school sports he could be relied on to bring victory out of apparently hopeless defeat. Of the races I enjoyed competing in, the relay was the one I liked most of all.

Since the sports field was next to the main road, there was always some passer-by stopping to lean on the railings and watch our games. Or, folk would gaze from the top deck of double-deckers, on their way to Cowpen or the Transporter.

It did not matter much which way you travelled. On the opposite side of the road you could look down on the Synthonia Sports Ground, an immaculate area of turf that even hosted a touring Australian cricket side!

CHAPTER FIFTEEN

S. A. & N. Ltd.

IT MAY SEEM STRANGE that so much space and time has been devoted to matters that were peripheral, when the great pulsing heart that kept us all alive throbbed audibly just across the road from the school! On the sides of factory railway trucks the bold letters S. A. & N. stood for Synthetic Ammonia and Nitrates. These two elements, used in the manufacture of fertilizers, proved powerful ingredients later when munitions were needed in the war effort.

Square miles of land, once ploughed and harvested as farms, now carried workshops, production plants, offices, railway-lines, pipe-lines, and roads leading past cooling-towers and reservoirs (misnamed by us bairns as 'resevoys') to coal and coke dumps. All this combined basically in the process of producing the means of artificially manuring the world's acres, to provide much-needed food for starving millions. Ours must have been the biggest chemical factory in Europe, if not in the world! Underneath it lay the essential mineral on which it all was founded − anhydrite.

Dust and stinks! Writing with feeling to me, in his letter of 27th February, 1988, Bill Jelley states,

> I'm speaking from experience. I worked on South Side from 1950 to 1966, as a maintenance-plater, so I worked at times on every plant on the site, and I realize the appalling conditions our parents worked in − the sodium plant, cyanide plant, chlorine plant, filled either with heat and choking fumes or chlorine gas, and the sinister cell-rooms, rows of cells, a clean environment, but an unseen killer, destroying lung tissue. There were deadly plants on North Side too, particularly, coal-oil and ammonia, and you had to be a superman to work in the packing-sheds.

Dad too spoke with feeling after doing maintenance work, like Bill, in the water-gas plant. To me these plants were just names. The only stint I did in the factory was for six weeks in a summer vacation in 1941, as I awaited 'call-up' to the RAF. Even then I only worked in the Stores Department of the Workshops Group, wheeling material to the various workshops – cold draughty places in winter, no doubt, but at least free of obnoxious chemical elements.

We were fortunate to live on the windward side of the factory. It was only when a shift of the wind to the east brought the fumes and the dust that we realized how awful the conditions were for folk living in Haverton Hill and Port Clarence. The dust, borne on the prevailing wind, was so insidious in its fineness that it penetrated inside the windows. It lay thick on the sills. Housewives just gave up the struggle!

The stink came from the nitric acid and sulphuric acid plants. It was often heralded by a dense cloud of yellowish vapour. My Scottish pupils must have been mystified that I never turned a hair when they ventured to drop a 'stink-bomb' in the classroom. More than likely I had smelt more 'rotten eggs' in my time than some of them had breathed fresh air!

Our road was the dividing line between the sites North and South. The North Gate was along Belasis Lane, opening directly to the Workshops Group with its Machine Shop, Tube Shop, Platers' and Boilermakers' Shop, Blacksmiths' Shop and the Stores. Dad and Eric worked in this section for many years, Dad in the Tube Shop and Eric in the Platers'.

The Main Gate was at the top of Roscoe Road, giving entrance to various processing plants for nitric acid, sulphuric acid, ammonia, water-gas and coal-oil. Towering above it rose the chalk-tower, two hundred feet of dusty corrugated sheeting.

About a mile up our road from the house was the South Gate. Opposite to it, sweeping up in flattering curves, were two giant water-cooling towers, King Kong's milk bottles as we called them, visible for miles around. When we passed that way we just had to stop. The concrete walls contained a criss-crossing structure of triangular wooden slats (if only they had been 'Toblerone' chocolate-bars!). Down them the scalding water from the factory processes cascaded in tinkling droplets, growing cooler and cooler as they fell. The cooling vapour rose wraith-like out of the tops of the 'bottles'.

Throughout the factory lay a network of railway-lines that linked into the national layout through the LNER (London and North-Eastern Railway) system. The factory's own shunting-loco-motives bore the names of rivers — Tyne, Tees, Tweed, Taff, Teifi, Trent and so on. Ro Arnott, whom I met recently, recited the whole list and corresponding numbers — a feat of memory, since he was going back fifty years to our childhood!

These little fellows, puffing away with Napoleonic pomposity, thought they were the equal of the big 0-8-0s that pulled the seemingly endless clanking coal-trains from the Durham collieries. We could spend hours on the bridge at the top of our road, waiting for them to appear. A warning-bell, that they all carried, told us of their imminent approach. As they passed under the bridge they swathed us in a smirr of hissing steam, or furious force of funnelled smoke.

All that was the 'Synthetic'. There was also The Beck (which is marked on old maps as the mill-stream), diverted from the main beck to power the wheel of the old mill which gave Mill Lane its name. Sluice-plates controlled its flow near the bottom of Billing-ham Bank, where it passed under the main road and then round the mound of New and Imperial Roads, bringing to the Boiler-house the very essence of its being. The other essential element, Vulcan's power, lay beyond The Beck in miniature mountain-ridges of coal and coke.

We had a front seat at the filling-in of the Bottoms. The white waste from the anhydrite mine-workings had been spread out to form the base for the coal and coke dumps. On dry days, if the wind was blowing in our direction, the fine white dust penetrated our houses, much to the housewives' annoyance!

This catalogue of the component parts of the colossal enterprise is not quite complete. Roads and railways imported the materials and exported their products. Nevertheless, there was another entry and exit, the River Tees. Ocean-going cargo-boats could moor at the Billingham Reach Wharf, off the Port Clarence to Portrack Road, on our side of the river.

Whatever pride the inhabitants of the township felt in the mighty industrial complex, however antipathetic their feelings were towards its domination of their lives, they must have experienced relief to know that the spectre of the 'dole' no longer hung over their heads. Pits might close and shipyards too, by the Tyne and Wear and Tees; the 'Synthetic', puling infant of the early 'twenties, was to exhale its pressured breath, resounding for miles over the countryside, when, two decades later, the 'purple alert' moaned out its fearful wail.

'Well, undoubtedly, ICI were very good employers and treat their workers fair and just.' So writes Bill Jelley. Part of that treatment was shown in the facilities outside work that were offered to employees and their families.

'All work and no play ... ' ICI were well aware of how this maxim runs. Beside and behind the pavilion of the cricket-ground, tennis hard-courts had been laid out in blaize. At the north-eastern end of the ground stood the Synthonia Club and Theatre, with bowling-greens adjacent. The Club was licensed. While enjoying their drinks, men could play at billiards and snooker. Tables were arranged for card-games and dominoes. There were reading-rooms and lounges, all comfortably appointed.

The Theatre facilities were second to none. Club members were provided with a programme of the season's activities – plays, films, lectures and the annual Scout Gang Show, since Synthonia had its own Scout Troop.

Under the floor of the theatre a small-bore rifle-range had been installed.

Beyond the indoor entertainment area were rugger and soccer pitches, with good changing-room facilities and stands for spectators. John Best, the Synthonia's First XV full-back, was capped for Durham County in that position. Bob Coulson, an old classmate, was a Durham County three-quarter.

Hockey, played by both men and women, was accommodated on the cricket-ground, with the 'hallowed' square cordoned off.

Annually, on the same ground, S. A. & N. held the factory sports. The factory departments and plants competed keenly for a trophy. The usual races were run. 'Tug o' War' was an additional event for the 'heavy brigade'. Furthermore, employees' families were catered for. A 'gala' atmosphere prevailed, when the children too competed for prizes, each entering in the appropriate age-group.

At Christmas-time the traditional parties took place in the theatre-hall, organized separately by each department. We had a slap-up feed, played party games, relaxed to watch a conjurer or ventriloquist act, and left for home at the end clutching bags of 'goodies'. That, at any rate, was the highlight of our childhood years. Good old S.A.(&)N.T.A!

CHAPTER SIXTEEN

'Heigh-ho! Heigh-ho! ... '

SEVEN TO EIGHT THOUSAND workers spewed forth when the buzzer went at half-past four for 'knocking-off' time. Some ran to the bus-stances; others walked alone or chatted to workmates on their leisurely way to homes nearby. Yet others, having dismounted from their push-bikes at the white line on the factory side of the gate, trundled their machines across the 'No-Go' space (a traffic safety-area), then remounted, a work-worn, care-worn, jocular, gloomy, youthful, aged 'peloton', the 'massed bunch' whose 'Tour de Teesside' was about to begin. For they came from Wolviston, Norton, Stockton, Thornaby, Middlesbrough, Greatham, Haverton and Port Clarence – and even beyond.

This torrent of humanity did not flood back into work with the quarter-past seven buzzer next morning. I do not think there *was* even a 'peloton'. The varying distances, the unwillingness to leave a warm bed, the reluctance to don the yoke, made for a long line of stragglers pedalling on the various roads into work.

If a man was just seconds late in 'punching the clock', which indicated on his time-card the instant of his arrival, he was 'quartered'. (Hanging and drawing did not quite come into it!) He simply lost a proportion of his day's pay.

One morning I was walking up Billingham Bank, giving our dog Mick his morning 'constitutional' before I went to school. It was nearer eight o'clock than seven, so the chap on the racer, coming up the bank, really had his head down as he pushed with all his might on the pedals. I was transfixed – could not utter a sound – yet I knew it must happen. It did! Crash! He rammed into the back of a car parked half-way up the bank! Until the last split second I had expected him to swerve; but his concentration had been too intense.

At No. 10 New Road lived old Bill Buckley. He had a push-bike and a unique style of mounting it. It had a back-step, a spindle that extended from the back axle on the near-side of his bike. Somehow, with surprising ease of movement that belied his years, he pushed off, put his left foot on the step, and swung over the back wheel and onto the saddle, his right foot connecting smoothly with its pedal.

He was a rigger, concerned with scaffolding, ropes and tackle. His was a most essential trade with so much building going on all over the factory.

Dad biked to work as well. He no longer needed the little motor-bike of Hartburn days. He stayed at work at dinner-time. Most workmen had a canteen or sandwich lunch. Some, living closer to home, biked back to snatch a meal in the three-quarters of an hour allotted to the dinner-break.

Then there were the 'walkers'. In our road you could have set your clocks by them. One pair kept the same distance one behind the other, day in day out. Mam nicknamed them 'Mutt and Jeff'.

'Monsewer', Tom and Ro Arnott's dad, always walked to work. A tall, upright, military figure, he was a foreman in the process works. From the 'Sec' I learned to pronounce his title correctly, 'M'sieu'; but to Mam he remained 'Monsewer' to his dying day. The title she gave him, but not in his hearing, showed that he was a cut above the rest; or he may have given the impression that he thought he was!

How far the walkers came, I have no idea. It could easily have been from Norton, a good mile across the Bottoms even to our house, with another mile to the factory gates.

Some of the men who lived beyond cycling distance came to work on motor-bikes. What a roll-call of illustrious names! A.J.S., Matchless, Rudge-Whitworth, Levis, Excelsior, Scott, Triumph and Norton – machines whose fortunes (and those of their riders) we followed in the papers and on the wireless when the annual T.T. Races took place on the Isle of Man.

B.S.A. was a popular bike, its acronym irreverently transposed as 'Bloody Sore Arse'! I often wondered why it bore an emblem of crossed rifles. Only donkeys' years afterwards did I discover that it was a product of 'Birmingham Small Arms'.

We could recognize most machines by their sound − or the lack of it (the hall-mark of the whispering 'Velocette'). The only foreign machine I ever saw in those days, and that rarely (because it was a prestigious vehicle) was the Harley-Davidson from the USA − a smooth, powerful ace of a bike!

Just as vehicles had their identification marks, so the grades of workmen had theirs. Tom Arnott senior wore a trilby − no 'Andy Capp' cloth cap for him! Only working men, not foremen or the management, wore caps. A skilled tradesman went off to his work in his blue overalls. His 'mate' or labourer, who fetched and carried for him, would go about in a jacket and trousers that had seen better days, dirt-stained with oil and grease or anhydrite dust, pock-marked with burns from the sparks flying off welding jobs, or from the spray of acids which rained down through the air in some of the plants.

The office staffs were white-collared, dressed in suits. The ladies of the secretarial departments, and the girls working about the offices, were attractively dressed in the practical fashions of the day or season.

The 'big white chiefs' were the ones most likely to drive to their place of employment in the status cars of the day − Armstrong-Siddeleys, Rileys, or the occasional Daimler.

But, surprisingly, there were others of them who walked to work - bright-eyed and bushy-tailed types, slim and wiry with athletic stride, keen products of the universities or top polytechnics.

Gradually, however, auto-mobility spread down to the tradesmen, especially the electricians, who were well-paid. Frank Dewhirst, a good neighbour in No. 12 and a lifelong friend, was one such. He may have kicked off with a 'Morgan' 3-wheeler. Later, he advanced to a 'Riley 9'. And at No. 14 lived Arthur 'Cock' Clements − 'Cock' because he spoke with the London twang and was on the cocky side to boot. He was another motoring enthusiast, for ever tinkering with an old bull-nosed 'Morris'. He boasted that he had got himself home, after a piston had gone on him, by removing the broken piece and shaping a bit of log as a replacement! I do not remember 'Doo' or 'Cock' using their cars to go to work.

'Well, Alf, what are you working this week?' 'Oh, I'm on days, but they are talking of putting us on to shifts at the end of the month.' 'Days' meant a 7.15 a.m. to 4.30 p.m. stint Mondays to Fridays, with a half day on Saturdays till 12.30 p.m. An average working week could amount to about forty-eight hours. Tuesday and Thursday evenings might see a man called out for overtime at 'time and a quarter' (for every hour worked, he received one and a quarter hours' pay). Saturday overtime came to 'time and a half', with 'double time' on Sundays. Since Dad belonged to the AEU (the Amalgamated Engineering Union) and attended union branch meetings, we heard a lot of the debate about the introduction of a forty hour week.

At our early age, shifts were of much more significance than 40 hour weeks, the 24 hour day being divided into 'six till two', 'two till ten' and 'ten till six'. We felt the effect of it when Dad was on this last shift, working through the night and going off to work when we were sound asleep in bed. He was trying to sleep during our play-hours! And he was not alone. Neighbours might easily be caught up in the system. Gone were the noisy games on the road. We had either to clear off up to the 'Rec' to play, or go down to The Gully or Foster's field.

This daily working routine and a week's summer holiday (the oft inclement Stockton Race Week, the third week in August — for many years without pay) formed the pattern of most men's working lives throughout the 'thirties.

CHAPTER SEVENTEEN

The Cast

THE STAGE is set. The 'noises-off' are in the hands of the sound effects lads — the hissing of steam; the rumbling of carts, lorries and trains; the clip-clop of horses' hooves; laughter; tears; the swishing of skipping-ropes; the rattle of bails falling; battle-cries and cries of triumph; all the rich music of childhood play and tragedy. Some of the players have already peeped round the side of the curtain — not to see if there is an audience, but just to let folk know that there is more to be seen of them! A few may only appear in bit-parts, or flit as ghosts against the back-cloth. Some may need to be satisfied with just a mention in the programme notes. The passing of years, or their early move from New Road to fresh theatres, is to blame.

The Thomases were the first people to dwell in No. 1. Joan and Tony are the only children's names I recall. She was an attractive lass, definitely 'smasher' material. When the Thomases left, the Jeffs moved into No. 1. They were a childless couple, fostering their Dalmatian pack, and attracting kindred spirits like Ro Arnott, who shared their fondness for animals and birds.

When I hear the haunting, trilling call of the curlew over moorland swamp, the place-name 'Brignall' flashes across my mind. After tea one summer's evening, Mr Jeffs took some of us off in his car to Brignall, a hamlet south of 'Barney' (Barnard Castle), 'twixt Greta and Tees, near the 'Meeting of the Waters'. There was a breath of illegality in the air about this expedition. Nothing serious, like a hold-up; perhaps poaching was nearer the mark. Yet even if salmon still made it so far up-stream, and that was doubtful when you saw the muck that poured into the lower river from ICI and all the other factories and townships along the river-banks, we were not equipped for the crime.

Jeffs was 'bird-nesting', eagerly backed by Ro! They were after curlews' eggs! In an effort to preserve the species, officialdom had 'blacklisted' these eggs, hence the illegality of our expedition. Whilst Jeffs and Ro hunted for eggs, the rest of us camped in the car and a little pup tent, spending a cold spooky night in a shallow quarry-hole, out on the wind-swept moor. I think the egg-seekers returned home empty-handed.

Billy McCabe lived at No. 2. He just flits across the stage in the shadow of 'Big Eggie' − Ray Eggleton of No. 12, our neighbour for a short time. Ray was a six-footer, taking after his mam. His tale is quite brief. He was the one who got stung on the head during a brambling trip to the 'Golden Gates' at Wynyard, Lord Londonderry's estate about four miles north of home.

At No. 3 was the Anderson family. There were children there, but they do not figure in this story. The Shipleys took over from them. Young Dennis nearly met a tragic end!

The road was becoming colourful, with the Greens at No. 4 and the Browns at No. 5! Les Brown was an only son, another tall chap who was one of the gang.

The Williams sisters at No. 6 were too old in one case, and too young and solitary in the other, to come among us.

By contrast the Hunters at No. 7 were almost overwhelming in numbers and nature. The eldest, Audrey, was soon to be working behind the bar in a hotel in town. Madge (Marjorie), sister No. 2, was another lass who was certainly attractive to males. Beryl, poor lass, with red-rimmed eyes prone to styes and yellow with matter, was a sorry sight as a girl, yet grew out of this into womanhood − a charming, caring person. Joan robbed Mary of any plumpness she might have had. Mary was a real 'Skinny-Lizzy', but had plenty of energy for the skipping games we all enjoyed. Billy and Gordon were on the young side for joining in with us. They did not share our interests, but figured more in the slanging matches which brought Mrs Hunter to the top of their steps in defence of her brood. Gordon was born in New Road, so he really was a babe amongst us.

Captain Hook in 'Peter Pan' was as large as life at No. 8, for Jackie Lambert's dad had lost an arm. They had fitted a contraption to the stump − a fearsome hook the mere sight of which put the wind up us. Jackie was a biggish white-faced lad with a tendency to precociousness. He once came down their steps into the street brandishing a real six-shooter! The trouble with him was that you were never too sure if a thing like that, in his hands, was loaded or not! Alan Glass and his parents were the next occupants of No. 8.

'Monsewer' Arnott and his family resided at No. 9. The eldest sister, Jean, was something of a mystery to us. She never seemed to be at home at No. 9 but made fleeting appearances from her Gran's in Station Road! Winnie ruled the boys' roost. She made sure they did their share of the chores before they had leave to join us in play on Saturdays. Usually, if we went round to their back door and asked, 'Are Tom and Ro coming out?', the reply was brief, 'Not till they've polished the knives, forks and spoons!'

Bill Buckley and his wife were an elderly couple who lived with their grown-up lad at No. 10. Risbon was something of a celebrity with us. We were living next-door to a champion amateur boxer of one of the lighter grades, bantam- or feather-weight. We shared with him his triumphs when we read that he had knocked out another opponent. He probably was a hero in his plant at the factory with his pugilistic prowess, as he would keep the plant's name to the fore in the sporting championships.

We lived next door at No. 11, the only family whose parents were the first tenants of the house and lived out their lives in it.

Our first neighbours at No. 12 were Frank and Doris Dewhirst, and their forbidding Alsatian, Von. They became cherished neighbours and lifelong friends. When they eventually moved over the river to the 'Boro' (Middlesbrough), the Eggletons took their place. Jim Sorley, his wife, and daughters Jean and Hilda, were our neighbours for a long time afterwards.

Jim Allison, a keen gardener, was at No. 13. Marjorie, his daughter, was another bonny lass. He and his wife had a younger daughter, who did not grow up amongst us as they also shifted house. The Cacketts took their place, Mrs 'doing' for Mam in

Mam's later years when housework became more of a problem as her eyesight dimmed with cataracts.

Arthur 'Cock' Clements was the first to come into No. 14. His eldest, a girl named Flossie (Florence), grew the longest hair I've ever seen. When she combed it out at the back it reached right down to her bum! Her younger sister, May, was at the stage of attracting lads of my age! Joyce, May's kid sister, was as old as our Joyce. Young Arthur, the apple of his father's eye, will appear later on, almost on the point of disappearing for good!

There were two Franks at the Michisons in No. 15 – father Frank (a bit of a wag, always ready to tease) and young Frank (who went seafaring later and, in Colombo, was entertained by a good Cingalese friend of my university days, 'Wally' Wallooppillai!)

Dennis Chapman of No. 16 was an early school pal at Billingham, but his family did not stay long. The Fullertons, another warring faction we had youthful dealings with, also moved on quickly from No. 17, to be replaced by the Corners, with son Ray and his sister Joyce – who must have had no trouble in attracting a good husband, for she was another beauty!

Andy Lamb at No. 18 was cousin to Alan Glass of No. 8. Mrs Glass was a Lamb with a strong 'Geordie' accent and a ready cheery greeting as she passed by along the road.

Here follows a gap, not in bricks and mortar but in memory. At No. 21 lived for a time the Roberts, a Cheshire family. There were boys amongst them, playmates on occasion.

At No. 23 the first tenants were the Timothys, whose stay was marred by tragedy.

Ron Davy was at No. 24. His parents were West Riding folk from round about Leeds. They spoke a cultured tongue, only with a broad-vowelled accent that lent authority to what they said. Mrs D. was a Gomersall. Her brother, 'our' Edgar, was a paragon! He was the cathedral organist in Dundee, which seems to attract fellow Yorkshiremen in that capacity. (Bob Lightband, a Keighley lad and an ex-colleague from Forfar Academy, officiates there now.) Visiting us in our Dundee home, Edgar confessed that at one stage he had been obliged to choose between making a career in music or in professional cricket, a not improbable choice for talented lads in his part of the world, where cricketers abound on the one hand, and Black Dyke Mills Band and Huddersfield Choral Society perform resoundingly on the other. His wife was a keen bargain-hunter. She once knelt at the altar-rails in the cathedral and there, chalked plainly for all to see on the soles of her brand-new shoes, bought in a sale, was the auction lot-number!

Cyril 'Stiff' Meachen, Stan, and young brother John, lived at No. 25. Their dad, Norman, was a little broad chap, another keen gardener. Their mam had lovely russet-apple cheeks. She spoke in a bleating kind of voice that would have fitted her well to be Larry the Lamb's mother in a favourite programme of the BBC's *Children's Hour*. But she always struck me as being like the mother of Rupert Bear, the newspaper-strip character whose adventures were to be followed in the *Daily Express* and feasted on in the *Rupert Annual*, a longed-for gift at Christmas time! She was such a kindly, caring soul!

Vera and Walter Pugh lived at No. 27. Walter joined us in some of our ploys, especially kite-flying.

At No. 31, really at the limits of our playmate zone, Bill Palmer and sisters Winnie and Connie could sometimes be coaxed to join us. Bill's father had been a seafaring man, so it was not surprising that Bill joined the Navy as a boy entrant. Theirs was an extended garden. Two or three standard houses like our own could have been built on it. Perhaps the terrain had not been judged suitable for building; so it remained garden-ground, largely uncultivated, cut in half by a path and trodden without permission to make a short-cut into the 'Rec'. This saved folk the extra yards to the thirty-two steps, the official route.

Over the gap, at about No. 34, lived Gordon Coulter and his big brother. Gordon joined us sometimes in games of football and cricket. Somewhere further along the road, where the houses sloped to Brunner Road, and possibly in this latter, lived Elvin Dove, whose name alone warrants his mention here. In March 1943, on board the troop-ship SS *Strathmore*, somewhere in mid South Atlantic, his accent gave him away. (In Hartlepool, folk tend to pronounce the vowel sound in 'work' to rhyme with 'err';

so the stock phrase runs, 'Me father werrks at the Werrks, and wears a perrple sherrt on the gerrders'!) Elvin had said something on this pattern. He was lounging on deck just yards away from me, with a bunch of soldier pals bound for India, whilst I was with some RAF cadets heading for Durban and training in aircrew duties somewhere in the Union of South Africa. We had not seen each other in the previous five years!

Imperial Road opened into ours, just about opposite Bill Palmer's. The Jelleys lived at No. 5 or 7, a family of boys (Arthur, Jim, Chris, Bill and George). We saw little of the first two, as they were either working or on the threshold of a first job. Chris played a little cricket with us. Like Tom Arnott, he was renowned for his singing voice. Mam once invited him into our house and accompanied him on the piano while he sang. Both Chris and Tom were choristers at St Cuthbert's, and were regularly called upon to sing the anthem at Evensong. I can even now see Chris attempting to retrieve a cricket-ball, hit into the beck and floating close to the bank. He lay in line with the stream, so had little to hold on to. He rolled as nice as ninepence, gently into the water! There is more to say later about Bill and 'Judd' (George, the baby of the family). Further down Imperial Road lived the Tuckers. Tommy was involved in some of our ploys.

At No. 1 Imperial Road (or in one of the 70s of New Road) had lived a lassie, Joyce Waters, who was tragically drowned at the 'water-fall', the man-made barrier in the beck, where the sluice-gates operated. During a freezing period of winter she had fallen beneath the ice on the beck.

The 70s were built on the other side of New Road, over from No. 26. They were on the slope below, so we went down steps to them. In the last house, No. 75, lived the Meads.

The Williams were at No. 73. As it was with the Jelley older boys, we had little in common with the older Williams. I only saw the eldest a couple of times. Jim, the next lad (a rotund figure), was nothing like his sporting brother Bill, the wizard of the left foot in our school 1st XI. Kid brother Alec went to the 'Sec' with me. We met every morning to catch the bus, the 'Workmen's Special', up at the junction of New Road and Mill Lane. Over that three or four hundred yards we kicked a ball to each other across the road to add interest to the stretch. Pa Williams was a Scot, whom I saw on rare occasions sitting in his armchair, puffing at a pipe.

The Worthys lived at No. 71 or 72. Brother Vic was to enthral us with story-telling later.

Certainly, it looks to be a formidable cast of players; yet there are amongst them no Gielguds or Vanessa Redgraves − just a bunch of amateurs who enjoyed lots of fun and much laughter, and shed some tears along the way. I trust that the show will arouse some emotion in a younger generation. I am sure the survivors of ours will not be disappointed.

CHAPTER EIGHTEEN

Gardening and Gardeners

PERHAPS one of the greatest changes for the inhabitants of the new Billingham was that they found they had their own gardens, both front and back, whether they liked it or not. In Maryhill, Glasgow or on Tyneside, dads may have rented allotments, just as they can still do in most of our urban areas.

The local Council had planned roads like Central Avenue (a dual carriageway) lined with trees and the central reservation planted with them too. Furthermore, by planting more trees in every second front garden throughout the estate, it had encouraged tenants to take an interest in their gardens.

The Council workmen planted a sycamore in the corner of our front garden, close to the top of the steps. The planners knew what they were doing, but Dad fancied he knew better! He decided to make it a central feature of our garden, so he moved it! It had never entered his head to look carefully at a sycamore growing in its natural state. He had not realized that the sapling in front of him would become a tall tree twenty or so feet high! Throughout his lifetime in No. 11 the sycamore flourished, casting its shade over the ground floor windows and finally darkening the upstairs bedrooms!

This garden was not a showpiece. In a lawn of sparse grass, that grew even sparser as the sycamore cut out its light, Dad dug two diamond-shaped beds, where he planted roses. They thrived on the clayey soil, old style varieties with lovely blooms and perfume.

A hedge of verbena separated us from No. 12. A low privet hedge grew along the front and from the top of the steps back towards the front door. It did not need to grow tall, since the public footpath was four or five feet below the level of the garden. Looking out from the front windows we could easily see who was passing by; but in the garden we could sit unseen and enjoy the sun.

I had my first success with a packet of seeds in the front. I sowed cos lettuce below the kitchen front window. Behind them a wall facing south, and open to the sun for the best part of the day, was ideal. Of course, a favourite flower was the nasturtium. We also enjoyed the abundant flowering of the tiny gems of Virginia stock, which coloured the border profusely without any attention.

Dad's interest in the back garden was sparked off by my reluctance to go up to the village one evening for a packet of fags. At the time I was at the 'Sec'. I moaned on and on so much about the homework I had to do that he said, 'Well, that's it! Don't bother! And the next time you see me smoking, I'll give you a shilling!' There and then he stopped!

What Mam had to put up with from then on, as withdrawal symptoms took over, I cannot say. He had smoked twenty a day at least. However, before the year was out he had bought a Sutcliffe's 8 feet by 10 feet greenhouse and, with Uncle Charlie's encouragement and advice, was soon into the way of growing 'Kondine Reds', a tasty variety of tomato. His health improved, and so did our diet!

The only snag was that we had to start gathering bags of sheep-muck, which he hung in a water-barrel, to produce a potent brew that had tomatoes fairly bursting out of their skins! (Fifty years on I still have to get round to gathering sheep-muck for my own tomatoes, and there are plenty of sheep handy!)

From tomatoes he went into chrysanths. These grew out in the back garden, then in late summer were transferred to the greenhouse to save them from the frost, rain and wind. We had the whole palaver to learn of disbudding, nurturing of crown-buds, taking side-shoots and pricking them out into pots or boxes to increase the stock, and so on. Yet, when in autumn we saw the size of some of the flower-heads of the incurved whites and yellows, and the colour of the bronzes and reds, with the clinical whiteness of Edith Cavell, we were quite proud of our share in the growing. And those blooms lasted, day after day, week after week, a cheering prospect in winter drabness.

Oh yes, I did catch him smoking again! It was during the war, and I was no longer a laddie. As was his wont, he was sitting in the 'lav' with the door slightly ajar. I came round the corner, smelt the stink of tobacco and caught a glimpse of the glow of the cigarette-end. With a laugh, I chaffed him about it. 'Well, Dad, what about that bob?' He had to laugh too. I did not take it. He admitted that, what with the war and the pressure of work and his responsibilities as a charge-hand, he had surrendered to the 'weed'. It was only a truce. Once things went back to normal he never smoked again!

Mam's interest in the back garden was partly floral and partly pyrotechnical! She was left in peace to cultivate her own border up the back garden path. There her flowers must have been an uplift as she possed, shook mats, cranked the handle of the old mangle, carried in scuttles of best Shilbottle, and lugged baskets of damp washing up the back steps to the clothes-line strung alongside the path.

The night of the Fifth of November (Gunpowder, Treason and Plot) was the occasion when Mam performed her pyrotechnical magic! Over the previous weeks, helped by our pals, we had gathered materials for the 'bondie', the traditional bonfire. We cajoled shopkeepers to give us old cardboard boxes. Scraps of timber were scrounged from over the beck. Dead branches were hauled over the fields from the Willow-garth. We combed hedge-rows and lanes. The fact that our garden was the site of the fire was the safeguard that none of the other gangs would raid it and pinch all the stuff we had amassed. This often happened on more open sites. Also, by the end of October, there were no crops of any consequence left growing in the garden.

In the back kitchen Mam prepared a supply of home-made toffee, a concoction of syrup, sugar, butter and vinegar – boiled in a pan. At the right moment, Mam would drop a spot of the boiling mixture into cold water to see how it was setting. Once it was right, flat cake-trays were filled and allowed to cool. Then, 'Let's have the little taffy-hammer and we'll try a bit for size!' This

was a light hammer that Dad used for tapping sprigs into shoes
when he did a bit of DIY cobbling.

The round slabs from the trays splintered into pieces, mostly
very angular, even sharp. We chose the biggest bits we could get
into our mouths (even if it meant we could not speak), with
cheeks wedged apart and throats letting the soft goo of the melt-
ing delicacy slip smoothly down. There would be choking fits as
someone was tempted into breaking silence, and the 'sludgy'
sound they uttered caused the rest to laugh.

Gingerbread was another accompaniment to the festivities,
baked that day and sometimes still warmish from the cake tin.

The fire burning brightly in the kitchen range had its part to
play in the drama. Already Mam, who should have been a black-
smith, had set the long steel poker into the heart of the blaze,
balancing it between the bars of the grate and the fender. Once
the end of the poker glowed bright red she withdrew the steel
expertly, swung away from the hearth and, having ensured a clear
exit through kitchen and back door, darted forth to the pyre. The
'guy' was in for a hot time!

Old newspapers and twigs for kindling burst into a blaze as the
poker plunged into the heap. Even on the dankest of November
evenings, and they seemed to be more often wet than not, Mam

never failed to get the fire going. We just stood and gawped at her skill.

Between us we had a fair array of fireworks, but nothing excessive. Our folk could ill afford throwing good money up into the air. Our limit was a shilling box of mixed fireworks − flower-fountains, volcanoes and Catherine-wheels − displays that were pretty, that did not go off with a 'bang'! and scare the younger bairns. We probably got the best fun out of 'sparklers' − which fizzed delightfully with their own enchantment and were safe to hold, so that we could trace our own imaginative patterns at arm's length.

We had seen 'Thunderers' and 'Cannon-balls' at a penny apiece in the trays displayed on shop-counters. They were not only frightening in the bang they made, but dangerous for young hands to hold and light! We were warned, and took heed! 'Jumping-jacks' spread consternation, and had the girls screeching when someone lit one and dropped it slyly near their feet. A sudden jump and a 'crack' left us wondering at Jack's next move, hissing away somewhere, invisible in the dark made darker against the leaping orange flames of the bonfire, now well alight.

A 'rocket' was an extravagance, but sometimes we had a six-penny or a shilling one. Then it was a case of, 'Go and fetch an empty bottle and make sure that it's standing upright and not likely to fall!' Rockets were in any case temperamental, even when their stakes had been set nicely in the bottle and the blue touch-paper was handy to light. A match was struck. We stepped well back, then ... whoosh! ... a blazing trail soared into the night sky, a moment of 'oohs' and 'aahs', a final flare-up and it was done! Perhaps next day we might find the burnt out case, a blackened tube lying on the road. We were not too disappointed, as we could always enjoy some of the expensive displays that flashed against the night, up at the homes of the wealthier 'Nesco' folk!

Neither the fireworks nor the 'guy' were our chief concern on these occasions. At an early moment in the proceedings we had poked potatoes into place, in amongst the embers forming at the base of the fire. Impatience had us nibbling at raw spud that had a special taste always associated with Bonfire Night – 'wood-smoked'!

The more persevering gourmets were little better off in the end. More often than not, from the middle of the inferno, they would retrieve a charred husk that had once been a proud 'King Edward'! Today, foil-wrapping has changed all that. The only things that came to *us* in silver paper were expensive chocolates. We were indeed highly privileged if we were allowed to take one!

Envelop the whole bonfire event in damp and chill, then you must wonder what the great attraction of it all was. We must admit that our tastes in entertainment were not so sophisticated as children's are today; but we also did not have to rely so much on others to amuse us. The event was traditional and came at what could have been a bleak time of the year. Or, perhaps, the real delight comes in this snug reminiscing in a warm room fifty years later!

None of this could have taken place at Uncle Jack's. The garden at No. 56 Raleigh Road, Norton, with its rustic rose-entwined pergola, a lawn as smooth as a bowling-green and borders resplendent in asters, stocks, nemesia, blue lobelia and 'Little Dorrit', was a living tribute to his patience and skill. Open to view on a corner site, it was much admired by all who passed. He was a real 'Mr Green-fingers'!

But, in our garden, he made one big mistake. He thought he would help his big brother, our Dad. There was a patch at the top of our back garden that did not readily yield to the spade. Jack thought he would bring a bit of life to it. He planted some sprigs of poplar. The last time I saw those trees they were umpteen feet high, and their roots had taken over the whole of that side of the garden! Fortunately they had not been planted long before the war, otherwise we should never have managed to dig the hole for the 'Anderson shelter', designed to protect us from falling bombs in air-raids so long as it did not turn out to be THE target!

In his last summer, at 82, he was advising me, 'Don't let flowers go to seed, Don. That's their whole purpose in life. If you want flowers, you've got to nip off the seed-heads. Then the flowers think, "Gosh, we'd better do something about this!" So they start putting out more flowers to ensure the survival of the species.'

Though he was half-blind with cataracts, he did not let that upset his gardening. The handles of all his tools were painted white, especially the hand-trowels and forks, all the better to see them. The heads of the flowers, whose virtues he was extolling, he held in the gentlest of caresses as if stroking the hair of a favourite child.

CHAPTER NINETEEN

Warfare!

THE BACK GARDEN, in its early virgin state, had been the scene of our first games – even of cricket with my first bat! Gran had bought it for me for being a brave boy at the dentist's! However, when we had smashed a couple of 'sixes' into neighbouring gardens lush with grand crops of potatoes and broad beans, irate gardeners had warned us to clear off up to the 'Rec' or else the ball would be confiscated. We took the hint and played elsewhere, and at other games.

The Second World War had not entered anyone's mind in those closing years of the 'twenties. We still saw living reminders of the first one! Jack Smith (no relation), a fine soldierly figure, only had to appear marching in the Road for us to scatter and hide behind steps and hedges. We peeped out, watched and listened. Jack talked to himself, stopped, and shouted some command to the platoon he imagined to be still following him 'over the top'. In the First World War, on a battle-front in France, the hellish pounding of German shells had left him shell-shocked when one had exploded close beside him!

On the sitting-room wall in Gray's Road hung a self-portrait of Uncle Charlie. On his left sleeve were his sergeant's stripes, and near the cuff a little matchstick of a stripe – a wound-stripe to show that he had been a casualty and entitled to a 'Blighty' – leave back home in England.

Outside the Zetland Park in Redcar, where we spent many a family summer holiday, a tank stood ineffectual guard of the park gates. Had it rumbled across No Man's Land on the Western Front? Had its guns blazed away at a fleeing German foe?

Back at the bottom end of New Road, before the houses began, we re-enacted deeds of valour, pretending we were soldiers of the DLI (Durham Light Infantry). Our 'Geordie' pals plumped for the 'Fighting Fifth' (Northumberland Fusiliers); some other lad had 'enlisted' in the Green Howards – local regiments all, with a proud tradition.

The steep embankments and drainage ditches, that formed the cutting for the road, lent realism to our make-believe. We were in the trenches. We climbed up the bank side and aimed our home-made wooden rifles at an imaginary enemy. Clods of earth became hand-grenades, to be hurled over-arm at ... There was nobody! That is the strangest thing about it all! We could have picked sides and fought it out against each other. We did not. We were all on the same side!

There were 'pretend' wounded to be gallantly rescued 'under fire' from beyond the trenches. With bits of corrugated sheet, or big cardboard boxes, we made bivouacs or camps under the branches of elder-berry and hawthorn bushes at the foot of the 'Gully'. There was drilling 'behind the lines'. We went in for semaphore signalling with flags, as explained with diagrams in my copy of Baden Powell's *Scouting for Boys*. Not even the mouth-to-mouth message, 'Send reinforcements, we are going to advance', finally transmitted as, 'Send three and fourpence, we're going to a dance!' ended up as garbled as some of our flag-wagging efforts!

For days on end, in the summer holidays, we met down at our camps to carry the game on, only retreating at the urgent call for meals, mams standing at the top of the steps shouting, 'Leslie, Tom, Ro, Eric, Donald. Time for dinner!'

Of that little army, those of us who in the end went away to the real war all survived. Tom Arnott died prematurely some years ago, at fifty. His experiences as a Guardsman at the landings on the Italian beach-heads, Anzio and Salerno, probably hastened his untimely death.

Yet, there was fighting – gang-fighting and fighting for fun. Ramsay Scott, of Old Road, was the leader of a group that he mustered from Cockie Burnett's family, some right tough nuts!

They had to be, living as they did over the road from the 'Gully' in two old railway-carriages, without obvious signs of water-supply or sanitation.

With one or two of Cockie's bairns, Scotty would terrorize us, Tom and Ro Arnott, Eric and me. We retreated up our steps. The odd stone was thrown, till an angry parent appeared threateningly, warning of dire consequences if any windows were broken. Scotty would lead his troops away to our taunting chant:

> Scotty Malotty, the King of the Jews,
> Bought his wife a pair of shoes.
> When the shoes began to wear,
> Scotty Malotty began to swear.
> When the swear began to stop,
> Scotty Malotty bought a shop.
> When the shop began to sell,
> Scotty Malotty bought a well.
> When the well began to run dry,
> Scotty Malotty began to cry!

These incidents were few and far between. Scotty was a bit older than we were, so he probably grew out of this   kids'stuff quite quickly.

The 'Roscoe Road Gang' was a different proposition. Antagonism would flare up over who was first to the football pitch on the 'Rec'. This situation eased when the bigger lads from our road came along. The Gang either took over one goalmouth or accepted a challenge match. These challenges ultimately led to our trying to form a New Road football team!

That Christmas we were each supposed to put in orders to Father Christmas for a blue shirt, or boots, or both! At seven shillings and sixpence a pair for boots with steel toecaps de rigueur, we were accounting for a sixth or an eighth of a man's weekly wage. You got boots when you were chosen to play for the school, or when they were part of your equipment at the secondary school for sports afternoons. Through lack of finance and uncertainty about who could be available to play on Saturday mornings, the team never materialized.

The other major confrontation we had with 'Red' and his gang was over the railings that Nesco had dumped round their cricket field, to fence it off from the 'Rec'. There were hundreds of these 'Toblerone' bars, creosoted palings of triangular section, six or eight feet long. We built houses or camps of them, starting with two laid parallel about six feet apart, then two on top at right angles and a similar distance from each other. That way we stacked them quite high, climbing up the sides as if we were going up a ladder. When the hay on the 'Rec' was cut we could roof the 'houses' over. Some had more than one room.

'Red' and his gang would come and pinch our stock of palings, or just knock the 'houses' down for pure devilment. That skirmishing, too, gradually tailed off as the joiners incorporated the palings into the fence proper. That building ploy lasted long enough to fill our summer days and give lots of pleasure.

When we fought for fun, we divided our group into sides to play 'Cowboys and Indians' or 'Cops and Robbers'. The Wild Western venture saw some of us trying our hands at making bows and arrows. It was a job to find branches that lent themselves to bow-making; either they were too sappy or too dry. Our best bet was to wheedle a bamboo cane out of a gardening dad. However, it was not long before parents, fearful of seeing innocent parties blinded by our arrows, put a stop to that game.

In the meantime, we had a crack at shooting 'spuggies' down from the branches of bushes and trees. The mere twang of the bow-string was enough to frighten off our prey!

Then we discovered we could make pea-shooters from the hollow stems of cow-parsley. 'Pluff'! When we blew green elderberries down a pea-shooter, that was the sound we made. Bill Jelley's chubby cheeks made the loudest 'pluff', so 'Pluff' became his nickname. Amongst us, his proper name was hardly ever heard. ... 'Where y' going, Pluff?' 'Pluff, have ya any worms for fishin'?'

Berries we found in plenty in the 'Gully', the scene for many a running battle between the sides we picked. The sloping lane gave a ballistic advantage to the warrior up the slope, and this was improved by the narrowness of the bore of the shooter.

Like nature's wonderful timing of the appearance of insects and blossom, the choosing of our shooters had to coincide with the unripe period of the berries, whilst they were hard and green. Haws were hard but big, so it was not easy to find the right bore of hollow cow-parsley. They were plentiful, too, but the thorns on the branches did not allow for a hasty snatch of ammunition whilst, short of 'ammo', we were in flight from a foe. The umbrella-like bunches of elder-berry gave us an ample supply of shot without the risk of scratches!

We exchanged many a 'ping' round the neck and ears, but nothing to compare with the 'stinger' our neighbour in Dundee received a good twenty years later, in the 'fifties!

Ian, my sister Joyce's oldest boy, was eleven at that time and judged old enough to go alone from Teesside on the train to stay for a couple of weeks with me, his Uncle Don. My family were all girls. The eldest was the same age as Ian. A brother-in-law living just outside Dundee had a couple of boys who were just the right age for Ian; so they were invited to stay with us in town.

We ought to have known better! Bringing up girls is quite a different matter from bringing up boys! The first sign of high jinks came at bedtime. Dutifully the boys went off to bed. Next minute our girls were screeching and screaming their heads off! We dashed upstairs to see what was going on. There the boys were, taking turns to crawl under a bedside rug made up from a lion-skin complete with snarling head and huge fangs. In the gloaming they were frightening the living daylights out of our girls, who were perched as high as they could get on the bed-head!

It was decided that a way of ensuring a readiness for bed the next night would be to take the bairns out into the country. I drove them out to Petterden, just north of Dundee, where there was plenty of scope for running about and climbing.

Up on a knoll I found a profusion of rowan-berries just asking for a pea-shooter! The boys soon caught on to the idea as I advised them on choosing the best stems for the shooters. A good time was had by all, and much energy expended!

Unfortunately, we did not declare an end to hostilities, so the boys returned to town fully armed! Our back-doors at Nos. 28 and 29 Lintrathen Gardens faced each other. At No. 29 Alastair appeared in the doorway. Suddenly he let out a bellow. Ian had taken aim and 'pinged' him a right one in the corner of his eye! Back into the house dashed Alastair. A second later he was back again, with a bucketful of cold water. He flung this in the general direction of the offender, little caring that our back door and pantry window were wide open to the flood! My wife was not at all thrilled to find rugs and food packets soaking! Much, much later, she consoled herself that we ourselves had not been saddled with laddies to bring up! A man like me, still harbouring boyish ideas, was enough!

CHAPTER TWENTY

The Roadway Our Playground

OUR GAME of 'Cops and Robbers' was probably based on ideas
inspired by visits to the 'Tuppenny Rush', the Saturday afternoon
matinée at Billingham Picture House. Like our heroes, cops or
villains, we had to be 'motorized'. An old tyre, preferably off a
motor-bike because it was lighter and more manœuvrable, became our car. We 'drove' it with a bare hand or stick, performing
many an intricate pattern of weaving and dodging. Gradually we
clocked up quite a few miles as the tyres became an extension of
ourselves.

On more than one occasion we bowled them along up New
Road, past the South Site to the Portrack-Haverton road, then
down to the river bank — easily a two-mile run. There we would

sit watching the activity along the river — tugs nursing a big ore-carrier from Sweden, positioning it alongside a wharf on the Middlesbrough side of the river; coasters making their way upstream to Stockton and Thornaby, or downstream away into the North Sea, and on to mysterious lands below the horizon that bounded our world seawards from the sands at Redcar or Seaton Carew.

As we sat we sang the tunes of the day — 'Painting the Clouds with Sunshine', 'Making Whoopee', 'Donna Clara', 'Ramona', 'O, Play to me, Gipsy', and 'Bye, Bye, Blackbird'. We were comfortably ensconced within the rims of our tyres, clear of the sharp hard stones of the embankment. The air of the river had a salty tang to it as the tide rose on the flood.

It gives some idea of the density of the road-traffic in those days when I realize that we ran those four miles on the main road, seldom having to pull into the side or mount the pavement to let vehicles pass, and often running along with a couple of pals abreast! It was not the danger of the road that worried our parents. More likely they were afraid we should fall into the river, with nobody on hand to save us.

We hit on another use for a big lorry tyre. George 'Judd' Jelley, who as a bairn had terribly bandy legs, could be curled up inside one and then be bowled down the grassy banks outside our houses, turning head over heels in a springy continuous somersault. The idea caught on; but one shot was enough for me. I felt really squeamish during my 'turn'.

The roadway in front of home was ideal for a number of our games. On its smooth surface we could roller-skate at will, until the road-men came to re-surface it and lay down fresh chippings. That was annoying for a day or two.

Since games with bat and ball could lead to broken windows and damage to flower-beds, 'Tip-cat' and 'Hot Rice' enjoyed a seasonal popularity. The 'cat', or the ball in these games, did not travel so far.

The 'cat' was a piece of wood, pointed at both ends. The aim was to tap a pointed end, get the 'cat' to rise in the air, then swipe it as far as possible from the base. The greater the distance, the higher the score. Since the 'cat' was marked on each of its four sides with I, II, III, or X, extra strokes could be made − except if it landed on X, when it stayed put. Runs were scored from the number of jumps needed to get from 'cat' back to base.

'Hot Rice' was more static. The players formed a circle round the batsman boy or girl (even mam or dad in holiday games at the sea-side). The ball was bowled underhand to hit the batsman's feet or legs below the knee. The player who put the batsman 'out', took over the bat.

On the smooth surface of the road, various patterns of hop-scotch were drawn. This was a girl's game, but boys often joined in sooner than stand about doing nothing. If there was no chalk to draw with, a broken bit of tile or brick came in handy. The basic design was a big square, divided into sixteen smaller squares and numbered. Players took it in turn to slide a flat stone or tin-lid into each square in sequence. After each successful shot the tile was recovered by hopping for it. The player carried on until the tile failed to reach its goal.

There was a design like a Swiss roll, with the spaces curling towards the centre. When your tile landed in a space, you put your initials in it, so that your space had to be avoided either in sliding the tile or hopping. This game became trickier as the spaces filled up! But one pattern, that I had never seen before, was introduced by our youngest Australian cousin, Iris. It looked like this:

Many years later I saw the same pattern in Scotland. Yet none of our girls ever saw it used in Billingham by the Scottish girls, who might have brought it down from Glasgow. They had plenty of space to draw it out on the school yard, but they never did! What a mystery! Had Iris introduced it to this country and one of the Billingham Scots taken it north on a visit to relatives in Glasgow?

The road played host to the usual seasonal games of skipping, tops and whips and, in the darker nights of Autumn and Winter, to 'Kick-the-Tin'; and to sliding when there was enough damp and frost to polish its smooth surface. Both boys and girls enjoyed these games.

The chant ... 'A slow-skip, a what-you-like, a "dolly" or a "pepper",' brings back memories of the rope being 'clicked' at a 'dolly' when the culprit, down on hunkers like a Cossack dancer, bobbed up and down to see how many skips could be made as the rope twirled. Girls had a problem keeping skirts clear of the rope. If you landed for a 'pepper' you had to skip as fast as you could, so fiery was the turning of the rope. A sharp twang on bare legs was the reward when the rope 'clicked' in this sequence. Girls had an ability to do a sort of 'running-on-the-spot', so that they negotiated the fiery rope with ease compared to our clumsy jumping with both feet together!

Girls, too, were especially adept at 'Dutch-skipping', which involved a double rope. To me it was a confusion of twirling ropes that I never managed to skip in. It was almost like trying to skip

inside a giant egg-whisk! Yet girls managed to jump over the bottom strand of rope and dodge the top one as it swung above their heads! I have always admired our girls for that particular childhood skill.

'All in together, The cow's in the meadow. When I count twenty, The rope must be empty!' Heads and shoulders bobbed backwards and forwards as the skippers tried to follow the arc of the rope and get in. When all were skipping in unison, the chant went on ... 'five, ten, fifteen, twenty!' Everybody shot out of the rope. The one who did not get clear took an end and turned.

'Raspberry, strawberry, gooseberry jam, tell me the name of your young man! A, B, C, D , E, ... ' Here the game was to 'click the rope' at the initial of your best boy- or girl-friend! Then the whole tale of your future life together was revealed! Was he to be a 'Tinker, Tailor, Soldier, Sailor, Rich man, Poor man, Beggar man, or Thief?' Was the wedding for 'This year, next year, some-time or NEVER!?' Would you be married in 'Silk, Satin, Velvet, Cotton, or Rags?' Was the bridal transport to be by 'Coach, Cab,

Wheelbarrow or Muck-cart?' Finally came the crowning piece, when the number of skips you made pointed to the size of your future family!!!

Autumn evenings favoured hide-and-seek, or its variant, kick-the-tin. Since both boys and girls played these games, as 'On' was counting, romantic pairs shot off behind bushes and garden hedges, across the road, over the fence and down to the foot of the bank side, or snuggled close together in the drainage ditches running down from the roadway.

Younger ones who were 'On' gradually lost interest in the game when they failed to find everybody in the darkness, which hid everything outside the glow of the sparse street-lamps. 'If you don't come out, So-and-So, I'll tell our Mam you were hiding with Madge!'

This ruse might be effective, but the chances were that out of the darkness, from an opposite direction, a less romantically-inclined 'loner', imagining himself as the wiliest of Indian braves, would sneak in, kick the tin and clear the base for the captives to go off and hide again!

Street-lamps gave boys scope for testing their arm and leg

muscles, as they shinned up the stem of the lamp to hang from the cross-bar below the light or, in a moment of devilment, to turn the gaslight down! Girls got the lads to tie a rope to the cross-bar, and turned the lamp into a maypole.

A popular figure at this time of the year, always to be found with a trail of kids at his heels, was the lamp-lighter. He carried a long pole with a hook at the end. With this he turned on the gas, and the lamp burned brightly. 'Give us a shot, mister!' was a constant plea; but many a mile he had to step out, so he seldom acquiesced.

Our lamp was the scene of a near-tragedy. One night, along with some of the lads, Eric had tied one of the younger ones, Denis Shipley, to the lamp-post. Somehow the rope had become fastened round the victim's neck. In the excitement the prisoner slipped off the edge of the kerb — a mere couple of inches, but he was dangling by the neck! Whether the colour of his face or his choking sounds had scared the rest, I cannot tell. A grown-up arrived in the nick of time. Parental relief that the game had not ended in tragedy probably saved the lads from a thrashing!

Since our lamp stood mid-way between Nos. 1 and 20, it became the meeting place for evening games and general banter. The grass verge beyond the pavement left extra room for play, even for games of marbles. In 'Killer' or 'Three-holey', three holes had to be negotiated in sequence – up, down and back up again – with opponents' marbles being used as 'stepping-stones', giving extra shots for skilful aiming. At the final hole one's marble became 'Killer', ready to pick off an opponent, who forfeited his marble if he was picked off. Any other 'Killer' picking off a 'Killer' won that opponent's 'bag'.

So the lamp gave forth its gleam, drawing us like moths to a flame. It was the 'block' for our games of Hide-and-Seek, Kick-the-Tin and Relevo, and a place of security when older ones began to tell eerie ghost stories, whose effect was heightened by weird shrieks coming from the hedges, where pals in the know had hidden to add their piece and watch the fun!

The 'Gully' was also part of our road playground, a training stretch for boys who fancied themselves as rally drivers. Surface water from Old Road flowed down the lane, wearing away the loose earth to leave miniature rivulets meandering backwards and forwards. Outcrops of smooth stone, and stretches of hard-packed earth with the water-worn hollows and ruts between, offered a challenging course for would-be 'bogey-drivers'. Considerable skill was needed to choose a smoothish course, which helped to lengthen the lifespan of a bogey and subject the human frame to less of a jarring!

A bogey was simply a couple of planks nailed together for the driver and passenger(s) to sit on. A pair of wheels on an axle were nailed to the rear, and another pair were fixed to a steering-board, which pivoted in front of the driver. We steered with our feet against the board, or with a loop of rope attached to each end of it.

Brakes? Mr Ferodo would have turned sick at the thought of the risks we ran! The pressure of a boot-sole on one or both rear wheels might help. (Postillion, I smell burning!) Or a driver dug his heels into the surface dirt of the lane. As a last resort we could always fall off, risking bruises and scratched kneecaps, to avoid going under a bus or car passing at the foot of the lane. Riders took it in turn to act as look-out, to warn others of the approach of road traffic.

More often than not, wheels and chassis parted company on a downward run, unable to endure any further the hammering the contraption was suffering. No pit-stop staff was on hand to carry out immediate repairs. Breakdowns meant a trudge to No. 11, a search for fresh planking, a rummage through a box of old nails and screws, or just complete abandonment of the bogey until a fresh axle of wheels could be found. Folk throwing out old prams were a godsend. One of our bogeys had wheels tyred with old rope, bound round and round the rims.

Bogey-racing was a summer sport. When winter came with frost and snow, the pavement of the 'Gully' became a 'Cresta Run'. A bogey was convertible. We removed the wheels and nailed runners lengthwise in their place. Dads would be inveigled into bringing home from work lengths of half-round bar, suitably drilled and countersunk to take the screws that fixed the bars to the runners. The thin slats off old metal bed-mattresses were not despised if steel bar was not forthcoming!

Uncle Charlie made us a solid, well-built sledge. For some reason, however, it did not go at all fast. Pals on flimsy bits of steel-shod board, knocked together in a backyard, left us standing at the post! I have a feeling there is some mechanical ratio between the weight of a sledge and the breadth of the runners! If some metals had had a better coefficient of slide, I should have liked to know. Now it is too late! Our grandchildren in the depths of Alberta have already taken to skis, even before being old enough to go to school! They do not need Grandpa to make sledges. In any case, plastic has replaced the materials we used. Even a plastic fertilizer-bag can give a thrilling descent where the gradient is steep enough!

Of course our attempts to convert the pavement of the 'Gully' into a 'Cresta Run' met with the strongest of opposition from grown-ups, warily treading a homeward path from the pub or just going plainly and sedately about grown-up affairs. How soon does maturity cloud over the bright memories of childhood fun! Some of our elders may have had a narrow squeak now and then as we hurtled past them on the pavement. I do not remember a sudden call for an ambulance to transport any of them to the Casualty Department! Now I am at the warily-treading stage!

Balance and careful placing of the feet were essential when we forsook the level that ordinary folk trod in their daily movement up and down the road. The field below our houses was separated from the roadway by a four- or five-barred fence. We lads could not resist the temptation to tight-rope walk the top bar, which offered a surface of a mere two inches for our progress but put us almost on a level with folk sitting on the top deck of the buses. Practice soon gave us confidence to negotiate the top rail as easily as a stroll along the pavement. However, there was one point that offered a challenge which defied all but the most agile. Eric was one of the few who accepted it and won.

Just about opposite our house, the top bar was broken. A stub of rail gave a wobbly take-off towards an even shakier landing, a tapering shaft which shook in sympathy with its broken counterpart. More often than not, a challenger would be seen leaping down to the safety of the grassy bank in the field. Today, one can hardly bear to imagine the physical damage we might have caused ourselves in attempting the reckless dare.

CHAPTER TWENTY-ONE

The Road – Haulage and Traders

NEW ROAD was not a major thoroughfare in the early days. As the factory was extended from North to South Site and the population grew, so the volume of traffic increased. Many more vehicles became motorized. A bypass road, from the junction of Central Avenue and Station Road to the bottom of Billingham Bank, relieved the pressure on the old village centre. An extension to the bypass over the Bottoms behind Rancliffe Woods, leading on to the New Tees Bridge, removed some traffic from New Road. However, this remained busy enough with heavy lorries bound for the two factory sites. The new bypass was approached from Sunderland along the A19, which still had to contend with the obstruction of the railway-crossing gates at the station. A road bridge west of the station resolved this problem.

We grew up with Clydesdales hauling flat-carts, and the squarish farm-carts, riding high on big wooden wheels a good four feet in diameter. The Foster family, Tom and Lol, were hauliers, as was Cockie Burnett.

One morning at two o'clock I stirred in my sleep, suddenly aware of a reddish glow reflected from the whitewashed ceiling above my head. Shouts of, 'Fire! Fire! The stables are on fire!' brought us tumbling out of bed. We gazed in awe at the sight of smoke billowing and flames leaping skywards above the stables, down in the field at the bottom of the road where Cockie kept his horses. It was a summer's night, the dawn made earlier by the blaze.

Folk were wandering down the road, curious to see what was happening. Some were reporting that they had seen horses lying burnt to death. That night a score of animals perished.

Familiar as we were with horses pulling bread-vans, coal-carts, milk-carts and even hearses, we were probably more familiar with their dung, a product much sought after by gardener chaps. At times there was a bit of rivalry over a steaming heap! We nipped out smartly to be first on the scene, a bucket in one hand and the coal shovel in the other. The fireside one was too posh, and liable to be scratched on the road-chips!

There was a 'going rate' for the treasure. Some wag had proposed, 'Thruppence a bucket, ordinary! Sixpence, hand-picked!!' Even as a grown man, with my own garden in Lintrathen Gardens, Dundee, I was not averse to using the old technique to retrieve what I judged to be rightly mine when a heap appeared on my stretch of the street! I have even gone to the lengths of warning off younger men from down the way!

Nowadays our equine friend is making a come-back on our byways. Comely Amazons in proper riding-habit amble along singly, in pairs, or with a riding-school, in Indian file. Their passage is clearly marked. I have often wished that I had remembered to put a shovel and a plastic bag into the boot of my car. One day, I shall. But I am warned that I had better be on my own!

In the early days, dairy farmers faced some competition to establish a 'round' in the new Billingham. Mr Jackson, driving a horse and trap, came from Wolviston way, a round trip of five miles even before he started to sell his milk in New Road! The trap held a big churn, from which he measured out the milk with special little ladles for gills, half-pints, pints and quarts. (What a tuneless volume is a 'litre', against that ascending scale!) The housewife provided her own jug or basin for her order of milk.

Rena was a Stockton lass, who drove the Co-op milk-cart. She set out on her rounds from the dairy at the top of Billingham Bank, opposite to Poole's garage. She would be coming up our road at breakfast-time, at about eight o'clock. Hers was a modernized cart. It had pneumatic tyres! Her horse must have appreciated that. If the weather was at all inclement, Rena was sure of a cup of tea and a biscuit at Mam's, which she enjoyed in the warmth of the back-kitchen where the gas-stove, cooking our breakfasts, took the chill off the morning air.

Her horse was a character! He was so used to the 'round' that he stopped at the steps of customers only, and at about No. 16 he began to cross the road towards No. 75, where Rena had her next customer!

The milk came in bottles by this time, stacked in crates on the cart, which was roofed over so that the milk and the driver were protected from the elements to some extent. The milk was bought with bakelite 'tokens'. Money was no longer left in bottles or handed over to the milk-girl at the end of the week to pay for the order. There was little to be gained by robbing her. The week's supply of tokens was bought over the Co-op shop-counter in the grocery department. At a pinch they would have come in handy in a game of tiddlywinks!

Another horse-drawn shop belonged to Mr Carroll, the fruit and veg man from Beaconsfield Street, Norton. He too had an established round. Folk in New Road were his first customers, as our road was the nearest to 'Beakie', less than a mile across the Bottoms. When the mushroom or bramble season came round, he would give us one and tuppence (nearly 6p) a pound for what we had picked. I have no idea of the price he re-sold them for. We had trudged as far as Norburn Beck on the other side of Wolviston, over fields and along hedge-backs, in our searches – five or six miles, there and back. We might have thought his offer a pittance, but we enjoyed being out there together.   Mushroom-fields and bramble-thickets were jealously guarded secrets. I have cycled as far as forty miles in the round-trip for a day's brambling in Cleveland, out by Hutton Lowcross or Upleatham way. Once, during the early days of the war, when in a moment of forgetfulness Mam let the brambles and the sugar boil away to an inedible tar, I saved up my college sugar-ration week after week till the waste was made up!

We lived only eight miles from the 'Pools – Old Hartlepool and West Hartlepool, where the fishing-boats came in. 'Caller herrin' was the cry of the man selling fish from his cart. For a couple of coppers we could buy a dozen of those nutritious fish, which Mam soused in vinegar. Home-made bread and a herring was a filling meal, though I was none too keen on all those little bones!

'Rag, bones! Any rags and bones?' was another street-cry familiar to us. We would pester Mam for a bag of rags or a jam-jar. These were exchanged sometimes for a penny or two, or sometimes for a balloon. I have heard it said that there were cinemas where kids could gain entry to their matinée performances in exchange for a jam-jar!

On Saturdays in the summer, almost as if it were timed to coincide with the end of our dinner, the lemonade-cart would arrive. Sometimes, if Dad felt a bit flush with his money, he would order a crate of mixed bottles − dandelion and burdock stout, American cream soda, sarsaparilla, iron-brew, tizer and lemonade − a rainbow assortment of twelve colourful bottles. Tizer was supposed to stimulate the appetite, the name being a corruption of 'Appetizer'.

Tommy Sera! Will we ever forget him? A little Italian, as broad as he was tall, wrapped up warmly in a long coat no matter how warm our summer weather! The very mention of his nationality must give away his occupation! He had no horse and cart. He simply trundled a heavy box-like barrow from his base in Haverton Hill.

It was an insulated box, because it held a freezer. A box of magic from which he could conjure up all manner of delights, from half-penny cones to tuppenny sandwiches and much more expensive concoctions; chocolate-covered marshmallow cakes to set off a layer of ice-cream inside. We were on 'cloud nine' if Dad treated us to an ice-cream sandwich − twopenn'orth of the delicacy, a slim packing between two paper-thin wafers − that we contrived to lick for a considerable time, until the wafer was a soggy sieve at the edges, releasing those last oozings of cream, as if reluctantly. In a moment of extravagance we might be treated to a dash of raspberry-juice over the ice-cream in a cone.

But if Tommy was outside it was no use pestering for an ice, no use saying, 'Mam! Tom and Ro Arnott are getting ice-cream. Can't we have one?' Over the year we might have been luckier than our pals, because we did go away to the seaside on holiday, to Redcar, and then ... the delight of Pacitto's Gold Medal ices, renowned at some international trade fair, like Paris!

I could not guess the miles Tommy covered on his rounds. He was probably heading for home by the time he came along New Road, as we often saw him after tea-time, and New Road led into Haverton. He was later superseded by younger chaps on tricycle barrows. In front, was a cube-shaped fridge-container, with handle-bars attached for steering. Behind was the saddle and the low-geared pedals we normally associated with a bike. The slogan was, 'Stop me and Buy one!' 'Eldorado' was the firm's name on the salesman's peaked cap and the side of the barrow.

Companies of national or regional importance also sent their vans, motor-driven, round our streets. The rival firms of Brooke Bond and Ringtons (tea-merchants), put in an appearance from time to time in an effort to drum up fresh custom. However, since tea-drinking smacks of faddishness, any change in drinking habits tended to be of short duration. So we only noticed at irregular intervals the red fleet of Trojan vans bearing Brooke Bond's products, or Ringtons' stylish multi-coloured vehicles offering a hint of Chinese porcelain in the design which set their fleet apart.

The peak period for traffic on our road was around tea-time, half-past four to five. The workmen came home then, mostly on push-bikes and a few on motor-bikes. The main outpouring of the workforce sped home via Billingham Bank, so that they missed us out.

A puffing and hissing, heralding the approach of a steam-traction lorry, had us dashing to the top of the steps. It belonged to a Tyneside firm, Gateshead way. Beneath its bow-front we could see red embers glowing between the front wheels. Ro Arnott recalls it stopping to replenish the water-tank at a hydrant near the 'Gully' junction with New Road. It rumbled its way home-ward on solid rubber tyres.

Durham County Council had a little black steam-engine, also on solid tyres. It was used chiefly to pull tar-boilers and other road-repairing equipment. Recently we have been reminded on TV of such vehicles through the antics of that oil-smudged charac-ter Fred Dibnah, aloft on his steam-roller, chugging through 'red rose' country to attend steam-traction shows where scenes of our childhood come back to life. Steam-rollers and, in due harvest-season, threshing-machines, were all part and parcel of road activity.

Bit by bit we became familiar with motor-cars and lorries. Danger from them was minimized because we had a long clear view of their approach and could hear them coming through the cutting at the bottom end of the road. On Wednesdays and Saturdays, market-days in Stockton High Street, we had a regular half-hourly bus service (2A) which ran up New Road to the terminus at Billingham Picture House in Mill Lane. The stops for this were at the 'Gully' and up near No. 27 (for Imperial Road passengers). As we grew older and bolder we became quite adept at jumping off the bus, despite the printed warnings on the platform. The speed, as the drivers changed up the gears of the old 'Leylands', was just about right by the time we reached Les Brown's, at No. 5. We had saved ourselves about fifty yards of walking!

Gradually, as South Site was developed, traffic increased in volume, size and speed. But by that time we were in 'longers' and had grown away from street-play. Secondary school homework now inhibited our freedom.

CHAPTER TWENTY-TWO

Shopping

I DO NOT THINK that I considered 'doing the messages' an inhibiting factor. It had its compensations in the chance it offered to me to change the scene and to meet new faces and new experiences. Just as Tom and Ro had chores, my regular job was to do the Saturday shopping.

Friday night was pay-night. Unlike many 'Andy Capps', Dad handed his pay-packet over to Mam. She took what was needed for running the household, possibly banked some more, and left Dad with his pocket money. So, on a Saturday morning, off I would go early with my list of 'messages' to the 'Village'. To ask a pal, 'Where are you going?' and to get the reply, 'Up to the village,' meant that he was either doing some messages or had a penny to spend on himself.

Billingham was now a considerable township, but the old-established shops, like Fletcher's, were on The Green or close to it in Station Road. As the town extended, blocks of shops were conveniently sited within walking distance of the local neighbourhood.

When a purpose-built post office along Station Road replaced the sub-office in Cooper's on The Green, it was at the end of a row of shops that were within reach of the residents in Central Avenue and the streets running off it. A similar row was erected opposite the Station Hotel, over the railway-crossing, offering a service to the 'clans' of 'Scotch Town'. In most cases the main out-of-town bus services were available and sufficiently frequent to allow folk an opportunity to shop in the centre by The Green, or to go further afield into Stockton, Middlesbrough, Darlington,

West Hartlepool or Sunderland. In our area, new shops had been built in Mill Lane and in the new Co-op block in the south-east corner of The Green.

I had all my messages arranged in order, so that the progression was a steady one from shop to shop, then back home again with the minimum of delay. Any hold-up was due to clientele in the various shops. Customers felt a need for a bit of gossip and back-chat with the lads behind the counter, and sometimes arguments arose about the quality of goods supplied or the service!

My round began at the old Co-op at the top of Billingham Bank, with its grocery and butcher's departments and the dairy alongside. Then I made for Fletcher's in the middle of The Green. This family business had living-quarters above the shop. The astute Fletcher lads made good use of a gable-end to advertise the produce they were famed for. You could be sure that Alf would not miss an opportunity of showing off a prime side of bacon, extolling its unrivalled quality and having you buying a few rashers – before you could say 'pork'!

He was a cheery individual, a brisk salesman, courteous and attentive to his customers' needs. His older brother John was not quite so forthcoming, but had all the same qualities of another good salesman. There was an air of purposeful bustle about the place. In the back shop, orders were being packed and addressed for delivery in the town and beyond, so well was the firm known.

Before the new Co-op block was built there was bakery and confectionery to buy in 'Waring's o' The Green', whose meat pies were a speciality. Mr Lancaster kept a fish-shop at the end of the row before the Smith's Arms. Cooper's, with the post-office, was just across the road. Sometimes I had to go into Station Road to Moffat's the chemist's. The shop opposite, Gillespie's butcher's shop, might be offering a better bargain in sausages than the 'Stores' (the usual name for the Co-op), so I would make the necessary purchase there. There was an ironmonger's next-door for odd items like 'segs' (to reinforce the heels of shoes and give us some extra wear).

Back across The Green I could cut through an alley next to the Black Horse, going down the steps and crossing the main road to

Haverton, to reach the newsagent's. Mr Burns supplied our daily paper *The Northern Echo*, *The Northern Weekly Gazette* and Arthur Mee's *Children's Newspaper*. (Mee was already well known for his *Children's Encyclopaedia*, whose agents tried from time to time to induce parents to buy this book of knowledge that no child should be without!!) At Mr Burns' I squared up our weekly account. He also sold us Brock's Fireworks in preparation for Bonfire Night.

The final leg of my round might take me down Mill Lane. Mam shopped at Hinton's, which had a good reputation as a grocer's. From there I could complete a circuit by crossing the 'Rec' and coming down New Road from Bill Palmer's at No. 31.

The Co-op undertook a big building programme on the block facing the park. It incorporated a butcher's, chemist's, draper's, grocer's, fruiterer's, tobacconist's and hairdresser's. Above the main departments was a function hall, where dances and parties could be held. In one of the ante-rooms Dad's union, the AEU, held its branch meetings. The old shop at the top of the Bank was closed, but its staff moved into the new set-up.

When I called at the new butcher's I still had to obey Mam's firm injunction, 'Make sure you get Charlie to serve you! He knows what I want.' I addressed him respectfully as Mr Middleton. A cheerful bald-headed man, expertly rubbing a dangerous-looking knife against a steel, he was the boss. Mam was a good customer, and though through the week she had her purchases marked down in his book 'on tick', she always paid up every weekend. My job was to get the order − a piece of sirloin, a leg of lamb, or whatever she could afford for a weekend roast − and pay the bill, so that she started all square for a new week. It was much the same routine in the grocer's, just round the corner.

By and large the CWS (Co-operative Wholesale Society) served all our needs, especially from the new Emporium in Wellington Street, Stockton. As well as the usual food outlets it had furniture, drapery, footwear departments and a restaurant. On the top floor, administration offices controlled the area branch-shops. Mam had to go there annually to collect her 'divi', the dividend paid on the year's purchases. She could either take it in cash, or bank it in her 'divi-book' to make interest that would be on hand for a major purchase. (The best 'divi' I ever knew was paid by the Dundee Eastern Co-op, where my wife and I were members in the 'fifties. It amounted to two shillings and tenpence in the pound, just a shade over 14%!)

Gran, Aunty May and Mam were all Co-op members, with their own 'check' or membership numbers. These were given at every purchase and recorded in triplicate on a pad, so that both the Co-op and the member had a tally of what had been spent when it came to working out the amount of dividend due to each member. Gran's number was 3150 (thirty-one fifty), and Mam's 20570 (two, aught, five, seven, aught — the way we said it).

For me, waiting-time in the 'Stores' was pleasantly relieved by the cash-trolleys trundling overhead from counter to central cash-desk. They were catapulted along wires. At the desk the container was unscrewed, the cash accepted, the change calculated — and put back into the container for it all to be catapulted back to the counter and the waiting customer.

In Stead and Simpson's, in Stockton High Street, they had a much more intriguing system of cash-handling. The money was put into big wooden balls, which rolled in a cylindrical cage-way all round the shop. As the balls disappeared out of sight behind Mam, we would duck behind her to keep track of them. I cannot remember where they finished up, but it was quite exciting to see them coming back with the change.

Later, the Billingham Co-op and the Wellington Street shop adopted a pneumatic system of rubber-tipped cylinders. The counter-hand inserted the cylinder into a vertical tube. We heard a pressurized 'gulp' (or 'suck'), and were left wondering whether we should ever see check-number or change again! A plop, followed by the rattle of the cylinder in a tray, and we heaved a sigh of relief. How unexciting today, by comparison, is the 'brass-rubbing' technique of the plastic-card handling machine of Access and Visa!

Only once was Eric entrusted with a message at the 'Stores'. He came home empty-handed, having stumped Charlie in the butcher's with a request for 'a pound of barley!'

It soon came round to Joyce's turn to take over my routine. She took to it like a duck to water. In later years I should not like to have been behind the counter when *she* was out looking for a bargain. *She* would stand no nonsense, and was as quick as the best of them with ready repartee.

One message we had to do at fairly frequent intervals was to go to Harkness's at the Bank-Top Garage to have the battery re-charged in order to keep the wireless-set running. That cost sixpence. We had to carry the heavy accumulators carefully, in case any of the acid spilt out and burnt a hole in jackets or trousers.

Some of the lads had Saturday jobs, delivering groceries and meat on heavy, low-geared message-bikes. They did not get much pay, but there was always the prospect of tips from grateful customers. There was also the chance, too, that others of us might be asked by a neighbour to 'run a message', when we were often rewarded with a coin. I knew *I* was not going to be spending *my* tips. I could hear Mam already, 'Now, that's to go into your bank, Donald!' To this day I am not over-fond of parting with hard-earned cash, though I am beginning to get the hang of Visa-cards!

'Down the town' − the phrase that meant 'in Stockton' − there were well-established shops and businesses to deal with all contingencies from the cradle to the grave. National firms like Boots the Chemist, Timpson's Shoes, Marks & Spencer's and F.W. Woolworth, were all represented along the High Street. 'Woolies' intrigued me with its offer of nothing costing more than three-pence or sixpence. Then how did a hammer cost a bob (one shilling, or 5p)? Well, the head was priced as a separate component at sixpence and the handle too, at another sixpence!

Though the CWS Emporium supplied much that we needed, there was plenty of competition all around. Bargains could easily be sought elsewhere. The Market was just such a source. Held on Wednesdays and Saturdays, it was spread from St Mary's (the Parish Church), down the middle of the High Street (the broadest street in England), to the Shambles on the south side of the Town Hall.

Shopping in the market could not be classed as a chore. There

was every variety of stall. Many stall-holders were local people, especially those who sold fruit and vegetables. Even to this day there are representatives of families who have traded there for generations − the Medds (long-established seed-merchants and market-gardeners), Fewsters (whose base was near the Mile House Hotel, out on the Durham Road), and Wyllie's (the tripe merchants whose stall should be standing below the Town Hall, on the south-west corner facing the Billingham bus-stance, with Dovecote Street just a few yards up to the right). I do not imagine that the naphtha flares still hiss and burn yellow above customers' heads; but the honeycomb tripe, gently cooked in milk, flavoured with chopped onions, will still be unbeatable. I was about nine or ten before I accepted this delicacy. Earlier coaxings had been of no avail.

George's stall was a great attraction during lunch-break on Wednesdays, when we were at the 'Sec'. From the school in Nelson Terrace we only had to walk a few hundred yards down Dovecote Street, and then thread our way north-easterly through the produce stalls, to George's.

He was a 'patter' expert from Leeds, keeping up a steady flow of sales talk, catching the sallies of his customers on the volley and cracking back a joke that left most of us helpless with laughter. There was no room for false modesty round *his* stall. A voluminous pair of ladies' bloomers would be held up on offer. 'I don't want a pound ... not fifteen bob ... ten bob ... no, not even seven and six ... Five bob the pair, missus − and you can have them in any colour your old man likes!' Then to his assistants − 'A pair on your right, Bill! Two pairs over there for his mother-in-law ... in black! All done at five bob? Right, let's have that fancy item in china, those bedroom utensils!' And a pair of gaudy 'guzunders' (chamber-pots) would be held aloft.

The Shambles seemed to me a misnomer. Nothing was tidier nor cleaner. Cleanliness was a legal requirement, as butchers, poulterers and fishmongers sold their wares there. 'Shambles' is a historic term for 'butcher's stall'.

Twice a week, Stockton High Street swarms with a seething, colourful mass of folk, edging their various ways through the throng, fingering cloth, smelling pot-plants, testing the firmness of fruit, listening to sales patter, bargaining, laughing, joking back, meeting, exchanging news, gossiping, crying ('I've lost me Mam!'), and even finding relief in the toilets close to the Shambles! Demolition and refurbishing of property may have taken place along the sides of the High Street; the market still goes on.

CHAPTER TWENTY-THREE

Accidents, Illness, Death and Streptococci

AIDS. WHAT AN ACRONYM! At least, with our A.I.D.S. of the 'thirties we knew where we stood. The AIDS of the present day, for the most part a self-inflicted scourge of mankind, is out of control.

For us, streptococcal infection was evident in boils, on faces and in awkward places — often on knees, where a nasty scrape could become infected and 'angry' with yellow pus. Before Fleming's discovery of penicillin, and the subsequent development of antibiotics, treatment of such wounds was primitive and drastic.

'Now, just sit still until the kettle boils! Pass me a saucer and the packet of pink lint!' Once the lint was to hand, a patch big enough to cover the area of the wound was cut out, put into the saucer and boiling-water poured over it. 'Now, you must let me put it on as hot as you can bear, otherwise it's no good!' We kept testing the heated pad, fearful of being scalded. On the patch went. We howled! A bandage was quickly and firmly wound round the injured limb. The last few inches of the bandage-roll were torn down the middle, a knot tied to stop further tearing, and the two 'tails' were used as ties to keep the dressing in place. We were usually consoled with the remark, 'It's all right, now. It'll be like a pig's foot in the morning!' Perhaps our attempts to understand what a 'pig's foot' had to do with the cure kept our minds off the throbbing. The worst part of the treatment was the removal of the dressing, which often stuck to the wound. The whole procedure had to be repeated until the wound was clean.

The saucer and the first aid kit shared the same top cupboard in the recess by the fireplace. Along with cups, saucers, plates, jugs and bowls stood bottles of Scott's Emulsion, Parrish's Chemical Food, Sanatogen, cod-liver oil, olive oil, a jar of Radio-Malt, phials of tincture of iodine, eucalyptus oil, camphorated oil, oil of cloves, a jar of Vick-brand Vapour Rub, a jar of aspirin tablets, a box of Beecham's pills, a roll or two of bandaging, cotton-wool and a packet of white and pink lint. A ribbed purplish bottle, denoting contents that were 'POISON', held picric acid, a yellow fluid used as an antiseptic dressing. H.P. Sauce, Heinz Tomato Ketchup and medicine bottles rubbed shoulders with each other!

On the shelf below the cupboard was a copy of *The Universal Home Guide*, published by Odhams Press Ltd. I still have the copy that Mam bought through one of the daily papers in the 'thirties. On pages 902, 903 and 904 I have just noticed such nostalgic remedies as Castor oil (ugh!!!), sulphur (flowers of, mixed with treacle to give Brimstone and Treacle, a remedy that was thrust down throats in the Spring to cleanse the blood!) and ipecacuanha wine − I quote, 'can be used in two ways. ... If you want to make a child sick ... (hardly surprising with a name like that). For a cold on the chest in children ... is useful.'

All three of us had spells in bed to recover from the usual complaints of childhood − chicken-pox, mumps and measles. I was usually the last one to contract the complaint and seemed to bear the worst of it!

None of my experiences of childhood illness were anywhere near the traumatic sufferings Eric underwent, when it was decided that he must have his tonsils removed. The doctor arranged to perform the operation at home on the deal kitchen table! It took every ounce of the combined strength of doctor, nurse and family member to hold him down. There was blood everywhere and the doctor's clothes were ripped. Mam was in an awful state, apologizing to the doctor and offering to pay for the torn garments. The doctor would have none of it. His comment was simple, 'The boy was only defending himself!'

There was no escaping the dentist, Mr Beaton. He held his victims in a rigid grip with the stump of an amputated arm. His calming injunction before he began to operate was, 'Once I start, you can spit, swear or sing!'

Joyce knew trauma too, once when she stood on a garden frame and gashed her leg so badly that blood was spurting out. There was an emergency dash for aid. On another occasion she was taken off to the Fever Hospital in Durham Road, suffering from scarlet fever. The trauma was to pass on to Mick, Uncle Charlie's dog we saved from a premature end at the vet's. He came to us the day after the sanitary officials had been through our house spraying every nook and cranny with formaldehyde, the statutory treatment after a fever case had been reported. It was bad enough for us to have to put up with the smell, but a thousand times worse for Mick with his super-sensitive snout!

Lockjaw (the very name struck dread) caused the death of one of the bairns in the road in the early days of folk settling into their new homes. Perhaps this made it all the harder to bear where there was a clean new environment and no suspicion of the deadly tetanus bug. As bairns we put young Master Timothy's death down to his eating of hoss-muck! I have no idea where this theory sprang from!

The shadow of death hung for quite a number of days over another lad in the road. Bill Palmer was in his early teens at the 'Sec' when he was suddenly whipped away into the Stockton and Thornaby Hospital. An appendicitis had deteriorated into peritonitis. In the 'thirties the very sound of that word rang like a death-knell.

Bill was a sturdy lad whose clothes were skin-tight on him, especially his short trousers. When we were in the 'phiz' lab (the Physics Department, next-door to the 'Boss's' study) we could easily hear the crack when 'Jackie' Kinnes applied his butter-pat to Bill's seat. That was the punishment for running up a forbidden total of detentions.

Bill's sturdiness pulled him through the dreaded operation, though he wasted away to a rake. He and his parents swore that his recovery was due to the qualities of the cold water from Billingham taps! For a period, that was all that Bill craved when his anxious parents went to visit him. When he left school he joined the Royal Navy as a boy-entrant. My last memory of him is of a jolly Jack-tar, as broad as he was tall!

Death did come to our immediate family and dealt a double blow. I was about ten at the time. I knew something was in the air, because Dad had called in a 'woman' to 'do' for us – make meals and tidy up the place. Mam was upstairs in bed.

One morning I was given the order to take an urgent message to Gran. Twins were on the way! This news shattered me! Was it because I saw the chance of my life-style being dramatically altered with two extra mouths to be fed? Could Dad afford to keep us all? All the way to Grandma's, I kept saying over and over to myself, 'I hope they don't live! I hope they don't live!' They were still-born. They were named James and George after Grandpa Barlow (Mam's dad) and her only brother, George.

That terrible secret wish lay deep inside me for nearly fifty years, until I knew the unspeakable joy of seeing for the first time my own twin grandsons, born on 3rd October 1980 in Edmonton, Alberta. I first set eyes on them when they were eighteen months old, at an interesting stage for them to learn some tricks from Grandpa! Only then did anybody learn my secret. I revealed it to my wife. Yet all the words I write or say will never erase that memory of my dead twin brothers.

Dramatic, yet not so intimate, was the death of Jack Eve, an old workmate of Grandpa Barlow's – like him, a tailor to trade. He had boarded with Gran in the early days, coming down from Spennymoor to work in Stockton. We met him most often at Christmas time in his retirement, though there are snaps of him in family albums when he joined us on the sands at Redcar.

Usually he stayed with Aunty May and Uncle Charlie during the festive season. With Uncle, Dad, and a neighbour Mr Rutherford (or cousin Ray, then old enough to join in with the adults), Jack would make up a foursome for snooker or billiards played on Uncle Charlie's table – not full-size, but slate-bedded and true. It was a dual-purpose table. Polished mahogany inserts could be set up over the cushions to turn it into a good-sized family dining table. On Boxing Day we all sat round to savour the goose and all the trimmings, with Christmas pud and mince-pies to follow –

traditional fare, beautifully cooked by Aunty May in her electric oven.

Once the meal was over, the womenfolk left the men to get down to the serious business of deciding on partners and playing for a prize — a luscious bunch of purply-blue Black Hamburg grapes, grown in Uncle's greenhouse.

On this particular occasion, Jack was staying with us at Billingham. Down at Aunty's he had been making himself useful, helping about the place. He had got a sweat on with all his physical effort and the extra warmth afforded by woollen vest and longjohns. He did not change out of his damp clothes, caught a chill which developed into pneumonia, and a few days later died in our bed. They had an awful job carrying the coffin down our narrow, steep, stairs, because Jack was a heavily-built chap. For long enough Eric and I did not want to go into that room, never mind sleep in that bed!

An incident that might have been tragic had its funny side. We were playing cricket down in Foster's field, where Cockie Burnett's stable had burnt down. The ball had been hit into the beck. For such a stroke, the score was 'six-and-out'! The 'corkie' (we only saw proper leather-encased balls in school-matches) was floating along in mid-stream.   Ro Arnott and one or two more lads had negotiated the iron palings, meant to close the bridge off

and stop access to the coke dump. On the plank bridge Ro was reaching down for the ball when suddenly he lost his balance and toppled into the beck.

It was pretty deep in the middle. The bottom was slimy and soft. With commendable presence of mind, Cyril 'Stiff' Meachen grabbed Ro by the hair and hauled him up and out with the help of the other lads. Ro was bawling with pain and fright!

Our Eric was a wiry agile lad, with a fondness and great ability for climbing trees. Our favourite tree, below the 'Gully' and near the beck, spread its branches − offering not only several routes upwards, but also downwards with an exit-drop, especially when the farmer piled his hay below which cushioned the fall.

One morning, before breakfast, we persuaded Eric to try a new route down for a 'dare'. The lower part of the branch hung over the rusty strands of a barbed-wire fence. He climbed down the drooping branch well enough, but caught his leg on a barb of the fence. From a jagged tear in the flesh of his calf, blood gushed! Consternation! I feel the creeps again just thinking about it! Yet, before the summer holidays were over the wound had healed cleanly, though the scar is still there. Our annual trip to the seaside and his constant paddling in the salt water effected the cure!

Despite the growing volume of traffic along the road, it caused few problems. We were growing older, and better able to take care. 'Cock' Clements' little son, called Arthur after his dad, had a near squeak however outside their front gate. He had run out into the roadway in front of a car. Fortunately the impact had lifted him up onto the bonnet. We do not remember much of what happened to Arthur junior; but we shall never forget Mrs Clements squawking in a high-pitched Cockney voice, 'Gawin fetch yer fawther! E's in the pab!' (translated à la Stanley Baxter of 'Parliamo Glasgow' fame − 'Hie ye hence and alert your progenitor, imbibing in the hostelry, that his presence is required forthwith!')

Another near miss caused consternation in our house and at 'Doo's' next door. Frank Dewhirst was a member of a local motoring club. He and Doris were younger than Mam and Dad, and 'trendy' folk, though the term was unfamiliar in those days.

Frank had invited Dad out for a club run, possibly a 'Treasure-Hunt', in his little three-wheeler Morgan 'Runabout'. Somewhere in the country, by Redmarshall or Bishopton, they had come out at a junction, when another car had struck the tail-end of the Morgan, throwing Frank and Dad out on to the road.

There was no sign of either of them when they were due to come home from the outing. Suddenly, a message arrived. The pair of them were in the casualty department of the hospital! There were no further details.

I have a picture in my mind of seeing Dad next morning with his head swathed in bandages. Both he and Frank had been concussed. Other injuries were simply superficial. That was the last time Dad went out in a three-wheeler!

In their teens, some of the lads owned bikes. Bill Palmer owned an 'Elswick' fixed-wheel racer. Anybody used to an ordinary free-wheeling model was in for a shock once aboard Bill's racer, especially if he tried to free-wheel down a hill! Whether this was the case with Stan Meachen or not, the poor lad came a terrible cropper. He and his pals were out for a run in the Cleveland Hills. Coming down Swainby Bank from Osmotherley via Scarth Nick, Stan lost control, failed to take a bend and went through a hedge. Some of his front teeth were dislodged!

John Metcalfe, the dentist who looked after our teeth, actually retired close to the spot where Stan had his accident. John's sister was a friend of Mam's, so I got off to a good start with dental care, knowing of John and being known by him. I trusted him and was not afraid; so much so that most of my teeth that I have had drilled have been done without anaesthetic.

Eric, Joyce and I still have our own teeth, though not the full thirty-two. How often did we hear as kids, 'Eat your food properly! Don't gulp it so! Give every tooth a bite! Chew thirty-two times!' Kids like us who had four meals a day — breakfast, dinner, tea and supper — would have had to be chewing whilst we slept! Meal-times were just a necessary evil — times pleasant enough, but they interrupted much more absorbing ploys.

Dad had had strong teeth, yellowed with nicotine; but some gum disease meant he had to lose them all. Mam had hers removed early on in our Billingham days. Menfolk little appreciate the drain on a woman's system when she is producing a family. She will make sure her family is fed, going without a proper diet herself. This plays havoc with her teeth.

With her own teeth out, Mam had little joy with her new dentures. More often than not, though she persevered for a while, her gums stayed sore, so that for longer and longer intervals she went about toothless. Gradually her gums hardened. Then she could masticate crusts with the best of us. With Mam as an example, I could appreciate at an early age how Eskimo women manage, having chewed their teeth down to gum level in their efforts to soften the sealskin to make garments for husband and children. (That is what they say in the text-books!)

'Our Edie, you can't go out like that! Where are your teeth?'... 'It's all right, May. I've got them in my handbag! I'll put them in when we get to Jack and Polly's.' That was Mam's way. When her teeth appeared for a trial insertion, we knew Mam and Dad were 'going out'. Having had a look at herself in the mirror, Mam would wrap the 'pot' teeth in a hanky and put them into her bag.

A person who elicited my sympathy, and possibly that of the other lads, was Vic Worthy, a younger man between our generation and Dad's. He had a wooden leg. When on watchman duty he got up from his sentry-box to tend the line of danger lamps, to re-fill the oil or trim the wicks, his wooden leg creaked, a painful sound that went no doubt in sympathy with the real pain he felt.

Round his brazier, we listened to his tales as he sat in his box, pale-faced in the firelight, with a greasy trilby on his head. He was a fount of knowledge, speaking on literature, history and philosophy. We plied him with questions. I often wondered why such an intelligent man was shackled to such a menial job. Perhaps with so many unemployed about, and his handicap, he was only too glad to take any job that was going.

Beyond the private level of accident and disaster, there were other tragic events on the local, national and international scene which reached the headlines. In an explosion on 15th April 1934, in the Ammonia plant at ICI Billingham, 11 men were killed and 20 were injured. Anxious questions were on everyone's lips, for those not working in the factory had little idea of its layout, and practically every working man in Billingham was employed somewhere in it. Relatives of workmen were only reassured when the exact site of the explosion was known.

Our road witnessed despair which touched the nation, for down it passed the Jarrow hunger-marchers, men desperate for work since the berths of their Tyneside shipyards were empty. They accepted humbly and gratefully packets of food, hastily put together, as they marched proudly on, heartened by the show of fellow-feeling. That was just at an early stage of their long trek. One is tempted to ask where that spirit is today?

The news of the terrible crash of the airship R101 near Beauvais in France was incomprehensible. All aboard were burnt to cinders in seconds!

Colliery disasters were often reported, many in the local coalfield, as at Seaham. The Gresford Colliery catastrophe on 22nd September 1934, during the night-shift, claimed 265 lives out of 400 miners employed in the mine!

At sea, in Liverpool Bay on 1st June 1939, the submarine *Thetis* foundered on a second trial voyage. 50 crew members and 53 civilians, chiefly employees from the Cammell Laird yard, were lost. Only four men managed to escape, and they hardly had the strength left to do so. The rest had died from asphyxiation!

Those are some of the less happy memories of childhood. None of us could foresee the shattering effect of those dread words of 3rd September 1939, when Neville Chamberlain addressed the nation over the wireless, to announce, 'We are at war!'

CHAPTER TWENTY-FOUR

St Cuthbert's, Festivals and Festivities

ST CUTHBERT'S CHURCH had stood in a prominent position over-looking The Green, until the Tower House was built in front of it. However, the Saxon tower of the church, over 1,000 years old, still proudly challenged the elements on top of the slope which rose from the flood-plain of Billingham Bottoms.

On Sundays, the first service of the day began at 8.00 a.m. This was a simple communion service without any music. A faithful band of parishioners attended regularly. At 9.00 a.m. Sung Eucharist was celebrated with a choir leading the praise. This was a more popular service, usually well attended, at which Vicar F.C. Tymms and his curate officiated. Then followed an interval during which the clergy had time to have breakfast before Matins began at 11. This service was often referred to as the '11 o'clock service'. Devotions for the day ended with Evensong at 6.00 p.m.

Midway through the 'thirties the congregation of the church grew, as did the town of Billingham itself. It was felt that the church was no longer big enough, especially for popular festivals like Christmas and Easter. Parishioners were asked to contribute towards the cost of extending the building. A five-shilling donation bought one brick or block of stone. Somewhere in the new part are three bricks marking the contribution we made as children.

The chancel choir area was widened to be in line with the walls of the main structure. As a result, the natural lighting of the whole building was improved.

The vicarage was on the north side of the church. There the vicar lived with his wife and two sons. The older boy, Wilfred, followed in his father's footsteps and was ordained.

I knew some of the church officials by sight. Mr Ayres was headmaster of the church school and lived in a big house on the east side of The Green. Mr Cowley was the sexton, one of whose duties it was to ring the 'curfew-bell', at 8.00 p.m. in winter and at 9.00 p.m. in summer.

Whenever we went cricketing up to the 'Rec' in those long northern summer evenings, we were given a stern warning to be home straightway after the 'curfew' had rung. One evening Eric came traipsing in a good half-hour overdue. 'Where've you been? Do you know what time it is? Why didn't you come in with the rest of them?' Eric had not been with us. None of us will ever forget his answer! In a tone verging on tears, he replied, 'I didn't hear the *perfume* bell!'

In our early days in Billingham, Dad's church attendance merely satisfied the canons of the Anglican Church, which stipulated that a communicant member should partake of Communion on the main Feast Days of the Church's year. We, on the other hand, attended Matins regularly every week. There was an inducement − a 'stamp' − a different one for each Sunday.

A picture illustrated the theme of that day. For Pentecost or Whit Sunday, the Apostles were drawn with 'tongues of fire' descending onto their heads. These 'stamps' were much the same in size as the commemorative issues of the Post Office, and gummed like them to be stuck into a special little book. If we had a complete set, which meant full attendance throughout the Church's year, we could expect a Sunday School prize.

Sunday School for younger children was held on Sunday afternoons in the School-on-The-Green, which was the weekday Church school. Mr Duncan was the superintendent. He was also a sidesman, to be seen regularly in church, handing out hymn- and prayer-books, ushering folk into pews, and taking the collection. He had a thin face, wore spectacles, and his Adam's apple was rather prominent.

The older children had Sunday School in the church. As the

time for Confirmation approached, for 16-year-olds, classes for intending candidates were also held there. At this stage I was in a peculiar situation. None of us had been baptized as infants. Now I had to be baptized before I could be confirmed. In the Prayer-Book there is an order of baptism for those of riper years; so all three of us were baptized together, standing sponsor for ourselves, without any godparents. We took Dad's advice and had 'Barlow' inserted as a middle name, just to distinguish which branch of the Smiths we belonged to!

Attendance at Sunday School led to a special day, a Saturday, the day of the Sunday School trip. Invariably this was to the seaside at Seaton Carew, about eight miles away. Everybody met up at Billingham station, on the north-side platform. Kids milled about. Warnings were shouted, 'Come away from the edge of the platform! You'll get sucked in when the express passes!' There were tears as some of us became separated from our families, or because warnings were not being heeded so that a crack across the lug stressed that adults meant what they said!

The excitement mounted as we saw the signalman, up in his high signal-box, move over to the big wheel which operated the crossing-gates. Then we knew that the train was approaching. Heads turned to the right towards Norton, to see who would be the first to spot the train. A rumble of wheels, a hissing of steam, a metallic squealing of iron rims braking on rails, and a clanking of buffers accompanied by a heady smell of hot oil and coal-burnt smoke heralded the rush for carriage-doors. 'In here, Mam! Hey, Tom! There's room for you and Ro!' Vicar Tymms climbed sedately aboard, having left the harassment to his curate and the Sunday School teachers.

Once we were off, the warning voices yelled afresh, 'Get your head back inside! You'll get a cinder in your eye! You're letting the cold air in!' At times mams must have wished that they could have removed the leather straps that hauled the windows shut and used them on unruly backsides. It was not a long journey. Besides, it was only natural for the bairns to get excited.

Seaton Carew station, built on the outskirts of the resort, was a good mile from the sands. We were dying to get on to the beach and down to the water to paddle, but could only traipse along, held back by the slowest member of the family.

Invariably the sea was grey, the sky was grey and greyness enveloped the whole place, borne in on a biting east wind from the sea. At some spot near the beach the bags containing a sandwich, a bun, a cake and sweeties were dished out. The grown-ups were told where the distribution point would be for the pouring out of Sunday-School-trip tea, as grey as the sky and sea! It had one virtue. It was hot, at least for throats inured to the scalding beverage through years of practice. For us kids, there were more warnings. 'It's too hot. You'll burn your mouth!' We ended up gulping chilled dishwater from sand-encrusted cups!

And the sea? Vicar had probably never even seen a tide table. Invariably the tide was out, and the sea with it, miles away on those flat, vast expanses that border the Tees estuary. All thoughts of paddling were gone. We could see ourselves disappearing to the water's edge, then unable to find our folk again. So we stayed put. We were told to use our buckets and spades to good purpose and dig a big sand-hole, so that the elders could sit in more comfort with a modicum of shelter from the biting wind.

Invariably it was a quieter, downcast, weary crowd that headed back to the station for the train home. Despite it all, we were already looking forward to next summer and another trip. For most of us in the hard years of the 'thirties, those outings were a treat indeed.

Through our 'stamps' we gained a knowledge of the seasons of the Church's year, starting with the four Sundays of Advent leading up to Christmas-tide. Epiphany (or Twelfth Night), 6th January, did not provide an occasion for the festival parties enjoyed by bairns in France. For us it meant the removal of all Christmas decorations, or 'decorootions' as Mam humorously said. The Santa Claus frieze from above the picture-rail, the cards on the mantelpiece and piano-top, the baubles and tinsel from the tree (in later years an artificial tree), the streamers and paper-chains, all made by ourselves from coloured paper − found their places back in the cardboard boxes that we had opened with so much excitement a fortnight before, to be stored away for next time.

'Pancake Tuesday' was the next eventful day. For one thing, we had an afternoon off school. As soon as twelve o'clock struck, we rushed home, trusting that for 'afters', instead of rice pudding with the skin on top, we should be tucking into thin pancakes. Once they were served, from the tin we spooned great gobs of Golden Syrup, which drooled down, golden tongues of delight, onto the brown-streaked, yellow layers, hot from the frying-pan. Mam certainly slaved over a hot stove for *that* meal, tossing out pancake after pancake, as fast as we could gobble them down. Yet, to this day, I have not had to complain of indigestion. My stomach must have been well lined with pancake.

Eight miles away, up in Durham County, the annual 'football-match' was taking place at Sedgefield. This involved the whole community. The ball was chased by the mob, through dub and mire, between goals sited at each end of the parish. Cautious merchants had boarded up their shop-windows in advance.

Next day was Ash Wednesday. For a long time I associated it with 'hash', the left-overs from the Saturday roast. They were usually our dinner-time lot on Mondays, heated in an iron pot along with savoury onions, potatoes and carrots or turnip, amid a lovely dark-brown gravy. With a plate of such 'hash' in front of me, I did not envy the gourmet his roast pheasant!

Ash Wednesday, of course, was the beginning of Lent, when we were exhorted to 'fast'. From Sunday School we received a little oblong box, with a slit in the top. This concertina-like box could expand as it received our offerings, the savings we made from our pocket-money when we did not buy sweets. There was no virtue in saving on sweets only to put the money aside to buy a ball of string for a kite or a new cork cricket-ball at some post-Lenten date! Our contributions were handed in as part of the Easter celebrations.

Fridays throughout Lent brought a change in our dinner-time menu. Fish took the place of meat. Often we sat down to boiled cod and parsley sauce and boiled potatoes.

Quadragesima was the First Sunday in Lent. It had been pre-ceded by Septuagesima, Sexagesima and Quinquagesima Sundays. Coming much more readily off our tongues were, 'Tid, Mid, Misere, Carling, Palm, Pace-egg Day', the sequence of the Lenten Sundays. Less reverently, and something we dared not utter inside the house (or rather in the presence of Mam and Dad), was the chant – 'Carling Sunday, Fart on Monday!' Since a carling is a brown sort of pea, traditionally the main item on the menu for Passion Sunday, no more need be said!

On Palm Sunday we came home from church clutching our little cross of palm-leaf, recalling the Lord's triumphal entry into Jerusalem, astride a donkey, on the road strewn with palms. We had processed up and down the aisles of the church on a token journey, following the example of the Master.

We knew about Maundy Thursday in Holy week, because in the papers next day there were photos of the sovereign doling out to the poor the traditional Maundy money, one coin for each year of the sovereign's age.

Good Friday was a statutory holiday. We really had no excuse for not attending some part of the Good Friday service, which went on from nine in the morning till three in the afternoon. I have to confess that I have only twice made the effort to attend that service, and then only for a part of the time. On each occasion I expected to see the afternoon grow dark or, at least, grey, in keeping with the shattering events of that Day nearly two thousand years ago.

Easter Sunday was a great day of uplift as we sang glorious hymns and 'Alleluia' refrains. Lilies decorated the altars in brilliant white profusion, balanced by the glowing vestments of the vicar and his curate. Perhaps, in a moment of inattention, our thoughts turned from the service to the image of hard-boiled eggs! Traditionally these were gaudily decorated either by brush and paint or, more economically, dyed in boiling water to which had been added onion skins or other plants that had properties of producing stains that pleased.

Since Easter Monday was a holiday, we also had the prospect of going to the Park, where we might roll our eggs down the slopes. Dad told us of a tradition of his youth, when lads 'jarped' their eggs. 'Jarping' sounded like a sort of 'conker' contest. Each competitor held his egg in his fist, so that the 'Challenged' offered as little of the top of his egg as possible to the 'Striker', who tried to crack the opponent's egg with the bottom of his. The egg that resisted unbroken was declared the winner. The loser handed over his egg to the victor! Some 'wide' boys got their shout in first for 'Striker', and went from triumph to triumph and the possibility of being 'egg-bound'! Earlier they had bought, or scrounged out of nesting-boxes in hen-houses, the pot eggs set to encourage laying!

April Fool's Day, a sinister day on the calendar as far as we bairns were concerned, was awaited with some trepidation. The morning, however, from the moment of wakefulness, was spent in wary alertness for the unexpected order to do such and such a thing. 'Joyce, mind you don't stand on the cat's tail. She's just behind you!' If Joyce so much as hinted that she was tempted to glance behind, she was greeted with a chorused, 'April Fool!'

Mam did not feel too old for pranks on this day. Milk was delivered to the back door and left on the step. Early one April Fool's morning, she took in Doo's milk, two pint-bottles, and swapped them for two she had prepared the night before, only they were filled with starch! It must have made her day to be greeted at breakfast-time by a shout from Doo, 'Oh, Miff (Doo's nickname for Mam), how could you? I had to pour Frank's tea down the sink!' And the pair of them had a good laugh over it!

Fortunately, the threat of being 'fooled' only lasted till midday, when we could relax again. Any late attempts at 'fooling' were treated with contempt.

Ascension Day, the Thursday ten days before Whit Sunday, was an occasion for church-going and the receipt of the 'stamp' for the day.

Whit Sunday saw a change of vestments worn by the clergy. The dominant colour was red, to simulate the 'tongues of fire' as the Holy Spirit entered the Apostles before they set out on their evangelical mission. We did have Whit Monday and Tuesday off school. Since the break just extended a June weekend, the long days were most likely spent playing cricket.

The Church season of Trinity took us right on to Advent, from the First Sunday after Trinity to the Umpteenth Sunday of that season, and completed the Church's year.

This long period of Trinity was marked with individual festivals, celebrated more especially by the Roman Catholic Church. 'Corpus Christi' was one, when there were processions through the streets, noticeable in towns like Middlesbrough with a large Catholic population.

St Swithin's Day, 15th July, was a day of omen. We wanted no clouds and rain that day, because it would rain for forty days and forty nights! In that case Stockton Race week, the third week in August, when we took our annual holiday on Teesside, would be a complete wash-out! I do not recall any celebrations of 'All Saints' and 'All Souls' Days, 1st and 2nd November, but 'Hallowe'en', 31st October, was most specially marked. It was Eric's birthday!

The 'Poppy-seller', knocking at the door on this November day in the 'eighties, has reminded me of an anniversary celebrated in a far different way pre-war. The solemn moment was always the eleventh hour of the eleventh day of the eleventh month, the moment when the terrible carnage of the 1914-18 War came to an end in the Armistice.

Every year, at that precise moment, the hooters or works' buzzers blew, and the whole nation came to a stop for a Two Minutes' Silence. Factory machinery was switched off. Buses, trams and other transport vehicles ground to a halt wherever they were. The drivers stepped down from their cabs. Activity in offices, shops and schools was stilled. Everywhere, folk stood in silence, heads bowed. Even in the fields, the ploughmen whoa-ed their horses, to join in the national moment of remembrance for those who had died in the war to end all wars.

Today the solemnity of that moment is only reached for me when, from the ceiling of the Albert Hall, the poppy-petals begin to flutter down on spectators and participants at the end of the annual televised British Legion Service of Remembrance.

Now we have a special day − Remembrance Sunday − the Sunday when the nation is silent again and the Queen is televised carrying on the tradition of laying a wreath at the Cenotaph in London. This new date is so much more convenient for Commerce, Industry and Transport. Our generation was brought up to respect the sacrifices made in World War I and we ourselves experienced the horrors of World War II, so it is not surprising if we are critical of the change from Remembrance Day to Remembrance Sunday.

Christmas in our childhood was not advertised, as it seems to be today, almost as soon as the children return to school after the summer holidays! We only became aware of the event when 'December' was on our lips. Our excitement, therefore, was more intense. Suddenly, shop-windows glistened with displays to gladden the heart of any child, toys in profusion, games in boxes.

Girls could gaze at dolls, mentally try on nurses' outfits, and dream of cooking on model cookers with all the pots and pans. For boys and dads (still boys at heart) there were train sets and, where the shop had space, railway layouts of 'Hornby' trains, Pullman express coaches and shunting locomotives. Close by, 'Meccano' displayed working models of lift-bridges, cranes, windmills and all manner of mechanical devices. A boy with an engineering bent might wish for a No. 1 'Meccano' set, which would mark a beginning and an entry into Dad's world. With real nuts and bolts he could assemble girders and plates, axles and cogwheels. Models made like this gave further scope for creative and more varied play.

In Robinson's Coliseum in Stockton High Street, a visit might be paid to Santa. In flowing white beard, snugly wrapped in his red hood and cloak, he sat and wrote with the tip of his finger-nail on his striped walking-stick, noting down the name and address of his youthful clients and the orders they expected him to deliver down the chimney. I could recognize handwriting, but I never saw any loops and squiggles on that stick. It must have been magic!

I may have been about nine years old before I discovered who Santa really was. A careless move by the old gentleman, delivering the goods; a boy half-awake with excitement to know 'when He passed'; this conjunction of circumstances gave the game away. But the boy was in on the secret and now enjoyed a feeling of superiority, of responsibility not to spoil the fun for the younger members of the family.

Back at home, away from the sights, sounds and smells of

Christmas in the shops, we had plenty to do. Decorations had to be made. Presents were wrapped in secret. Either a tree was bought, or the old one was restored to its place of honour and duly adorned with tinsel and baubles stored away from the previous year. The cards that the postman brought were set out on the sideboard or the piano-top. Sprigs of red-berried holly were draped around the pictures. A bunch of mistletoe hung from the lamp in the centre of the ceiling.

The crowning-piece of decoration was the frieze that went round the walls of the room, above the picture-rail. It had served since my early days in the Hartburn house. There was Santa, driving his reindeer team above the roof-tops. In the next panel he was halfway into a chimney with his sack full of gifts; then he was seen filling the stockings by a child's bed. With the reindeer scene the whole sequence was repeated, so that wherever we gazed upwards we could see the benevolent gentleman smiling down on us.

There was work to be done in the back kitchen, chiefly in the preparation of vegetables and sauces and the cooking of the duck. Duck was our Christmas extravagance. The Christmas pud, like the cake, had probably been made months beforehand and allowed to mature, as the rum or brandy or sherry filtered its way into every pore of the mixture. I have known cakes to have been made in January, a whole year in advance! Were the ingredients cheaper then, like the goods of the post-Christmas sales? Two cakes were usually baked at the same time. The second was to celebrate New Year.

Christmas Day never dawned. It was already on the go a good hour or so before there was a hint of light, as we suddenly felt the weight of a filled stocking or, on more affluent occasions, a filled pillow-case, pressing down on our feet. 'Ooh's and 'Aah's, cries of, 'I've got a ... ! What have you got?' 'Mam, look what Santa's brought me!' Then muffled warnings, 'Don't get orange-juice on the bed-clothes!' 'Mind where you put the pips! I don't want to be treading on them in my bare-feet!'

As usual, Mam would be up first to light the fire. Once the room was warm, we came down for breakfast. We then spent the rest of the time playing with our new toys on the clip-mat in front of the blaze. Mid-morning a fire was lit in the front-room, which only came into use on special occasions.

Mam had her own technique for expediting the lighting of the 'room' fire. Onto the big shovel, that she used to bring coal in from the coal-house, she would rake a bed of red-hot coals from the living-room fire. Having opened the 'room' and kitchen doors in readiness for the ceremony, she would warn us all to keep out of the way. Then she moved with alacrity and caution, holding the shovel at arms' length, for a fair heat rose from it, as also did wisps of smoke!

This burning heart of the new fire, now transferred to the sitting-room grate, was nourished with some bits of stick and coal from the scuttle, so that in next to no time the front-room too glowed with warmth. Later, the grown-ups lounging in the easy chairs would have to move them back, as the heat made itself smelt in the distinctive odour of hot furniture polish on chair-leather.

In our early married days I tried the same technique with success, but my wife was less happy to see the plumes of smoke rising from my burning-offering, and anxious for her carpets lest an ember fall! An odd dark patch on a 'Readicut' rug testified to her well-founded anxiety!

So the day passed in playing and feasting, with our having recourse to chocolate pennies, apples, oranges, tangerines or grapes in between meals just to keep our strength up! In the warmth of the fire and the family circle, ours was a rare content-ment.

On Boxing Day there was more bustle. We were getting ready for a trip to Gray's Road, where we were invited to share dinner with Uncle Charlie, Aunty May and Raymond. Jack Eve was there too. They needed us to help them demolish the goose that was served up at this meal.

But for me, the outstanding feature of this day was the invita-tion I received to stay on for the remaining days before New Year's Eve, to be company for my cousin (an only child) and share in his toys. This did not affect Joyce to any extent. She was seven years younger than Ray, and a girl! Eric, however, felt out of it, and this feeling grew more and more intense with each succeeding year of the invitations.

After Mam, Dad, Eric and Joyce had left for home, it was time for bed. We had all had a long and exciting day. Ray and I slept in his bed in his room. For nearly a whole week, we only came down from it for meals! Anyone entering had to tread warily, as the whole floor-space was a pattern of 'Hornby' rails, rolling-stock and depots for goods to be carried by the trucks, cranes and lorries made from 'Meccano'.

Ray had worked out a timetable, or rather a distance-table, to cover the journey from King's Cross to Aberdeen. (We were ardent admirers of the LNER.) Place-names like Hitchin, Huntingdon, Peterborough, Grantham and Newark belonged to a country beyond our ken. Doncaster touched off a spark of recognition, to be fanned by York, and kindled into a blaze of knowing with Darlington, Durham and Newcastle. Morpeth, Berwick and Dunbar had an honourable mention on the way to Edinburgh. With the Forth and Tay Bridges, two tremendous leaps across their firths, we were arriving in Aberdeen in a trice.

The names were logged in an exercise-book, in a place-column. Alongside, another column indicated in due proportion the number of circuits needed to cover the stage between each station – King's Cross to Hitchin (one circuit of the track); Hitchin to Huntingdon (two); and so on.

Aunty May had sewn little sacks for the open trucks. The farmyard animal set found itself dispersed the length and breadth of the kingdom, loaded and unloaded into and out of cattle vans. Small wooden building-blocks were piled aside in timber-yards, and 'Lott's' bricks simulated the granite exports of the city of the Northern Lights.

The goods train, hauled by a black LNER 4-6-2, would pant impatiently in a siding, whilst No. 360, the green express aptly named *Yorkshire* (a model of the 'Shire' class of LNER passenger-hauling locos) did its quota of circuits, to dash its passengers from King's Cross to Edinburgh in the luxury of a Pullman coach! There were spectacular crashes as this train failed to take a bend.

The weakness of the goods train was derailment, when couplings jammed or the leading bogies jumped the points. Day after day we played on, unaware of sun or rain outside!

One vivid memory of a stay at Ray's brings into focus a snow-covered garden, mistiness above the trees, and a stirring reveille of Christmas carols played by a Baptist church group, joyously blowing silver cornets, horn, trombone and euphonium. 'O Come, All Ye Faithful', 'Hark the Herald Angels', 'It Came upon a Midnight Clear' — all the old favourites. Looking out of the window, we joined in lustily.

Having lived most of my life in Scotland, I still feel a bit touchy when Scots rave on about Hogmanay. I do not think Mam was far out when, having experienced the Scottish version, she said scathingly, 'Hogmanay! — What hogs men are!'

We in the North Country were not behindhand when it came to celebrating the departure of the Old Year and the arrival of the New. The fire was lit in the front-room in the late afternoon, so that there would be a cosy atmosphere to welcome folk who would come over to our place. We bairns sat in the firelight, gazing at the wonderful shapes formed by the flames or dying embers, trying to decipher what they were, seldom in agreement as we all had our own interpretation of the magic.

After tea in the kitchen, we moved over to the front-room to await the guests. No specific invitations needed to be issued. A chance remark was enough, on meeting in the market or before coming home from a visit to friends round about the festive season, 'If you are free and fancy coming in, we'll look forward to seeing you on New Year's Eve.' The invitation was even extended a year in advance, as folk left for home after the fun, bidding us not only 'A Happy New Year', but also, 'Good Morning! We'll be over next year.' Or, 'Don't forget, we'll be looking forward to you coming next time.'

When intending visitors had finished their teas, they would get ready and head for No. 11. The Thompsons (Father, Mother, Renee, Gert and Joe) would troop across from Thornaby, a good four miles. Jessie and Frank Yellow might come over from Park Avenue, next to Ropner Park in Stockton. Aunty May, Uncle

Charlie and Ray came from Gray's Road. For quite a few years we did not have permission to stay up till midnight, though the bedtime hour was delayed so that we could enjoy the fun till ten o'clock.

With Jessie in the party, we were sure to be treated to a few piano-duets played by her and Mam. Fingers rattled over the keys. They even got to the point where hands were crossed onto the other's territory, but there was no fumbling or nudging. Much of the music was invigorating, played with verve. Jessie, bright-eyed and laughing, would thump away in the final bars to sound a definite close. Everybody clapped. Favourable comments were passed, 'By, wasn't that good!' 'Ee, our Edie, why don't you play us another one?' 'I fairly enjoyed that!'

The familiar party games were played – 'Potted History', 'How? When? Where? and Why?', 'I Spy ... ', 'Happy Families', 'Mixed Pickles' and THE football game.

One year, the 'Doos' passed over to us a horse-racing game. The course was a row of metal troughs or slides, sloping uphill to the finishing post. Each slide held its own little horse and jockey, wearing self-coloured silks – red, green, blue, yellow, black and white. The horses were impelled up the slope by ball-bearings, kicked upwards by a square-shafted rod, rotating at the foot of the game. A flywheel attached to the rod kept up the momentum. The ball-bearings reacted independently. Gradually the kick of the rod faded and a new pull-start was needed. Away shot the balls again. The horses took fright. Black went into the lead. My 'blue' seemed to be jibbing. The atmosphere became electric as the horses neared the winning-post. No photo-finishes here! The first horse home tipped with its front hoof a little metal marker in its own colour. This shot upright to proclaim the winner. We had placed our bets in matchsticks. Winner took all.

When at last we were allowed to stay up, we felt the excitement mounting as the hands of the clock moved towards twelve. Unknown to us, one of the party had disappeared outside. As the clock struck the magic hour we heard a rat-tat-tat at the front-door. 'Go on, Alf! Go and open it!' More than likely it would be someone like Uncle Charlie, with dark hair, carrying a lump of best Shilbottle, sticks and paper, to ensure warmth for the coming year and something to eat and drink to show that we should not starve either. Manly hands were shaken. Kisses and hugs were distributed among the fair sex and us little 'uns.

Ginger wine, or cordial as it was called, was the ultimate in beverages on these occasions in our household. It was made from a strong essence, diluted to taste with tap-water. To us it was an elixir. I never saw beer or whisky about the house. Mam did not approve of alcohol, having known the effects of strong drink on folk from her experience of serving drunks in Grandma's tobacconist's shop in the Great North Road in Darlington.

On one occasion, however, Mam had been given a bottle of home-made rhubarb wine. It had lain in the sideboard for years, forgotten. I do not know how or why it came to light on this particular New Year's Eve. It was uncorked. A clear liquid glug-glugged into a glass. 'Here, May. Try this!' Aunty May took a sip. I have never seen anybody's eyes roll as hers did! They were normally slightly full in their sockets, but this time they just about popped clean out! 'By, our Edie, where did you get that stuff? Ee, it hasn't half got a kick!' 'We were convulsed, for Aunty tended towards the strait-laced!' She was not putting on an act. 'Are you all right, May?' was Mam's anxious cry. May's wide grin was ample reassurance!

The New Year cake was cut and handed round. Knowledgeable comments were passed amongst the ladies, sometimes with requests for the recipe, or hints on variants that had met with approval in other cakes. Stilton was sliced, and relished as a necessary accompaniment to a good piece of fruit cake. Strong cheese and fruit cake does not sound to be the right mixture, but it is well worth trying!

From this moment on we, the novices, found ourselves fighting against drooping eyelids. We wanted to see the whole night out, to keep the fun going; but, gradually, the grown-ups got round to reminiscing, the fire began to die down, a coolness crept into the room and the spell was broken. First one, then another, sought coat and hat. Farewells were said, and thanks. The chill early-morning air sneaked in every time the door was opened. Soon we were only too glad to crawl upstairs and snuggle down under the blankets in our cold beds, lying close to share each other's warmth till we drifted into oblivion.

CHAPTER TWENTY-FIVE

Party Time

BIRTHDAYS for us children were celebrated mostly as family affairs. Rarely were pals invited in. We had enough close relatives in the area to cater for. Joyce's on 24th March came roughly at Easter-tide. Mine was on 21st September, to be followed almost six weeks later by Eric's at Hallowe'en. Since this was a festival traditionally kept in the North, I tended to lose out on a full-scale party, especially as we grew older. We preferred to have a better 'do' on Hallowe'en. Provided that I had my birthday presents and a special tea to mark my day, I was satisfied. Mam's birthday was 17th May, and Dad's 26th June. Inside the 'extended family' there was the coincidence that Uncle Jack was sixty on the day our youngest daughter, his great-niece, was born, 19th August 1959!

Hallowe'en was a tailor-made party-time, with all the extra fun and games that were only played then. Despite those attractions, nobody was going to be disappointed with the sound basis of any party, a good tuck-in!

Like most North-country mothers, Mam could bake well and was used to our appetites. The main dish would be a knife-and-fork affair. A salad-bowl brimmed over with shredded lettuce, onion slices, tomatoes (more than likely from Uncle Charlie's or Dad's greenhouse), sliced hard-boiled egg, a pinch or two of salt, a dash of malt vinegar and a sprinkling of sugar! 'Sugar? Ugh!' That was the reaction of my Scottish wife when confronted with this highly palatable mixture! There would have been more 'Ugh!' if she had seen us washing the lot down with pint mugs of steaming Bournville cocoa! Oh, there were lashings of tea − but Ray, Eric and I were real 'cocoa-nibs'.

The 'ughiest' thing, which I shall never forget, happened at my 25th party, on the eve of my departure for France to study there for a year. Max Rallon, my French pen-pal, was also fond of cocoa. In order to aid the digestion of a tomato-and-egg sandwich, enclosed between two slices of Mam's home-made brown bread, Max proceeded French-fashion to dunk the lot in his bowl of Bournville!

The usual dessert at parties was trifle and jelly. Cakes followed − plates of rock-buns, maids of honour (little pastry tarts filled with jam and topped with a sponge mixture), gingerbread and walnut-loaf (both to be spread with butter, as they came into the 'bread' classification). Finally − and we still found room for it − came the birthday cake, the same rich fruit mixture as we were to enjoy at Christmas in the pud and Christmas cake. It was coated with icing and marzipan, and lit with the appropriate number of candles for the years. These tiny coloured candles were set in their little holders shaped like flower-heads.

Whilst the table was being sided and the washing-up done, there was an interval which allowed for some much-needed digestion. Then, when everybody was ready to join in, the fun and games began.

'Potted History' was a favourite. We all sat round in a circle with the 'reader' in the middle. Each of us had a number of oblong cards with a phrase or a word printed on them. The 'reader' read the story out to us. It sounded so straightforward, until there came a pause. This was a blank on the written page, and a signal for the first of us to read out whatever was written on the top card in our hand.

'Mary, Queen of Scots, was led to the block, where the executioner chopped off her ... ' [Number 1's contribution from the top card was, 'Size 12 wellies!'], whereupon the executioner was heard to say, 'That's the first time my ... [player No. 2 rallied round now with 'Stick of rhubarb'] was sharp enough!' The hilarity often reached such a pitch that tears streamed down our cheeks, or we fell off our chairs and rolled helpless with laughter on the floor.

To calm the proceedings down, the adults would suggest a game

of 'How? When? Where? and Why?' One of the party was sent
outside the room, whilst the rest of us decided on some object
inside the room that the 'outsider' had to discover by asking
questions – 'How do you use it?' 'When do you see it?' etc. We in
the know tried to give veiled answers to make the interrogator's
job harder. Sometimes, one of us blurted out a simple give-away
answer, only to be met with a chorus of, 'Oh! Our So-and-so,
you've gone and given it away!'

Often we had a game of blindfold 'Sticking the Tail on the
Donkey'. The sheet with the donkey painted on it was pinned to
the wall or door. Then came the palaver of blindfolding! 'Ooh,
you've tied it too tight!' – 'I can see our Mam's head!' The binder
would counter with, 'How many fingers am I holding up?'

Once all parties were satisfied, the victim was spun round three
times and pointed roughly in the right direction. When the tail
was pinned on some part of the animal's anatomy, the cry went
up, 'Mam, it's my turn now!' – 'No, it's not! You went first last
time!' This contest could easily end in tears!

What really set the seal on Eric's birthday party was the Hallowe'en part, when we played the traditional games. The big enamel basin, that Mam made the bread in, was half-filled with water
and set on a sheet in the middle of the room. Out came the bag of
rosy apples, enough for all the bairns and some of the grown-ups
who still felt like bairns. There, temptingly in the basin, bobbed
the apples. Two or three of us got down on our knees by the basin
and, with hands behind our backs, tried to get a grip with our
teeth and mouths on Macintosh Reds or Cox's Orange Pippins.
We gasped for breath as we snuffled water up our nostrils. Quiffs

drooped wet over foreheads. Sometimes we must have felt
tempted to try and drink the basin dry, to make the job easier.
Heads got bumped. Chins dripped water. Yet still those apples
bobbed out of reach. *They* were the lucky ones, who managed to
come to grips with the fugitive fruit. In the end the losers were
consoled with their share, for they had made a good try.

I do not remember tackling 'Treacle Scones', though that is
another traditional game, having much the same ingredients of
hampered effort, elusive goal and undignified activity. A string is
stretched across the room, from which are dangled other strings.
To the ends of these are tied plate-sized scones, liberally coated
with black treacle. The object is to eat away one of the scones. If
the dangling string does not offer enough problems, a sudden tug
on the main string makes amends. All good clean fun, did you
say? Try licking treacle off the back of your ears!

CHAPTER TWENTY-SIX

Wet Weather Fun Indoors

WHEN WE WERE forced indoors by the weather, we would sometimes invite pals along; but, usually, families were big enough to
need the indoor space for themselves. On these occasions, card
games were popular.

We played 'Pairs'. The pack of playing-cards was spread face
down over the table top. We took it in turn to find a 'pair'.
Success came from remembering where cards lay. Once all the
cards were 'paired', the player who could then recall who held
which 'pair' became outright winner of the game.

We played 'Rummy', 'Donkey', 'Old Maid', 'Beggar-my-
Neighbour' and 'Snap' if there were younger less-skilled players
involved. If Grandma or other family relatives were visiting we
played 'Bezique'. Dad taught us 'Cribbage', a game he had often
played aboard ship. In this game our mental arithmetic was put to
the test, as we had to seek out combinations of the 'pips' on cards
to make up totals of fifteen. When the scores for 'runs' and 'pairs'
were added we were entering the realms of higher mathematics.
All the calculation had to be done fairly quickly and 'pegged' on
the score-board. We did not 'peg level' with Dad so often!

We also had a set of dominoes, which taught us to 'knock' with
the best of them! At one time, we were caught up in the craze to
play the new game of 'Tiddlywinks', where we tried to nip the
discs into the 'cup' from all directions. Very often we were searching about on the floor for errant 'winks'! All these games filled in
many hours from one meal-time to the next. I suppose we learnt a
degree of self-control through some of these frustrating games, of
which 'Snakes and Ladders' was a classical example. Happy

shouts proclaimed the scaling of a ladder; but oh, the groans of disappointment when we had to slide down a snake! Especially galling was the moment when we fell foul of the last snake on the board, round about square 98, with only two more squares to go for victory! On occasion, this loss was too much for a frustrated player. In a tantrum of defeat, the whole board would be flung off the table! That usually spelt the end of that session, with a warning that, if there was any more of such nonsense, the offender would be heading for an early bed!

I am sure that family will remember the unusual game of 'Mixed Pickles', which had been bought one year to provide part of the Christmas fun. Each player had a pair of what for want of a better word might be called 'chopsticks'. They were in fact like short knitting-needles, fixed into wooden handles, with which we had to lift the 'pickles'. These were beautifully turned pieces of wood representing an onion, a mushroom, etc., all awkwardly shaped lumps whose centre of balance was hard to find! The aim of the game was to transfer each 'pickle' to the central 'pickle-jar'. In such games, facial expressions revealed the mental and physical contortions racking a player. The family phrase of encouragement then was, 'Keep your mouth straight!' 'Mixed Pickles' certainly had us twisting our mouths as we strove to balance and retain those 'pickles' on the 'chopsticks'!

From some remote corner in No. 4 Oxford Terrace, Mr D.F. Smith retrieved an old game, probably of Victorian origin. It was a racing game for four players, each of whom had a pig and a wooden ramp of saw-toothed stairs. These led to a central sty with four doors, one for each pig. We had to race the pig up the ramp by pulling on a string from its tail-end. This allowed the back legs to engage in a stair on the ramp. As the legs were spring-loaded, the pig was pushed upwards. 'Porky's front legs held him steady on an upper stair. It needed a canny touch to pull just hard enough to move the pig without hauling it clean off the ramp.

Instructional and constructional games accounted for a lot of our indoor play-time. We did have some toy soldiers, but there was a general move to play down warlike themes after the horrific experiences of the Great War. Farmyard sets took over from the soldiers.

Farm layouts could be bought, and machinery and stock acquired, as funds allowed. Darnborough's in the High Street was the place where we browsed over exquisitely-modelled hens, ducks, geese, pigs, sheep, lambs, cows, bulls, horses, cats and dogs. The farmer and his wife employed milkmaids carrying milk pails attached to a yoke, haymakers with pitchforks and shepherds with crooks. All were painted in their true colours. The human beings were dressed in the workaday fashions of the time. We used the models to make Ray's 'Hornby' railway layouts look more realistic.

'Meccano' was the foremost constructional toy. The basic No. 1 set could be converted into a No. 2 by the purchase of a 1A. Set No. 7 was the ultimate! Again it was in Darnborough's that we spent odd coppers on spring-clips, nuts, bolts and washers. Cogwheels, ratchets, worm-drives and rubber-tyred wheels for vehicles meant a longer period of saving up pocket-money or birthday monies (when they did not go into the bank!). That was the beauty of 'Meccano' or the farmyard models. A copper or two bought something tangible and lasting which extended the range of our play ideas.

Seven shillings and sixpence ($37\frac{1}{2}$p) bought me a clockwork motor that formed the central piece of a working model of a farm tractor. Instructions on how to make these models appeared in the *Meccano Magazine*, to which we subscribed every month. Hanging in my garage there is a little spanner, from one of my 'Meccano' sets, which I sometimes find a use for still!

Lott's Bricks gave much pleasure. Many types of building were laid out in plan form in the booklet that came with each set – villas, bungalows, signal-boxes, town halls and half-timbered Tudor-style houses. Again, as for 'Meccano', there were bigger sets of bricks which allowed for a wider range of buildings.

The different-sized blocks of stone (some coloured dark-red, others an off-white, with black-striped blocks for the Tudor-finish) all carried a letter-code on the plans, as well as being drawn to scale. Appropriately marked roof-sections could be set in place to complete the structure. These construction sets called for patience, careful handling of the pieces, and an ability to read plans (which, at advanced stages, sometimes needed the advice of grown-ups before we understood). The modern 'Lego', which slots so firmly together, makes construction a 'piece of cake' as compared with the handling of finicky bits of Lott's bricks, which were so easily knocked down or nudged out of line.

Yet, despite all this cosy pacific activity, the warrior beast was lying dormant, ready even to bend 'Meccano' to his will. There was a craze to buy elastic bands at 'Woolies', which we used for firing ammunition made from folded scraps of paper. This catapult warfare was chiefly waged on the top decks of school buses taking us to the 'Sec'. It was the girl-passengers who bore the brunt of the firing!

Back at home, we used curved 'Meccano' strips to form our catapults. Then, on wet days, confined indoors, we turned the kitchen into a battlefield. Forts were set up at each end of the room. A couple of chairs and the table, all draped with the table-cover, formed one fort. Across the room, Dad's armchair and the settee reversed, with their cushions strategically placed, made another stronghold. We picked sides, since Ray was often with us, and Joyce was forced into the conflict. Really, injury could have been serious, as we were fighting at point-blank range and could send a stinging shot of paper pellet from taut elastic!

Decoy hats would be raised to attract a shot, whilst we fired from another corner on an unsuspecting enemy. There were howls and shouts of, 'Hey, our Donald (or Eric)! That didn't half hurt! You aren't to aim at our faces!' A truce would be called whilst opponents foraged in 'No-Man's-Land' for fresh supplies of ammo.

Throughout all this turmoil, Mam was working in the back-kitchen, or would cause a 'Cease-fire' whilst she attended to something in the kitchen, our battlefield. So long as the furniture in the room was back in place before Dad came home, and no damage had been caused to ornaments, we were free to resume the conflict another day. I am pretty sure that other mams did not allow the freedom in their houses that our Mam did!

Another game of a similar warlike nature came into the house as a birthday present. It was a firing-range. Cardboard figures of

Red Indians stood against a background representing forest. We took up position at the other end of the room, armed with a 'gun' that fired wooden beads as bullets. If our aim was true, we could knock a figure over at three or four yards. The time came when we started to use the 'guns' on each other! In this case, however, the dangers were more apparent, so that Mam and Dad soon put the kybosh on that idea!

A popular game with all who played it was the football game. For us it was something special, as Uncle Jack and Dad had thought it up and had even had ideas about taking out a patent on it! A sketch of its layout is easier to understand than a description.

Two players faced each other across the box, holding a two-foot length of ¾″ dowel. The football was a big 'glassy', about 1¼″ in diameter.

The start was like a 'bully off' in hockey. Each player poked a 'shooting-stick' through the central hole on his side of the box. The referee dropped the ball between them. The object then was to manoeuvre the ball to the opponent's side of the box. In this way, a player might find a blind spot where his opponent could not play the ball because he could not get sufficient angle with his stick to reach it. A skilful flick might take the 'glassy' over the opponent's stick and through a partition-hole into the scoring-square.

The manoeuvring was one skill; but more important was the speed with which a player moved from hole to hole along his side of the box. Often, in their excitement, players would think they were jabbing the stick through a hole only to find that they were a fraction away from it and striking the box-edge.

Speed was particularly vital when an opponent was in the scoring-square. If there was no defence he had an open goal; but, again, excitement could bring disaster, as with frantic swings at the ball the attacker failed to score, only to see that the defender was now in place and had wedged his stick into the goal-hole! A wary withdrawal might lead to a frenzied bout of fencing, as the defender tried to poke the ball back out of the square.

Seeing Uncle Charlie's billiard table, we were inspired to have our own game. We began with the dowel-rods of the football game, using them as cues. The big 'glassy' from the game, and two pot alleys, were pressed into service as we crawled about the floor playing 'billiards'. We used the pattern of the lino to give us 'pockets' to aim at! Or, to have more comfort standing upright, we moved up onto the table, where the sitting-out player kept the balls in play by using his cue as a sort of cushion.

Dad realized how earnest we were about the game. We had the surprise of our young lives one Christmas when we went downstairs to breakfast to find − not a meal laid on the table, but a quarter-size billiard table instead − cushions, baize, balls, cues, chalk, scoreboard, the lot! There was even a small spirit-level for setting up the table.

Flat-irons were heated in front of the fire to smooth the nap properly. That Christmas it took us all our time to drag ourselves away from the game. We even lost interest in food!

Over the succeeding weeks we became quite adept at billiards and snooker. Our Eric had a fluent style of play that led him into some fluky shots, hard to bear if they turned the game in his favour! But we all had our fluky moments. By and large we played on a friendly enough basis. Unfortunately it was not always possible to level the table exactly. When it was stored away it could only be left leaning against a wall in the parlour. Its laminated wooden bed took on a slight warp, so that the right-hand balk-pocket developed a droop that led to an otherwise wide ball curving gently home! Local knowledge is a great thing in all games!

Forts were not the only structures we made indoors. We also

played at camping — using the chairs, the table, the clothes-horse and, perhaps, the step-ladder, to make exotic abodes that would not have shamed a desert sheikh.

The same furniture could just as easily become a bus, train or boat. Tablecloths stretched up masts as sails, or were spread overhead as saloons aft, where we could shelter from the storm. All this indicates that Mam's kitchen furniture was practical, strong, and of little sentimental value. We did not hash it about. With it we had great scope for imaginative games that we enjoyed without the need for adult intervention or supervision. Always, the main thing was to see that everything was back in place before Dad came home from work.

One other source of fun came to hand in cast-off bits of material. This time, play was incidental to the making of a clip-mat. Two chairs were set back-to-back, four to five feet apart, and the mat-frame set on top. The sacking or hessian for the base of the mat was stretched on the frame. We sat underneath, sorting out the material, separating coloureds from blacks and blues. These dark colours were traditionally used to edge the finished pattern.

As we were old enough to use scissors, we were allowed to cut up the clips and pass them up to Mam, or even Gran or Aunty May, who would turn their hands to the task if they were visiting when there was nothing else on the go. May would very likely say, 'Get the mat out, Edie, if you've nothing special to do. We might as well be prodding as twiddling our thumbs!'

Like washing-up, it is one of those activities one can take part in without having to concentrate too hard, so that one can chat away or let one's mind wander.

Above our heads Mam would be prodding away, piercing the hessian and pushing one end of a clip down, then making a hole alongside and passing the other end of the clip through it, tugging the two ends even. When we became a bit obstreperous we would pat the underneath-side of the sacking and bounce the clips about. 'That's enough of that nonsense! Any more of it and you'll get a clip all right — across the ear!'

Eventually we reached the stage when we took a hand in the

clipping. Then we had the pleasure of pointing proudly to a piece of pattern that we had done ourselves. The prodder was usually a sharp-pointed piece of bone, wedged into the end of an empty cotton-reel for a handle. In small fists it was quite awkward to work, so that our efforts did not last long.

The finished article was thick and warm to walk on, or to lie about on in front of the fire. Clip-mats were the main covering in the kitchen on top of the lino. It was only in the front-room that we had a carpet. Upstairs in the bedrooms there was a slip of a bedside rug. Oh! the shock of the cold lino in winter, if we stepped just that inch or two wide of the rug!

CHAPTER TWENTY-SEVEN

Cultural Pursuits

As WE PROGRESSED with our reading in school, we began to take an interest in books at home. I vividly recall two titles, *The Swiss Family Robinson* and *The Gorilla-Hunters*, because both books helped me to pass two lengthy spells of illness in bed. The theme of *The Gorilla-Hunters* escapes me now, but *The Swiss Family Robinson* has probably inspired me to this day in my mechanical improvisations. It had been one of Dad's Sunday School prizes, a thick volume of five to six hundred pages of close print and innumerable etchings, which showed stratagems for dealing with wild animals and pirates attacking the abode of the ship-wrecked family, their bridge-building exploits and the like.

I have little interest in reading a book more than once. Perhaps the length of 'The Swiss Family' put me off. Besides, there are so many other good books to find time for. *Robinson Crusoe* was one, Grimm's *Fairy Tales* another, a thick book delightfully illustrated in colour. Many, many years later, I was to visit Strasbourg and climb up onto the Cathedral roof. I was thrilled to look down on the surrounding houses. Their gables, roofs, dormer-windows and even the colour of the brickwork seemed as if taken straight from the story-book I had read so long ago!

Books were fairly regular gifts at birthdays and Christmas. Then the 'Annuals' would appear in our stockings − Tiger Tim's and Rupert Bear's − amassing between one set of covers the sort of daily or weekly adventures of those characters whom we met in the newspaper or weekly comic, plus puzzles and pictures to colour.

Mam allowed us to have a weekly copy of Tiger Tim's comic,

The Rainbow; but later she did not agree with the Dundee-produced series of *Adventure, Wizard, Skipper, Rover* and (the last member of the team) *Hotspur*, each one appearing on a different weekday. She considered them 'trashy'! However, it was easy to get hold of a copy, perhaps a cast-off from a pal. Then, by swapping, we laid hands on the whole series.

How we devoured those yarns of Morgan the Mighty, the wonder goalie! A dozen years later, I was to be teaching in Morgan Academy, Dundee, which may have given its name to the hero of our youth. His story was most likely written by a former pupil of the same academy, since many former pupils from the Dundee academies (grammar-type schools) found employment with the D.C. Thomson press empire.

The Wolf of Kabul and Clickey-ba' (a fearsome cricket-bat which he wielded in tight spots with devastating results, overcoming tremendous odds) is another memory of magazine characters. A long-running series of yarns told of the man who drove a machine that could bore its way through the Earth. Fantasy? Today, hydro-generating stations are hidden inside mountains, with the use of machinery working on similar principles which takes all the slog out of navvying.

The Magnet recounted the adventures of the pupils of Greyfriars (Wharton and Co.) and the fat boy (Billy Bunter) who would have sold his soul for a cream-bun!

There is one big difference between all these papers and the modern 'comic'. In our day, pictures were few, but words there were in thousands. Today we wonder at the illiteracy in the nation, whose children and youth are fed on a pap of wordless TV images and comics that are a series of dramatic pictures accompanied by a text consisting of single utterances like, 'Wham!', 'Zing!', 'Zapp', and 'Gr-r-r!'

The Children's Newspaper was edited by Arthur Mee of *The Children's Encyclopaedia* fame. This weekly paper, delivered through the letter-box, was meant to give us an interest in newspaper-style literature to take us into the grown-up world of the 'dailies'. The present generation now has access to *Early Times*, an admirable publication of which Arthur Mee would certainly have approved.

Our early interest in the dailies was often limited to the children's page. Mam was interested in the crosswords, many of which were competitive, offering valuable prizes to be won. These competitions, like 'Bullets' in *Tit-bits*, which also offered good prizes, were no doubt meant to attract readership.

Though many of the answers to the clues of the crosswords were short, often of only three or four letters and seemingly easy to find, the catch was that there were alternatives to many of them, so that the chances of getting the right answers throughout the grid were almost as problematical as getting eight draws on the pools!

A clue might have read: 'caress (3)', meaning three letters needed. Was it 'pet' or 'pat'? That critical middle letter was blocked off by black squares, so that the puzzler was helpless and could only make a guess, taking a chance. We used to quiz Mam about her progress on a puzzle. The answer was usually the same, 'Oh, these alternatives!' Yet one week she did win a prize − a half tea-set!

The newspapers too attracted readers with offers of books and road-atlases. I have inherited *The Universal Home Guide* and *Home Gardens*. The latter is still a mine of information, running to 556 pages and giving, for example, lists of trees and shrubs to suit various sites − north-facing, shaded, sunny areas, etc. A cutting found inside, taken from the *Daily Mail* of 16th November 1935, is a good indication of when it was published and offered for sale.

The *Home Guide* is a meaty volume of 1152 pages, covering DIY, Family Health, Legal Matters, Etiquette − and a useful section on Sport that I had recourse to recently when I sent nephews a copy of the rules of croquet. They had picked up the equipment either from a relative or at an auction, but had only the vaguest notion of what the game was about!

At the age of eleven, we were able to join the Children's Section of the Durham County Library, in Chapel Lane, where it was housed in the infants' department of the church school. It was run by two or three ladies. Forms were filled in by parents and signed. When we had our own cards, we were able to choose books from both fiction and non-fiction shelves. The book-slips were duly stamped with the date of issue and retained at the counter in little pocket-envelopes which bore our names. The date of issue was also stamped inside the book-cover. We had a fortnight to read the book. Failure to hand it back in time incurred a fine of one penny a week for the time overdue.

Since the library had to share room with the school, it was only open on Monday, Tuesday and Thursday evenings. Avid readers aimed to take a book out on Monday night, read it and return it on Tuesday. The Tuesday book could be read at a more leisurely pace. On Thursdays we withdrew a fatter tome, since we had the extra days of the weekend to get through it. There were always plenty of borrowers of all age-groups. Eventually the need for accommodation was so great that a proper library was built in one of the avenues off Station Road.

I preferred school stories, Richmal Compton's series of the misadventures of that lovable rascal William, books of humour like Sellar's and Yeatman's *1066 and All That*, *And Now All This* and *Horse Nonsense*. From them it was a short step to P.G. Wodehouse's Bertie Wooster and Jeeves.

An interest in boats and sailing led us to the non-fiction shelves, where we unearthed Joshua Slocum's account of his voyage single-handed round the world, and a trilogy on the same theme by the Frenchman Alain Gerbault. I was to use extracts from *In Quest of the Sun* (*A la Recherche du Soleil*) in my teaching of French to senior Scottish pupils!

We studied closely Major Raven-Hart's *Canoe Errant*, an account of canoeing in Europe. The author paddled from the Channel through the French canals into the Rhine, and down the Danube to the Black Sea. He made reference to German 'fol-boots', which could be collapsed and carried in a rucksack. This interested us especially, as we were thinking of building a Scout kayak ourselves.

It has taken me practically all my working days to return to that joyous reading. The discipline of studying the classics, in our own and foreign literatures, stunted rather than fed an interest in books. I feel I have time to browse freely now that books are no longer part of my stock-in-trade.

Music was another interest that entered our home. We often fell asleep to it at bed-time. Mam had learnt the piano in her youth, gaining her 'letters', L.R.C.M. She was qualified to teach, like her old friend Jessie Yellow. But what time did she have for piano-playing as she brought up a family?

However, when she was in the mood and probably less worn out, she would go to the piano in the front-room, once we were all in bed, and play. Chopin, Beethoven, Mozart, the 'hits' of the day and airs from *The Desert Song*, *Show Boat* and other musicals, all mixed into the programme, would resound up the stairway. We sang along with the bits that we knew, or hummed some of the classical themes; but before long we drifted off into slumber, relaxed and happy. Now those memories are revived as I listen to much the same sort of music on the radio on a Sunday morning, after the eight o'clock news, while preparing to meet the day.

Our next door neighbours, the 'Doos', were members of Middlesbrough Operatic Society. Many an evening, in the period leading up to the week of performances, Frank and Doris would come in with their music and ask Mam to play the accompaniment on the piano. They let rip with their parts, only to stop to argue about and discuss the timing or the emphasis on this note or that. Mam would try to offer advice from her own musical experience. So it went on, with tunes repeated, often to our delight, not only because of the melody but also because whilst Mam was playing our bedtime was being delayed!

Much of this music we heard again on records, when Dad bought a gramophone. It was a piece of furniture enclosing a clockwork-driven turn-table mounted with its sound-box in a cabinet. It had storage space below for a few records. The spring of the drive was kept tight by cranking a handle. Usually there was enough tension, when the spring was fully wound up, to let a twelve-inch record play right through at 78 revs per minute.

The selection was a mixed bag on His Master's Voice, Columbia or Decca labels − 'O for the Wings of a Dove' sung by a wonder-boy soprano, the 'Light Cavalry Overture' by Suppé, and the odd hit-tune of the day on ten-inch records. I was reminded of one of the latter when, in the 'sixties, during a game of 'Scrabble', a Welsh friend led off with 'Goosey'! This was immediately challenged by Doug from Aberdeen. Possibly I became Lewis Jones' friend for life when I backed him up by singing the opening lines − 'How do you feel when the bells begin to peel? − Ever so goosey, goosey, goosey!' The rest of it goes on: "Walking up the aisle in a kind of daze, Don't you get the wind up when the organ plays?'

In every age new techniques are developed. One of the problems in the musical world of the 'thirties was to discover a long-lasting needle which would also reduce wear and tear on the groove of the record. With each box of steel needles there was a reminder to 'use a fresh needle each time' a record was played! A fibre needle, which could be sharpened, was launched onto the market. For this a special sharpening device was required!

Many of the tunes we heard on record were featured in the programmes of the dance bands of the day as they entertained us over the wireless waves at 5.15 each evening. Henry Hall and the BBC Dance Orchestra (signing off with 'Here's to the next time!'), Jack 'Agony' Payne, Ambrose, Joe Loss (and, jokingly, 'Dead Loss', his brother), Geraldo and his Orchestra, and the Dorsey Brothers, were all household names. My first recollection of a 'hit' was 'Show me the way to go Home', sung by buskers to a ukulele accompaniment as we sat in a sand-hole on the beach at Seaton Carew in 1925.

The melodies and rhythm really affected us. When cousin Ray was at our place for tea, a wild jazz session would start as the table was being laid. With spoons, knives and forks, we would proceed to tap on the plates, saucers, cups and jugs − as well as jam, chutney or pickle-jars and the H.P. Sauce bottle − lah-lahing the tunes to a ceramic or metallic backing rhythm. But just let Dad appear at the front, drawing up on his bike from work, and the silence was almost deafening!

Another musical (?) descendant, out of 'Comb' by 'Paper' was 'Gazooka' or 'Kazoo', having the lines of a submarine. The conning-tower held a piece of thin tissue paper. We hummed into the stern end of the vessel and out from the bows came a 'zizzing' sound of the tune. When the tissue tore or wore out, we simply unscrewed the conning-tower, cut a disc of thin grease-proof paper, and fitted it back into place. Kazoo bands were and still are, in the North-East, a feature of weekend summer galas when bandsgirls, kitted out in colourful uniforms, parade and play for trophies.

All of this may tend to give an impression that musical memories are of gaiety, love, life and laughter. But the dark clouds lowered. Literally! Their dark masses pressed down over Rancliffe Woods, which waved and tossed below a frieze of high-voltage electric cable suspended between tall pylons. A sudden zig-zag of steely-blue, a cardiographic dance along the power-lines, a swish, then an overhead clap of awesome thunder had us bairns cowering close to Gran, Mam, Aunty May and Aunty Laura. The fear of death was upon us. There was no escape. The whole storm-scape was open to our view through the bow-fronted window of the sitting-room. Sheet lightning lit up the background sky. As if to appease a god, thundering from the heights of an anvil-shaped storm-cloud, our elders struck up the dirgiest of hymns — 'Abide with me', 'When Mothers of Salem', 'Lead Kindly Light' or 'O God our Help in Ages Past'! It was all too much for us. We dashed out of the room, rushed up the stairs, dived into bed and hid under the safety of the blankets!

Visual stimulation came with the building of the Billingham Picture House at the top of Mill Lane. It was a rare refuge on wet Saturday mornings, and a cheap price for parents to pay to have some peace and quiet to themselves. The 'Tuppenny Rush' was a noisy stampede, driven into the corral of the wooden seats at the very front of the cinema. There, for two pennies (not even equal to 1p today!), we had to crane our necks up at an awkward angle to follow the adventures on the screen. If I had to watch like that today I should have a permanent crick in the neck. It just goes to show how resilient children are.

The programme consisted of a cartoon, a comic film, and the SERIAL! This was a long-running series of adventures, in which the hero and heroine were beset by 'baddies' of the deepest dye.

We were held spellbound. The music rose to a climax, then ... the film stopped! A caption appeared on the screen. (No, not 'Don't switch off your set ... !') Simply, 'To be continued next week!' It was always at some tense moment for our stars. We were left wondering, leaving the cinema arguing, 'Will they escape?' 'Will she drown?' 'Will the train stop in time?' Although the sequel from the previous week ought to have reassured us, we were too caught up in the drama to realize that all would be well. Out from the cinema we poured – hot, faces flushed, blinking in the broad daylight. Of course, we would be pestering for the coppers for the following week. Those Saturday matinées played havoc with plans to run a regular football team and play matches against other sides.

Other trips to the 'pictures' were something of a treat, as they took place at the 'First House'. 'Second House' was far too late for us to stay up. In any case, the film had to have some educational value, incorporating something of the 'documentary'. *Africa Speaks* is the vivid title of a film that epitomized the kind of show we were allowed to see, because big-game animals moved about in their natural surroundings.

Also acceptable were Walt Disney's cartoons of Mickey Mouse and Company, as they were not likely to corrupt. Our Eric could watch those films, come back home, and give an account of the whole episode, word for word, blow by blow, imitating to perfection the voice of such a character as Donald Duck. Mam and Dad knew their money had been well spent, and we enjoyed as good as a Second House when Eric got going with his mimicry. Not only that! He had the knack of sketching Mickey, Minnie, Donald, Goofy and Co. so that you would have been hard-pushed to tell which had been drawn by Eric and which by the maestro himself!

My first cinema visit took place about 1926, when I was taken to Stockton Empire to see a film starring Tom Mix, one of our cowboy heroes of the silent days. Happily, TV's revival of the 'Golden Oldies' stirs memories of laughter that made our sides ache and had us rolling in our seats, when Laurel and Hardy, Harold Lloyd, Buster Keaton and the Keystone Kops were involved outrageously in the most hilarious yet also most gripping incidents. How could we ever forget the 'genius' of Charlie Chaplin, though we did not know the meaning of the word? I remember him better in his full-length films of more recent date, such as *Modern Times* and *The Great Dictator*.

In the comic film world we had our own local-boy-makes-good – Will Hay, born in Stockton. The trio of Will Hay, Graham Moffat and Moore Marriott promised evenings of hilarity in film stories based on Narkover, the school disorganized and mismanaged by its head, Will himself. I wish I could remember the clever details of the 'history' lesson Will gave to the class when the inspector had arrived unsuspectingly as they were 'studying form' for the afternoon race-meeting. Suffice it to say that the 'Black Prince' removed his 'silks' at 5-1 favourite, to don the sinister armour of the sixteenth century royal heir, the Black Prince, who battled against the French.

Tears of laughter ran down our cheeks at *Oh! Mr Porter!* (a farcical railway mix-up) or *Wind-bag the Sailor* (a side-splitting, seafaring adventure when, amongst other things, according to Wind-bag, they must have 'sailed past Norway in the night!'). Now, fifty years on, when I have seen these films revived on the small screen, I wonder what we saw in them to make us laugh so. On the other hand, sketches we concocted in our student days in the 'forties would have put us on a par with David Frost and TW3, the Two Ronnies, and Monty Python's crowd; but TV cameras were not on hand then. Tempora mutantur ...

Indoor cultural pursuits led us on the rare occasion away from Billingham to the Dorman Museum in Linthorpe, Middlesbrough. Models of ships built in local yards, like Smith's Docks in South Bank and the Furness Yard at Haverton Hill, were a particular attraction. Dad or Uncle Jack would take us over to see them, no doubt on account of their close connection with both places and firms, as Uncle had worked in Smith's Docks and both he and Dad had sailed with boats of the Ropner Line bearing names that ended in 'pool'.

In his last years, Uncle told me an interesting fact or two about his life connected with shipbuilding and sailing. In 1917, working as a cabin-boy, he was rescued off the Norfolk coast by Henry

Blogg, the renowned coxswain of the Cromer lifeboat. In the 'seventies in the same town, Uncle and a Dutch skipper, who were the only surviving seafarers from long years ago to have been rescued by Blogg, received an invitation to a dedication in honour of the lifeboatman. It was a proud day for Uncle. In the Cromer lifeboat-station I have seen with my own eyes the details of that 1917 rescue, inscribed on the board that records the calls answered by the boat and its crew.

During Uncle's time in the shipyard, whalers were built for Salvesen's. The harpoon-gun was mounted on the foredeck, on a post which went the full depth of the ship down to its base on the keel-plate. This mounting was housed in a metal casing. It was Uncle's job to squeeze into the space inside the casing to inspect the post. He was the only skilled man in the yard small enough to carry out the claustrophobic examination, which was important as the gun-post bore the shock of the recoil of the harpoon-gun.

In 1931 we experienced real travel adventure. We were taken on a trip north to Tyneside to the Newcastle Exhibition held on the Town Moor, one of the handiest show-sites in any city, as it is close to the city centre and the population of Geordieland. Even before we arrived there we had the Tyne Bridge pointed out to us, a masterpiece of bridge construction by Dorman Long and Co.

The smell of wood-smoke, and its blue clouds rising above a 'kraal', led us to the African Village, one of the sights of the Exhibition. There, right enough, were real black men and native women, dressed in animal skins just as we had seen them on the Picture House screen in *Africa Speaks* or as 'extras' with Paul Robeson in *Sanders of the River*. I can still see that slightly menacing skinny figure of the black fellow, who must have wished himself far enough away from the drizzle and grey skies of Tyneside.

In the industrial section of the Exhibition we saw a bottling-plant. Bottles clinked past in a maze of circuits − being filled, corked and labelled en-route! 'Andrews Liver Salts' had a similar display. A tin of it stood handy in a cupboard at home, to tune up sluggish systems! It was quite exciting to put a spoonful of the powder into a glass of water and suddenly see it dissolve into a burst of bubbles. But the drink itself was disappointing, as it did not live up to its promise like the other fizzy drinks we enjoyed, and the bubbles kept getting up our noses!

On a platform of Newcastle station, as we were waiting for the train home, Dad found a labelling-machine, with which we stamped out our names on a strip of metal. Those name-tags lay unused about the house for years.

The Boys' Brigade and Scout movements are very much part of our British culture. These organizations provided us with further opportunities to work off surplus energy. Eric was a Cub, then a Scout, and ultimately ran a troop of his own. I did not join the Scouts. I had plenty of homework from the 'Sec' to fill up my spare time. Furthermore, the extramural activities that the 'Sec' offered, through its sports teams and the Literary and Historical Society, satisfied me and fitted into my weekly programme. Though I was not a Scout, I was much taken with the ideals of Scouting; so, for one of my Christmas boxes I asked for a copy of *Scouting for Boys*, written by the founder of the movement, Lord Baden-Powell. One phrase from the book still sticks in my mind – THE camping slogan, 'All you leave behind is your thanks!'

There was a cultural side to Scouting in the Scout Gang Show, put on by the Synthonia Troop and played to packed houses year after year. The audiences did not consist just of fond parents and relatives. Such was the appeal and quality of the performances that folk flocked from all over Teesside to be entertained, and returned home eagerly awaiting the next year's event!

There was no doubt that it owed much of its success to Mr Brown, a top-notch producer. He had a pair of 'naturals' for the comic sketches in John 'Tin-ribs' Tinning and his 'feed', Dougie Wilson. They were a well-matched pair, 'Tin-ribs' somewhat rotund and Wilson a tall slim stooge. They were the heart of the show, ably supported by the rest of the troop, a well-drilled cast. Oh that we could still enjoy their fun! Luckily our generation, familiar with Scout Gang Shows, have happy memories rekindled every time we hear the opening line of the original Gang Show signature tune, 'We're Riding Along on the Crest of a Wave'. Long may their successors ride that heady surf!

CHAPTER TWENTY-EIGHT

Activities away from 'The Road'

THE 'REC' offered not only space to play football and cricket but also recreational equipment provided by the Council – swings, a maypole, and the 'Ocean-wave'. The Gang Show song may have had us riding the crests. The 'Ocean-wave' had us down in the troughs as well!

The cone-shaped contraption really lived up to its name. Metal rods splayed down from the peak of the cone. At the bottom end they were attached to a circle of wooden seats with a hand-rail. The peak not only rotated, it rocked as well. So we could swirl round the mast on a 'calm sea' or, by making a lesser or greater rocking movement at the same time, we could combine the gentle rotation with a sickening swaying which was not at all amusing for the squeamish!

Of course, we found other uses for the 'Ocean-wave'. The open grid of bars gave many a budding 'Tarzan' the chance to show off to the girls as he swung across and around the rotating 'Wave'. The girls could be impressed in another fiendish way, and reduced to a screeching mass of hysteria, as the bigger lads used their strength to swing the 'Wave' around at a terrifying rate and rock it as violently as possible. Accidents happened, but it was a wonder there were not more serious ones.

The Maypole, a metal toadstool about twenty feet high, could change seasick 'circumnavigators' into giddy 'aviators'! To its dome were attached long thick ropes that dangled about three or four feet from the ground. Half-a-dozen of us at a time could take a rope and swirl in the air as the dome was set circling. Somebody had the hair-raising idea of taking a rope over the top of the other ropes, so that when the maypole rotated he got an added acceleration that sent him flying high into the air and at a faster rate. It really took some nerve to hold on as one emulated a rider on a fairground 'Chair-a-plane'.

A stand of six swings completed the mechanical amusements. Again, it did not take long for someone to find more excitement on the swings than was normally the case. It was a gentle matter for a big brother or sister to push a timid younger sibling on a swing, just as high as the rider wanted to go. A daring swinger, however, would stand on the seat and, using the extra leverage of his legs, swing himself up until he was horizontal with the top strut from which the swing hung. I have a hazy recollection that one of the bold boys even tried to 'loop the loop'!

A swing could always be a source of hurt, especially when little ones forgot and turned their backs. If a descending swing caught them a heavy blow, they might be knocked flat on their faces and suffer a nasty bump on the back of the head into the bargain. With a bunch of kids all milling around wanting a turn, it was not surprising that such accidents occurred.

Our other flying experience in the 'Rec', though more passive, was none the less exhilarating. The kite-flying craze took possession of us one summer. I had seen a design for a 'humming-kite' in a little monthly paper, *The Junior Craftsman*, that we ordered in the woodwork class at the 'Sec'. I still have the 1935 copy in which the instructions are given for making it. I had tried the familiar pear-shaped kite without success. Some lads had box-kites, bought in a shop and therefore beyond our means.

We pestered Mam for brown paper, scissors and paste, which she mixed for us from flour and water. We needed lengths of Dad's garden-canes, carefully slit down the middle, to give us lightness yet strength too. One of these lengths had to be bent to form a 'bow' to accommodate the 'hummer'. Once we had the 'tailings' adjusted and the kite trained not to nose-dive, we spent hours up in the 'Rec', clear of obstructions like telegraph-wires, wireless-aerials and trees, playing our kites as a fisherman plays a fish.

It was not long before we were spending pocket money on balls of string, vying with each other to see who could get his kite to fly the highest. The kites 'hummed' beautifully. We threaded the round cardboard tops off the milk bottles on to our kite strings to send 'messages' up to the kites. There was no selfishness. We shared with pals less fortunate who did not own kites, so that they too could feel the thrill of the lively string and the tug of the dancing paper hexagon trying to take wing into the blue beyond.

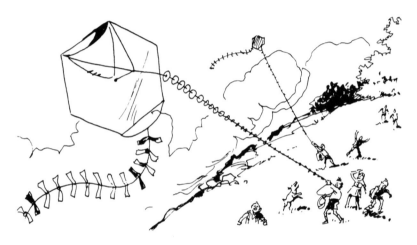

Cricket accounted for the major part of our summer playtime, possibly because most of us owned items of equipment. My share was a bat, ball, and stumps with bails − the reward for 'passing the Scholarship'. Quite often a 'Scholar's' prize was a new bicycle. In my case that was out of the question, either because such a purchase was too expensive or because traffic was becoming heavier and faster so that Mam and Dad decided to go against tradition. Instead they bought a set of three-quarter-size stumps, steel-pointed and topped with brass ferrules to hold the bails. Best of all was a bat of my very own, a three-springer, with three bands of rubber in the handle. They reduced the shock of contact when a hard ball, bowled at speed, struck the bat.

It cost Dad 7s. 6d. (37½p), the equivalent of a good three hours of a man's working day! It was not autographed. To own such a bat, branded with the names of Herbert Sutcliffe, Walter Hammond, or best of all Don Bradman the Australian Test star, was to set the owner in a class apart. Often that could be more a sign of affluence than competence. Many a less fortunate pal swung an ordinary bat with greater skill. If one of the special bats should fall to his lot, he could give the lucky owner a dazzling display of what the bat could do in the hands of a real batsman.

Non-players knew that the season had arrived by the smell of linseed oil which we rubbed over the willow blades, taking care not to let any drip on to the splice. Ironmongers found themselves having to stock extra rolls of insulating tape as the solid hump of the bat was firmly bound with generous strips of the tacky stuff. I can still recall the feeling of dismay when my own bat, in somebody else's hands, took a fast ball on the edge and was dented! In its time it must have scored thousands of runs, which meant thousands of moments of pleasure for all of us who wielded it.

Cricket on the 'Rec' followed a ritual. We sounded out Tom and Ro Arnott, hoping that they had finished polishing the cutlery. Then we collected my gear. I always hung on to my bat! The others shared out the stumps. At No. 25 we called on Stan Meachen, who also owned a stout bat. We gave Ron Davy a shout at No. 24. Like the Meachens, he could walk out of his back gate into the 'Rec'.

We trooped a hundred yards up the slope to the flattest area of the playing-field. It was not the smoothest, but was as good as any other part where we were likely to find a wicket. We set the stumps up at the regulation distance, as near as twenty-two of our paces could make it, then we chose the sides. 'Ginger' Reed, the Jelley lads, Bill Palmer, Walter Pugh, Ray Corner, Les Brown and one or two more drifted along.

The captains, often the lads who owned the bats, tossed for first choice of players. If they did not have a coin they drew straws, or threw the bat into the air and called 'Face or Hump'. A side with Stan and 'Ginger' in it was well on the road to victory! Both had a good eye for batting. Both were fast bowlers, 'Ginger' being probably the more deadly. Another toss for innings, and we were ready to start.

Once it was known which side was to field, a clamour arose. 'Bowler, top end, no sixes!' 'Bowler, bottom end!' Somebody might intervene with, 'Sixes!' This meant that two fielders were to take turns to bowl from the bottom end, whereas the bowler at the top end would bowl unchanged until a batsman was 'out', when the calls rang out again! Bowlers acted as wicket-keepers. When they fielded the ball they bowled it back at the opposing batsman. In this way the game proceeded almost non-stop. No time was wasted on 'overs'! Generally it worked out that those who could bowl had a reasonable stint at it. Everybody had a turn with the bat.

Though our junior by at least two years, our Eric was no mean bowler, specializing in all kinds of spin and lobbing up tantalizingly slow balls that, with his own suppleness and, on occasion, the help of a nicely placed bump or hollow, had most of us guessing – or looking at a shattered wicket!

But he could be mean in another sense. If things were not going right and he felt he was not having his fair share of the bowling, or if he did not agree with a decision (often the thorny LBW), he just sat in front of the stumps. Mahatma Gandhi and his 'passive resistance' was not in it! The chances were that Eric also had the *ball* in his possession. My only counter was to threaten, 'Look, our kid. If you don't pack in I'll just tell our Mam, and you'll have to go home. That will be the end of that!' Perhaps out of pure cussedness he would throw the ball away, mope a bit, and finally make his way back into the game. Such instances were rare. Perhaps he was just fed up with being bossed about by me and some of the other older lads.

The beck, that flowed at the bottom of the field across the road from our houses, was not at all like the becks and gills of the moors that tumbled their way over rock and peat, offering ice-cold water to slake the rambler's thirst.

On old maps it appears as the mill-stream to the mill that gave its name to one of the main thoroughfares in the township. So it was of uniform depth, cleared periodically of excess weed by the beck-men to ensure a steady flow, not to the mill (now demolished) but into the boiler-house of the factory.

Beyond the beck was the coke dump. From home we had seen every stage of its development. Refuse from the anhydrite mines below the whole factory complex had been hauled out in tipper-wagons pulled by the little locos. This white clayey substance had gradually filled in the low-lying field area between our beck and the main stream that flowed below Rancliffe Woods. Ro and 'Pluff' used to go down to where the locos were shunting. They had chatted to the drivers, who allowed them the heady excitement of a ride on the footplate. How we envied them! Gradually a ramification of sidings spread over the area. Coke was dumped alongside in parallel miniature ranges. Huffing puffing cranes arrived, with their grabs loading and unloading the coke, tons at a time as it was needed.

It was needed all right, not only by ICI but by the unemployed of Stockton and district! They came on foot, pushing old prams and barrows. They pedalled their way there on bikes. They filled their sacks by hand with great chunks of coke of a quality that, it was soon discovered, was not meant to burn on household fires. The draught was not fierce enough! Away they trundled their loads, pram-covers hiding sacks, sacks hanging conspicuously over cross-bars or handle-bars of bikes! Such a traffic developed that the factory authorities put up a fence at the bridge at the foot of the 'Gully', where at odd times a policeman patrolled.

We ventured across the bridge once or twice to scramble up and down the 'hills' of coke that shifted under our feet as we climbed, dodging from 'valley' to 'valley', playing hide-and-seek with one another. However, we did not play long on the coke dump. It had not lost its attraction, but parents had noticed the scratches and scuff-marks on our boots. Breeches-seats were beginning to wear thin! We were warned in no uncertain terms. We took heed of the warnings!

Yet I do not remember any special warnings about going down to the beck. Perhaps the dangers had been pointed out the first time we had ventured there. Perhaps, too, we were safe enough, as we were only the length of a back-garden away from friends and neighbours. It was quite a different matter if we went to the bottom of Billingham Bank to play at the 'waterfall', the name we gave to the spot where the main beck spilled excess water over the sluice-gates. Tragedy had already occurred there!

Along 'our' beck there were a few places where the bank had crumbled and formed a wide enough platform for us to fish from. There we thronged in noisy proximity. In front of us, minnows and sticklebacks spawned in profusion. A garden-cane or a stick from an elder-bush, with a length of black thread tied to an end, served our purpose. Worms from the garden were used as bait. Some of the lads speared these on bent pins; but many of us simply tied them by a slip-knot, delicately drawn taut round the worm's middle to hold it on the line and just avoid cutting it in two!

It demanded a fair amount of skill to judge whether a fish had swallowed enough of the worm to be held by its greed, so that we could whip our catch up out of the water. We did not need accessories like floats, as the beck was so clear we could easily see our intended victims.

On fine sunny days we fished from breakfast till teatime. By our side we had a jam-jar, filled with beck-water with a sprig of weed floating in it. Our catch was made to feel very much at home! On occasion we caught so many tiddlers that we had to transfer them into tin baths or pails, which we kept 'round the back' (at the back of the house). How often we were dismayed to see our 'aquarium' turned into a morgue as the poor little things died off overnight. On the odd occasion we caught a bigger red-breasted fellow. Now, thanks to TV nature programmes, I know that they were male fish; but we had been thrilled to catch a 'salmon-trout'!

'Pluff' surprised us with a technique completely beyond our ken. He put his worm inside a 2lb. jam-jar which he lowered into the beck, surmising that since the water was so clear for us to see the fish, they would easily see the worm and swim into the jar! It did happen, but not often enough to encourage us to adopt his original technique!

Of all of us who fished there, only one remained true to the sport, Ray Corner. He tended to be a 'loner', not one for joining in many of our team games. He went on to take up fishing in a big way. He acquired the tackle and a motor-bike, on which he rode to competitions all over the country, winning quite a few prizes on his outings.

Above the 'waterfall', the main beck broadened out into a deepish pool below sheer banks about three feet high, close to the narrow wooden footbridge at the bottom of Chapel Lane. On hot summer days, crowds flocked to the spot, some to swim, others to watch the dare-devil antics of some of the swimmers. On the Billingham side of the beck, hedges provided enough privacy for changing in and out of 'cossies'. Daring lads raced over the flat field space towards the beck to perform exciting dives in front of admiring spectators, many of whom were lassies! We watched somersaulting, leap-frogging, jack-knifing and, often, honest-to-goodness belly-flopping with resounding 'crack' and deluges of displaced water!

We ourselves were put off by the muddy colour of the stream as the bottom was churned up by the disporting throng. When swimmers emerged from the pool we noticed their feet and ankles coated in a greyish slime. Ugh! However, *our* chance to plumb those same depths was yet to come!

Billingham Bottoms − this geographical term conjures up all sorts of coarse imaginings − were the flat low-lying fields through which the main beck flowed. In the autumn, if the weather did its bit and brought heavy rains, we awoke to acres of flooded meadows. All we prayed for, then, was for the sky to clear at night to give us hard frost and freezing daytime temperatures. Inch by inch, the ice formed and thickened till it bore our weight − not only our odd few stones, but the tons and tons of Teesside humanity as the crowds thronged down to the fields at the foot of Beaconsfield Street. Stockton, Norton, even Thornaby and Middlesbrough bottoms, knew the pain of sudden contact with unyielding ice as skaters lost their balance or bairns their footing in the run-up to a slide or in some acrobatic caper as they shot over the ice.

From the cupboard under the stairs, Mam had unearthed two pairs of old-fashioned wooden skates like the ones Dutch skaters may still wear on their frozen canals. Upwards from the heel of each of these skates protruded a thickish screw, which we turned until it was firmly embedded in the heel of one of our boots. Toe and heel straps helped to keep the skates in place. The only snag was, that with all the strain and stress that we put on the skates, the screw-holes enlarged or the layers of leather in the heels of our boots tore away from the welts. That was an end to *our* skating, at least until we could persuade Dad to get out his last and tack-hammer to nail the heels back again. I was always intrigued to see how he could hold a mouthful of sprigs, and tap them home one by one without any disappearing down the wrong way!

One Christmas I put in a request to Santa for a pair of all-steel skeleton-skates. A little spanner adjusted the heel and toe clamps. The heel clamps had serrated edges, the better to grip into the heel of the boot. However, they still had a tendency to work the layers of leather apart at the heels, but repairs were carried out before too much damage was done.

Working in the machine-shop, Dad was able to get one of his mates to trim up the edges of the blades on a lathe, so that I became the proud owner of skates that were hollow-ground, possibly the sharpest pair of blades on the ice!

I envied some better-off kids, who owned proper skating-boots which laced up well above the ankle, so saving the wearers from many of the sprains and twists I was prone to. Their lightweight chrome-plated skates were screwed firmly and permanently to the boots. The toes of the blades were serrated, so that the skater could come to a sudden halt, pirouette, and do all manner of wonderful manœuvres. Little wonder that, as my skill improved, I grew envious of those lucky kids equipped with proper skating gear!

Edna 'Ginger' Dickinson's dad was a good skater. Her family lived on the NESCO estate, so they were of a different social standing from us. But my interest in skating and her dad's willingness to tutor me broke across the social barrier. He was very patient and soon had me doing my inside and outside edges on either foot, forwards and in reverse. Oh, I took quite a few tumbles, staving my wrists a time or two.

Since polio put an end to a lot of this kind of sport for me I have regretted not being able to show my daughters how to skate, to know the exhilaration of gliding effortlessly over ice, pirouetting and swerving, out in the cold crisp air of a sunny winter's day, on a tiny patch of natural ice or with acres of such freedom.

The 'Bottoms' attracted their quota of 'characters'. I can see one old gent now. He must have been in his sixties. His speciality was 'The Vine', a series of forward and backward movements on the edges of his skates that left a tracery of vine-leaf pattern on the ice. Hands in pockets, he would waggle his skates forward, then back, almost like a piston. Admirers stood around watching this artistic and nonchalant performance.

There were the dare-devil types who would attempt to leap over all kinds of obstacles. Space a-plenty allowed us to whirl like dervishes in hectic games of ice hockey, though most of our pals were playing at a disadvantage, not having skates of their own. We evened things out by pairing off the skaters against each other, between the teams.

It was into this scene that Dad decided to intrude his presence – not openly in broad daylight, but with the cover of darkness to hide any embarrassment. There were enthusiasts who came down at night to skate. They drove their cars into the fields, shining headlights onto the ice in order to enjoy the special atmosphere of skating in the romantic gloom.

On this occasion, Ray was with us to lend a supporting arm on one side whilst I did my bit on the other. We had to cope with quite a bit of drunken leglessness as Dad tried to make the skates go his way. However, despite thumping falls on the ice, he gradually got the hang of it. We let go of him! I can still see the determined clumping sort of movements his feet made on his first solo run.

We all staggered wearily home the long mile from 'Beakie' Street to New Road, sometime about midnight. I trust Mam did not give Dad any playful love-taps on his poor bum. More than likely she would have chided him for being so daft as to attempt the skating at his age! (He would have been in his forties then.)

I was not aware of it at the time, but the fact that Dad had come to us to learn something, and not to amuse us, probably indicated that we were stepping out of childhood.

'Stiff' Meachen, one of the older lads, introduced us to a couple of spots in the countryside where we spent hour after hour of the long summer days. 'What about going to the Willow-garth?' was 'Stiff's' suggestion. It lay below the railway embankment and the 'Ninety-nine Steps', about a mile across the fields from the bottom of Billingham Bank. Fairly recently a new road was driven right under the embankment where the 'Steps' used to be, to form a bypass to the original Bypass Road. The 'Ninety-nine Steps' took us up and over the main Stockton − Newcastle railway line. From there a path led on to Norton Quarry, a forbidden playground of tipper-wagons that we pushed along narrow-gauge railway-lines. Beyond the quarry, the walk led out to the Golden Gates of Lord Londonderry's estate at Wynyard.

The Willow-garth (or 'Willoy' as we called it) was a wasteland, cut off from the main meadow by a drainage ditch along which stretched a line of willow trees. This jungle of tall reeds was crossed by secret trails, zig-zagging to avoid swampy pools where frogs spawned.

An old willow with a low-spreading branch was 'base camp'. There we dumped our haversacks or 'bait-tins' ('bait' being our lunch). We divided into sides and set about hunting our opponents. For this type of game, the 'Willoy' was a boys' paradise. The narrow trails between the reeds were ideally suited for laying traps. We knotted long grasses at ankle height across the trail, then ambushed the unsuspecting victims, pouncing on them as they fell their length. When we misjudged a jump from one patch of solid ground to the next, our feet got soaking wet. We just wrung the water out of our socks and hung them up at 'base' to dry in the sun.

As a break from chasing, we would try and imitate 'Tarzan'. The hollow re-echoed with that famous call − Aah-ooh-a-o-aah-hoo − as we swung from a rope tied to some high branch. We were all keen Johnny Weissmuller fans, following his adventures at the 'Tuppenny Rush' sessions.

A quieter ploy was to make reed-whistles. We had to take turns to borrow 'Stiff's knife. The critical factor was the exact length of the slit that we cut in the upper wall of the reed. It was quite a finicky job to cut it just right and get a high-pitched 'peep'. Failure gave us a reedy 'raspberry' for our pains. Still, there were ample supplies of reed to let us try again and again.

During another interlude we panted to the top of the 'Ninety-nine Steps' to watch the trains go by, or in more serious moments to do some train-spotting, notebooks and pencils 'at the ready'. Articles in the *Meccano Magazine* explained how locomotives could be identified by their wheel-bases, and what classes they belonged to. We also knew how to tell what type of train was being pulled from the positioning of the headlights, above the front buffers and below the funnel of the engine. An express train carried two lamps, one above each buffer. The Flying Scotsman, No. 4472, was the great attraction as it came thundering past, not having stopped in Billingham station. A long straight stretch of track across to Norton allowed the driver to show off the machine's paces.

In the appropriate columns we noted the details, 'wheel-base: 4-6-2; number: 4472; name: The Flying Scotsman'. The details of another favourite read, '4-4-0; 360; Yorkshire; Shire class'. The work-horses of the LNER, which pulled the heavy coal-trains from the collieries, were 0-8-0s, and the shunting locos 0-4-0s, both types having no bogie-wheels – just main driving-wheels. Today I can hardly understand how train-spotters bother watching out for what seems to be relative uniformity in locomotive body and movement. Oh! the nostalgia, to smell the coal-smoke and hot oil, hear the hiss of steam and see the thrashing of con-rods powering the huge driving-wheels along!

The other place of boyhood enchantment where 'Stiff' led us was Norburn Beck. The O.S. map marks it simply as North Burn. It was the 'Willow-garth' plus! To penetrate to the heart of the vale, we had ahead of us a hike of a good five miles. Perhaps there would be ten of us traipsing along beyond the station, up the A19 to Wolviston and another mile further up the Sunderland road, to where the beck flowed under the highway.

Yet we were never bored. We 'car-spotted' distinctive makes like Morris, Austin, Bean, Singer, Riley, Daimler, Armstrong-Siddeley, and even a Lagonda 'open-tourer'! Or there were motor-bikes to note, all good British makes, machines that thrilled the crowds at the Isle of Man T.T. Races. Where are they now? In another game, each of us decided on a digit, 0 to 9. We had to keep a running total of the score as we recognized our digit on a passing number-plate. In the early days of the 'double-decker', a new form of bus transport, we vied to see who would be the first to spot the most recent number in the series of Corporation buses. 'I've seen No. 33!' 'Oh, there's a 34 and 35 out now!'

Once we reached the beck, all thoughts of the trek were behind us. It was 'over the stile, across the field and down to the beck side'! Norburn was something we had to respect. Below steep banks lay dark pools of uncertain depth. There were narrows where the stream rippled over pebbles. Here, if we failed to clear the water in one jump, a nimble skip on a part-submerged stone could save us from getting both feet wet!

As, near its source, the beck flowed through a wooded area and, like our own beck, was liable to overflow its banks in heavy rain, the estate had erected floodgates at certain points to trap debris brought down by flood-water. Such a gate was to be found on arrival at Norburn. Here began an 'initiation ceremony'.

We had to cross from one side of the beck to the other, balancing on top of the beam from which the gate hung. This was the first 'funkie'. If we funked it, we were not really fit to join in the Norburn trek. An elm preferred a branch conveniently over the gate, so that we had a little more security at our first test.

There were two or three more of these gates, offering us further chances of redeeming ourselves. Other 'funkies' might involve us in climbing a certain tree, where the test was for us to swing ourselves fearfully across the beck, holding on to a drooping branch. Further along the stream, a headlong rush down a slope was the approach to an attempt to clear a testing width of the beck. Risks we ran, of that there is no doubt. If anything serious had happened, we were in a relatively isolated spot, not within a mile of a habitation. How often do these considerations occur to laddies?

Our goal was the best part of a couple of miles up the burn. At this spot the valley bottom was quite wide. Wooded slopes on each side gave ample scope for hide-and-seek, one team against the other. A broad pool, between two pebbly narrows, beckoned invitingly on warm summer days. One of the bigger lads must have tried it one day and found that we could all 'bottom it'.

On one memorable occasion, conditions were perfect. The sun was hot. We had been riving about, up and down the slopes, dodging through the trees, lathered in a right sweat. We had our 'cossies' with us, so this was it! We dared each other to swim across. Perhaps there were three or four yards of water deep enough for us to get our feet off the bottom and splash our way over.

One of the lads could swim. At least, he managed a 'dog-paddle'. Eric and I had tried the 'water-wings' method in Coat-ham Baths − to no avail. This time it was sink or swim and keep yourself afloat by sheer will-power or fear of drowning. In we went and pushed off, arms and legs going 'like the clappers' in a frenzy of movement. We made it! We had really swum! From that moment we never looked back. The next time we went to Redcar on holiday, I set out the first morning to do one length and double each day's effort. Either I miscalculated or I felt it was enough to end up with 'round figures'. By the end of the week I had done thirty lengths.

That primary skill has been my saving. When at the age of thirty-five I contracted polio, swimming gave me a feeling of normality, as I could move through the water unimpeded, whereas on land I could only hobble along, encumbered with a caliper-brace. I taught my daughters to swim. That was one sport-ing activity I *could* share with them, when much else that I might have shared, like skating and skiing, was impossible. Little won-der that Norburn holds so many happy memories!

Trips to Norburn were day-long outings, so we had to be sure that adequate provisions were either packed before departure or available en route. Our main stand-by was the good old 'banger'. Mam would give us a 'bob' to buy some in the butcher's shop in Wolviston village. We usually carried a frying-pan, and a billy-can for boiling water to make a brew of tea. We were quite adept and sensible about lighting fires, setting up the hearth with stones from the beck, where water was at hand if, suddenly, we had to dowse flames. There was plenty of kindling from the woods, so we soon had a fire blazing merrily. We knew where we were with sausages! We could see the skins browning and could slit them to find out if they were anywhere near done on the inside. Holding in one hand a sausage between two 'doorsteps' (thick slices of bread), and in the other a mug of tea, I would not have called the King my uncle!

I first saw cheese being toasted over an open fire when Bill Palmer accompanied the gang on a trip. He speared a chunk of 'mousetrap' on a stick and held it to the flames. The cheese kind of oozed. One bit turned a smoky-black. I did not fancy sampling it, nor did anybody else! Bill was left to relish the rarebit alone!

We had to make several expeditions up to Norburn before all of these delights were revealed. Eventually, as a result of our explorations further upstream, we discovered a farm-road that brought us out onto the Sedgefield — Wolviston road, west of the village, so that we could make a circuit adding variety but also many extra yards to our day's outing!

For some reason, Dad had decided to come with us one day, a day tinged with sadness. Perhaps he wanted to see what we got up to at this fabulous place, or perhaps he was in that 'I'll-show-them-a-trick-or-two' mood. We spent a great day together. As a bonus, we agreed to show Dad the circuitous route home.

Passing through a sunlit glade he noticed, by the side of the path, a browny-yellowish form. It was a hen-pheasant. She could not fly. Dad picked her up. She had no feet! They had been chopped off by the cutting-machine in the harvest-field! Had she just flopped down in that spot? How long had she mutely borne the pain? Dad put the poor bird out of its misery. Later, back at home, we had pheasant for tea! At least, we did not come across lead-shot in the flesh, as we did when Dad and Uncle Charlie returned from their Saturday outings at Sadberge where, with their double-barrelled shot-guns, they bagged hare, rabbit and partridge, to be shared out afterwards.

The open country lying north of home was within four or five hundred yards of New Road. In it the Willow-garth, Norburn,

Wynyard and the Golden Gates were accessible goals that we could reach on foot, though the feet were often dragging by the time we reached the back door again.

At this stage, the South never beckoned. We should have had miles to traipse through town or across an uninspiring industrial zone, with the metropolis of the 'Boro' to negotiate into the bargain! A year or two later we had bikes ... Then we turned our backs on the North Country and headed south for the Cleveland Hills and North Yorkshire Moors, where mysterious dales lay beyond moor-tops, which toppled over cliffs into bays by the North Sea. As our legs stretched, so did the miles and our horizons.

Within a decade of our childhood, many of us were to be called away to the War, some never to return, and many to settle far from home. All of that is another tale.

CHAPTER TWENTY-NINE

Jack and Polly

UNCLE JACK was not the luckiest of people, though he would have been the last to bemoan his fate. At the age of five he had been orphaned. He was shipwrecked in 1917. In the dark days of the early 'twenties he was unemployed. However, he had taken the advice of his big sister, Eva, and sailed out to Australia. Ernie Pidd, Eva's husband, found work for Jack on the Victoria State Railway. He might have made a go of it but he was forced to return reluctantly to England, where he had left his betrothed, Mary 'Polly' Britten. He had intended finding a place for the pair of them in Australia.

Polly, however, was typical of many North-country girls. (Did we not sing of one − 'A North-country maid up to London had strayed'?) Even to this day, many are caught up by the 'tribe' or 'clan' of their home-town or village and will not budge. This is easily understood when one realizes how close-knit communities were, and still are, in our part of the world.

Up in Durham County there are still mining-villages of long rows of terraced houses, now nicely spruced up and often highly modernized, where folk can have 'a bit crack' over the garden fence. From Whitby up to Berwick-on-Tweed there are still fishing villages, like Staithes, where a couple of family names practically account for the whole village population. Is there any wonder that Polly put her foot down, in much the same way as Mam had done for Alf, and insisted on Jack coming back home if he was to marry her? Come back he did!

Throughout the lifetime of the pair we had many a happy visit to their homes − in Norton, Ormesby, and finally on the Hardwick housing estate up the Durham road, between the First- and Second-Mile Houses. Until a few months before Jack died, in his 83rd year, I used to drop in on him during my forays south of the Border.

There was a very good reason for my interest in visiting. Aunty Polly was a great cook, able to make a tasty meal out of the scantiest of ingredients, a skill she had had to acquire throughout much of her married life when she had had little but the 'dole' to live on.

She also had nimble fingers and clever artistic ideas, which helped to bring in a little extra cash. From frilly paper and cheap toy dollies she made cake-covers, ladies in crinolines whose voluminous skirts enveloped beautiful iced cakes. Attractive draught-excluders lay behind doors − cheeky dachshunds made from old stockings stuffed with oddments of cloth, complete with pointed noses, tiny legs, sharp ears, pleading eyes and a tip of a tail. She was rarely to be found empty-handed.

Uncle Jack was knacky too, turning his hand to all sorts of things. During the 'thirties he picked up odd jobs at the homes of the 'big-nobs', sharpening their lawn-mowers and then trimming their lawns. He tinkered with bikes and soldered pots and pans, doing anything that occupied his time and boosted his 'dole-money'. For one lengthy summer spell he worked in New Road, re-painting the gutters along the eaves of our houses.

Though Jack and Polly had no family of their own, they were fond of kids. During one visit, Uncle Jack brought out for our entertainment a toy he had made himself. It was a wooden 'Lowry-esque' creature for, being made from a piece of ply, it had little thickness. Its arms, legs and feet were pinned together at the joints to allow free movement of those members. This 'dancing puppet' had its own 'dancing-floor' which was shaped like a fat exclamation-mark. The puppeteer placed the board on a chair and sat on the narrow stem. The bulbous other end protruded in front of him.

Holding the doll by a piece of dowel fixed to its back, and keeping its feet just in contact with the 'dance-board', Uncle Jack would begin to sing or 'tra-la-la' the hit-tunes of the day, beating out the rhythm on the board, which was springy enough to set the doll's feet in motion. The 'vibes' worked their way up the creature's spine to jerk arms and hands alive in turn.

You can bet it was not long before we all wanted a shot with the doll! Naturally we did not have Uncle Jack's finesse, his delicateness of touch, nor his expertise. In our excitement we were tempted to get the doll high-kicking, so that a loosely-jointed agile leg might even kick the doll's cap off! It only needed one of us to start that caper, and we were hard at it to outdo each other!

Two outdoor events are unforgettable. On the first occasion, Uncle Jack had promised to take me to the South Gare Lighthouse, for a day's fishing off the breakwater at the mouth of the Tees. There was no prospect of catching a bus to our destination, as buses did not run within five miles of the place. No, he would take me on the crossbar of his bike! I was no longer a little nipper at that stage, and no lightweight either, wearing a fair bulk of warm clothes for what might be a cold day by the river. There was no seat on the crossbar, no foot-rest on the frame. I had to ride majestically, like the Queen, side-saddle(-less!), on a piece of 'inch and a half' tube of best British steel for the 'Best British Bike', a 'Raleigh'!

I cannot recall the earliest stages of the route which eventually led to the Black Path, a cinder-track winding its way amongst the coke-ovens and blast-furnaces of Teesside iron-and-steel works. Men working in that zone used it as a short cut, so it was familiar to Uncle. We were also clear of road traffic, and possibly of the police. We could have fallen foul of the law, as it was illegal to cycle like that, endangering not only the passenger but other road-users if an unexpected wobble were to take the machine out of control.

At Warrenby we left industry behind and headed over a waste-land of tall grass, remnants of slag-heaps, and an area of swamp, till we reached a road to the lighthouse and the concrete surface of the breakwater.

As for the fishing, I remember we scouted about for bait in a mussel-bed below the wall. Uncle baited the hand-lines. I threw mine over the side and gave a tug, only to find that the hooks were entangled in the seaweed that coated the sides of the breakwater and the blocks of masonry protecting the sea-wall. That was the end of the day's sport! Seaton Carew was away across the other side of the river. Its grey sky, grey wind and grey water found no difficulty in leaping the breadth of the Tees. We ate our own 'bait', sandwiches and a 'fatty-cake' washed down with a flask of hot tea, as we sheltered out of the wind, behind the wall atop the breakwater.

Yet the day was not all gloom. Quite a few ships entered the river or made out to sea, whilst the pilot-boat stood off. Small local river-craft chugged close in to the shore, all offering rec-ompense enough to a lad who would run four miles, from the house down to the river at Billingham Reach Wharf and back, just for the sight of such ships and water-borne activity.

By the time we reached home in the evening, my bum was sore. I did not want to sit down for ages!

The second episode was the most memorable event of the 'thirties, as far as we were concerned − the Silver Jubilee, in 1935, of King George V and his Queen, Mary. At school, Jubilee mugs were distributed to every child and, of course, a holiday was royally proclaimed.

At that time Uncle Jack and Aunty Polly were living at No. 56 Raleigh Road, Norton − off Norton Avenue, just past the Moderne Cinema. The house was on a corner site with spacious garden ground. During the period of his unemployment, Uncle had transformed the area into a beautiful garden, for that is where his great interest lay. The lawn was neat amid multi-coloured flower-beds. Roses climbed over a pergola made from branches he had 'rescued' from the country. In patriotic mood, he had edged the borders with the blue of lobelia, the white of 'Little Dorrit' and the red of asters and stocks.

Mrs Bradley and the 'twinnies' (her twin daughters) from next door had helped with the bunting and baking. It was a lovely sunny day. Games were organized outside. There were small prizes to be won and a bran-tub to be delved into. The game, however, that attracted us all, was laid out indoors on the deal kitchen-table. It was the FOOTBALL GAME!

Most of the local Raleigh Road kids had never seen it before, so they were slow to get going. We had them quite baffled with our expertise; but, gradually, some made progress and began to offer a serious challenge.

At one point in the competition, for we were playing a knockout for prizes, someone noticed that the table was quite red! Then one of the players looked down at his knuckles. They were skinned and bleeding! He had scuffed them across the rough deal surface of the table, but he had been so excited and engrossed in the match that he had not noticed or felt anything! Of course, we were used to playing on a narrower supporting surface, so that our knuckles never met any obstruction. Still, none of the competitors were put off by the sight of gore, nor did they play with less abandon. Too much was at stake. It is of little consequence today to wonder who was the champion; but I am sure that all who played have never forgotten that day.

The best, however, was still to come. We had enjoyed a wonderful party, with all kinds of sandwiches, cakes, jellies, trifle and ice-cream. This was ladled out in mouth-watering dollops, bigger than we had ever seen, not skimped out as old Tommy Sera and other ice-cream men did.

Back we went to the games. Time wore on. The end had to come. But what an ending! The ice-cream churn, just like the one that the men wheeled round the streets in their barrows, was still half-full! We were all given spoons and left to it. What a treat!

Since it took a fair spell for anyone to lick down a good spoonful, everybody had time to get in on the action. We spooned and licked, even trying a few bites; but, like the widow's cruse in the Bible, the churn did not show any sign of emptying! The earlier foundation of a good tea was being buried under a mound of ice-cream. Nevertheless, we had to cry 'Quits!' As the saying went, 'Our eyes were bigger than our bellies!' I should never have believed it possible that I, never mind the others, had to jib at another spoonful of ice-cream. I can almost feel my stomach distending at the recollection of that day!

You may wonder how the memorable day was financed. It was all done thanks to our host and hostess, along with kind neighbours, who had scrimped and saved from their 'dole-money', a mere pittance. A modern miracle? Call it what you will; to me it is as vivid a memory as the well-known story of 'The Feeding of the Five Thousand'.

Times were to change. With war-clouds on the horizon, work picked up again in the shipyard at South Bank. Jack went back to his old trade, but his misfortunes were not over. He was to be caught up in the War in an incident which involved me too; but more of that anon!

CHAPTER THIRTY

Mr D.F. Smith

HIS FULL NAME was Donald Fothergill Smith. As a token of gratitude for his help in the past, Dad and Mam had decided to name me after him. I am his namesake. This bond was cemented by the gift of a golden half-sovereign and a silver christening cup.

My earliest recollection is of an elderly grey-haired gentleman with a silvery-grey goatee beard, who had a very precise way of articulating, whether it was because it was his nature or because he had to be circumspect in accommodating his set of teeth. He lived with a spinster sister, whom I only knew as 'Miss Smith'. Happy wrinkles lined her face. Her lively brown eyes missed little.

He owned the Nebo sweet factory in Green Dragon Yard, a labyrinth of passages off Finkle Street, near the Town Hall in Stockton. Whenever the stories of Charles Dickens appear on TV screens, the sets for the towns of that era remind me of Green Dragon Yard. Though I was taken there on one or two occasions, I never saw anything of the sweet factory. All I can recall is a dingy office, with little natural light, hemmed in amongst old buildings of soot-begrimed brick.

I used to think of myself as something of a cyclist, having ridden some fair distances both at home and abroad. Yet, I have to take my hat off to D.F. As a young man in his father's drysalter's business, his rounds took him as far as York and back, a distance of one hundred miles − which he did on a bone-shaker over roads that must have been little more than farm-tracks!

He owned two houses, a town house at No. 4 Oxford Terrace, Stockton, and a country house, Urlay Nook, perched above the old quarry hole, just up from Castleton station in the old Cleveland. From this summer retreat he commuted daily by train to Stockton, carrying on his business at Nebo. This routine must have caused him some inconvenience, as he would have had to wake early to catch the eight o'clock train. The path from the house was a steep, stony, hill track. Even the main road, leading down to the station from the other end of the house, was negotiated by the 'United' buses only − in bottom gear! At the town end of the journey he had a tidy walk from Stockton station along Bishopton Lane, then half the length of the High Street. He was still stepping it out in his nineties!

Oxford Terrace was a continuation of the High Street, more or less the pedestrian way north towards Norton, forking off from the A19 where this main road takes a dive under the Portrack railway-line at Tilery. The footpath went through a low tunnel under the line, then sidled along the A19 in front of Blair's Engineering Works, later the site of F.D. Hill's window-making factory.

From the front room of his house, D.F. could have looked across at the billboards flanking the main road there, to enjoy the humour of the 'My Goodness! My Guinness!' adverts. The classic zoo-keeper stood gazing in amazement at his ostrich charge, snootily eyeing him as his Guinness, glass as well as stout, descended its undiscriminating gullet, though it could hardly have been unaware of the 'pure genius' of the beverage. Later the billposters, with seemingly haphazard 'slap, slap', would paste up the sections to make the picture of the Guinness Toucan, doing only what a toucan can do. Beverages did not come in cans in those days, otherwise the House of Guinness might have turned the poster into a visual pun. Possibly all of this would have been lost on D.F. He was a teetotaller!

Visits to No. 4 were not frequent. Each time we went we were sternly warned to be on our best behaviour. I was particularly critical of the supper-time cocoa Miss Smith offered us. It was dark, not over-sweet, and made with the minimum of milk! It smacked of frugality!

There was a touch of the same thriftiness at Urlay Nook.

Though the fare was good and sufficient, slices of buttered bread were never served on a big plate on the table. Instead, the whole-meal brown loaf sat on the bread-board and the bread-knife alongside, so that only the slices needed were cut from the loaf. We cut for ourselves and took butter from the butter-dish, enough for the slice. Why the butter had to pass to the plate and then to the slice, rather than directly to the bread, has always seemed a contradiction, when economy was being practised at the bread-board!

During one of the last visits to No. 4 I was to participate in an educational experiment of D.F.'s. He had a workshop and some tools for woodworking. His idea was to encourage some of us to acquire skill with tools, and also, in a social experiment, to gather together boys of different upbringings so that we could exchange points of view. I felt ill at ease. There was not the same feeling of freedom I was used to at home. My companion, Veitch, an older boy from the senior forms at the 'Sec', was rather taciturn. When he did speak, it was often of matters that went over my head!

From the days when Dad and Uncle Jack were boys in the orphanage, D.F. had maintained his interest in the welfare of young men and boys. He was District Commissioner for the Boy Scouts. Another early recollection of his interest in our family and me goes back to an invitation he gave us to see a 'Scout Gang Show', performed in the hall of St George's Church, off Yarm Road, Stockton. For historically-minded readers, all I can say is, that one of the hit-tunes of the show was,

> Chick, chick, chick, chick, chicken,
> Lay a little egg for me.
> Chick, chick, chick, chick, chicken,
> I want one for my tea,
> I haven't had an egg since Easter,
> And now it's half-past three.
> So, chick, chick, chick, chick, chicken,
> Lay a little egg for tea!

Castleton, lying in the valley of the Esk in the North Yorkshire Moors, meant a break with the holiday tradition of earlier years.

Castleton was in the 'South-country', beyond the densely populated industrial belt of Teesside. We could not trudge to it as we had done to Norburn and Wynyard. Bikes were essential, or the trip had to be made by bus or train.

Gradually the time came for us to want to break away from the traditional Stockton Race Week holiday, in 'digs' in Redcar with the family. The break was clinched when D.F. offered a group of us the use of a tent. His Scouting interest had led him to buy a cottage-type patrol-tent. It stood about six feet high, with three-foot walls. The ground space was six feet wide and eight feet long. Made of good quality green canvas, it had a fly-sheet which rendered it perfectly rainproof. We spent the best part of that summer holiday camping in a field below the Whitby railway-line, about a quarter of a mile from Castleton station, within a stone's throw of the River Esk.

Memories of this camp may be intermingled with episodes from a series of camping holidays that we spent there from 1936, not only in D.F.'s tent but also in a tent that was my own. During one of these holidays we met up with the Paton twins, Stan and Les, who lived in an estate cottage just above the line, two or three hundred yards away from our camp. Their dad was the game-keeper.

Donald Paton was a dour Scot from Scone in Perthshire. His wife was a gentle Yorkshirewoman. Hers was a hard life of relative isolation on the side of Danby Low Moor, between the villages of Castleton and Danby. Florence ('Flo') Paton, the eldest of the family, must have been a blessing to her mother as she grew older, someone who could understand a woman's needs and interests and share her problems in what was very much a man's world.

Donald was a dedicated keeper, who thought nothing of staying out into the dawn hours, in all weathers, in order to rid his beat of all vermin, foxes, crows and the like that would ravage his stock of game-birds, pheasants, grouse and their chicks. His favourite dogs were a pair of Yorkshire terriers, which he carried in the capacious pockets of his keeper's tweed suit. They were afraid of nothing, game even to tackling a dog-fox in his earth, despite the terrible injuries his fangs could inflict.

There was a field, behind the keeper's house, large enough to provide a crop of hay to feed a cow and its calf. Hens clucked about the door. Townsfolk may paint a picture of an idyllic life. Unfortunately Mrs Paton was not country-bred. She had to face the chores of milking, feeding cattle and hens, and all the seemingly endless tasks of a croft. We tried to do our bit, giving a hand in the field at haymaking or mucking-out the byre. In this way we made it easier for Stan and Les to come away and join us in our games and fun.

We spent many a happy hour with them in the pine-wood, west of their house, chasing each other and peppering our adversaries with pine-cones that lay in profusion under the trees. Some 'pine-chats' were right stingers, being fresh and hard and easily four or five inches long. If one of those caught us behind the ear, we knew all about it for quite some while afterwards. Since the wood was on a steep slope, an afternoon's chasing, dodging up, down and across, left us with good appetites and without any need for rocking when it came to 'lights out'.

One teatime we had the pleasurable surprise of receiving a tall enamel quart-jug of egg custard that Miss Smith had made for us all. To go with it she had brought a big pan of stewed gooseberries from the Urlay Nook garden. Half-a-dozen of us supped bowl upon bowl of this delicious dessert, till we were too stuffed to move. We just lay in the evening sunshine, digesting!

On a later occasion we had another gastronomic surprise. Ron Davy was camping with us. His mother and Mam had bought a seven-day runabout ticket on the railway. For ten shillings (50p) this allowed them a week's unlimited travel in their chosen area, the North Yorkshire section, which included the Stockton − Whitby line.

A train pulling out from Castleton station was hardly making any speed by the time it was passing our field. We had been warned by letter to watch out on a particular day for the early train. Along it came. We were lined up along the stone wall below the track. Suddenly, a carriage window was pulled down. Out flew a couple of brown parcels, stoutly wrapped. At the window, giving us a cheery wave, stood Mam and Mrs Davy. Above the rattle of the train we heard a shout, 'Mind what you're doing with the parcels!' Inside, we found a fruit loaf and a cherry cake!

In a sense, the railway company got its own back on us. We drew our water supply from a stream that sprang from the hillside in the wood. Naturally, it made its short way down to the river by the most direct route, which was under the track. One day we could not make out why there was an oily film on the water in the pan. The water had a funny taste too, a sort of tarriness. It was quite a while later before the truth dawned. During the night it had rained heavily, so much so that creosote had been washed off the sleepers carrying the rails. At one spot, this pollution had dripped into our stream. We had to carry water from the Patons' until the stream cleared again.

Though Ron's mam had shared in our camping to a slight degree, his dad played a closer part. He cycled over from Billingham on his tall twenty-four-inch frame bike. He had come to spend the weekend camping with us. We had a great time, for he was keen to let us see how well he could cook. He was no mean hand at it, so we fed well. But the best of all was at camp-fire time, after supper, when he regaled us with stories of life in the trenches during the First World War. That is where he had learnt some of the skills of cooking and making-do with bits and pieces. I thought his flapjacks were masterpieces!

Our Dad was not to be outdone at the camping. He too had had some experience, probably as a boy when the orphanage kids had been away under the guidance of Mr D.F. Smith.

Since the River Esk flowed close by, it added another dimension to our fun when D.F. offered us a flat-bottomed rubber-sided punt, which we could paddle in the deeper pools on this stretch of the river – and even through some shallows, because the punt did not sit low in the water. Really, the Esk was little more than a moorland beck, so we were in no great danger unless it was in spate after heavy rain, or had we ventured into very deep pools where the river ran through a gorge.

From our camp-site we could look across the river up to Castleton village, only about a quarter of a mile away. At this point, however, the river ran deep, so we were faced with a long detour past Patons' cottage, out to the Danby – Castleton road, then up to the village. It was some traipse, especially with a load of provisions.

Then we had the bright idea. We had not read *Scouting for Boys* for nothing. What if we made a rope-line ferry? We had no difficulty in finding rope. We tied the ends to a tree on each side of the Esk, at points where there was a reasonable landing-place, because elsewhere the banks were steep and lined with bushes.

All this was made easier with the aid of the punt. We became quite adept at hauling, learning that the craft tended to be unstable on account of its flat bottom and relatively high sides riding so far out of the water. The cross-current was another unfavourable factor. Once these problems were mastered, shopping no longer became a chore.

One afternoon Dad appeared on the scene. The ferry intrigued him. He would show us how to cross 'in the shake of a lamb's tail' (one of his expressions). I mean to say, he was a man! We were only kids! We had nothing like his strength. 'All right, Ray. You are the oldest,' said Dad. 'You come across with me and bring the punt back. I'll go up to the village and fetch a treat back for you all.'

'The best laid schemes ...!' Ray was in the bows, whilst Dad hauled from the stern. We had to use the right terminology, because we were in the company of a former ship's engineer! Oh, Dad could pull well enough! Too well! They were in mid-stream as Dad was about to give a third heave on the rope. We knew what was coming! His exertions had most likely caused him to shift his point of balance. Next minute she had overturned! Under he went!

Ray was closer to the opposite bank and in shallower water. He got wet too, but had not gone under. He just stood there dripping and howling with mirth. We were so convulsed, we almost rolled in on top of them. A gasping porpoise of a man emerged, thrashing out with a side-stroke till he found his footing. The last we saw of him was of a bedraggled figure, squelching its way across the field. What Mam said to him, or what explanation he gave to D.F., we never discovered. All the same, I bet Mam had had a good laugh!

Dad was lucky to find a dry set of togs to change into. We baled out the punt. Ray changed into some of our stuff. Back in the tent together, we relived the whole episode – Dad's herculean gestures, dives and floundering – to an accompaniment of roars of laughter. To my knowledge, Dad never camped again.

During most summer visits to Castleton, a much more attractive spot than Oxford Terrace, we met from time to time Alice Garratt, a niece of D.F.'s. If we had been young undergrads we should have found Alice to be charming, entertaining company. However, since we were just so much younger, we felt overawed by that well-educated, much-travelled lady, who became headmistress of a girls' school in Middlesbrough. In more recent years the age difference has counted for little, so that we have been at ease in her delightful company.

She and her brother, who was a banker by the time we first met him at Urlay Nook, had been taken under the wing of D.F. and his sister. But for this pair of kindly philanthropists, life for many of us would have been, and would to this day be, much the poorer.

Though D.F.'s invitations and seasonal greetings (as can be seen in a note of Christmas 1925) were written in an angular spiky hand, which was still legible in his last years, there was nothing spiky or hard in his attitude to those in need, unless they were scroungers. He expected folk who received help to use it to learn to stand on their own feet. Is there not in that philosophy a lesson for our society, which tends to lean on the Welfare State?

To my dear little namesake
Donald Smith,
Wishing him and his father
and mother a very

Happy Christmas

Dec 19th 1925

CHAPTER THIRTY-ONE

Holidays at Redcar

As I LOOK BACK on childhood summer holidays at Redcar, I feel that their attractiveness lay in the fact that for one brief glorious week, no matter what the weather, the joys of childhood were experienced to the full. There was the adventure of the journey. It was good to be back in old 'digs', among folk we knew. Or there was the excitement of going to a *new* place.

The wide sands, the rocks, the safe beach for paddling or swimming − all beckoned invitingly. There was the prospect, too, not only of meeting up with old friends from previous holiday friendships, but of having Mam, Dad, uncles and aunts − even Gran, down for a day − to join in our games of rounders or cricket (or at least to be relied upon to pay for an ice-cream or a donkey-ride).

An unexpected treat might be our good fortune, like an afternoon or an evening Pierrot show in one of the theatre halls. The grown-ups might have us tagging along on the golf-links, giving us the odd chance of an easy putt. A new attraction, like a boating-lake, might have to be sampled. Even the food had a special appeal, either for its novelty or, more likely, from the sharpening of appetites as we breathed in the good salt air.

Holidays in the 'thirties meant that many factories and offices in an area closed down for the holiday week when it arrived. Ours was Stockton Race Week (the third week in August), when punters nationally were attracted to the racecourse on the 'Wilderness' − as the open land between Middlesbrough and Thornaby was called. A general exodus then took place, the mass of Teessiders heading for the coast from Seaton Carew south − through Redcar, Saltburn, Whitby and on to Scarborough. Others, preferring the tranquillity of the Lakes, went west.

By this time Dad, who had started with ICI in 1924, was probably on Staff grade, which meant that he had his holidays with pay. The generality of workers had no pay that week, as they were not working, so they had to save up throughout the year for that one week of relaxation.

Of the preparations for our holidays I can say little. At times, if Mam and Dad thought they had found a good landlady, they booked those 'digs' for the following year before we left to return home. Mam had to pack our own bedlinen and towels. Cooking facilities were available, but only for re-heating pies or fish and chips and making pots of tea. Mam wanted to be on holiday like the rest of us. We all shared one big bedroom. Mam and Dad had a double bed. All three of us bairns shared another. This was seldom a problem, because we were not very big then. Mind, there were the odd complaints about one or other of us kicking somebody in our sleep, or pulling all the bedclothes to our side of the bed.

The packing before we set out remains a mystery too. At that time of the year shorts, a shirt and sandals were about all we needed, with a jersey for the cooler moments. Swimming-costumes certainly took up more room than the skimpy fashions of today. If these had been on the go then, the pier and its 'What-the-butler-saw' machines would have been deserted; but the penny-in-the-slot telescope would have been bunged up with coppers in next-to-no-time, leering eyes scanning the beach for scantily-clad or topless torsos.

The journey itself to Redcar could be by bus or train. The train offered a direct service and more space. By bus, we had to change at either Stockton Empire or in Middlesbrough bus-station. Mam could be left in charge of the travelling, as Dad would be working until 12 noon on the Saturday. He would follow later.

On one of these bus journeys, Mam was trying to make it as economical as possible. She may have forgotten our different ages. She did know that Eric and I were well past the age for free fares, allowed for children up to five years old. The conductress came along for Mam's fare. 'A whole and two half-returns to Redcar,' said Mam. Pointing to Joyce, the conductress asked, 'How old is she?' 'Just five,' said Mam. Up piped Joyce, 'Ee, ah'm not, our Mam! Ah'm six!' Consternation! From some passengers came sympathetic grins ... righteous glares from others. Mam paid up. I could have disappeared under the seat for shame.

Once we were settled into our 'digs', we were not long in hankering after a run down to the sands. There, in the fine spells, we played much of the time clad in just shorts and sandals. Dad never seemed to learn his lesson. In glorious sunshine he would sunbathe far too long, to end up with a redness of skin any self-respecting lobster, bound for the pot, would have given its right pincer for! Mam had to baste him delicately with olive oil or calamine lotion. He could not lie comfortably in bed. Finally, he began to peel. We offered to remove some of the extensive patches of white dead skin that he could not reach at the back! Our Eric had the sort of pigmentation everybody envied. He tanned a healthy brown.

However, Stockton Race Week was notorious for the mixed, often poor, weather it introduced. Fortunately, Redcar was well provided with alternative forms of entertainment when the drizzle or driving rain or chill breezes under grey skies drove us off the beach. All along the Prom, shops and amusement palaces, cafés and ice-cream parlours, stood cheek by jowl. Towards the end of the week, when funds were running low, even these refuges were out of reach for some; so desolate groups hunched together in the lee of the shelters along the Prom, gazing disconsolately through the glass partition to the windward side, mesmerized by the grey tossing sea and heavy breakers crashing over the Red Scar Rocks to thunder onto the beach.

In such circumstances, one big attraction was the Rock Shop. We could go inside and watch the whole process of the making of Redcar rock. The mixing-machine twisted and twirled the mint-flavoured candy dough. This was pulled out into a long strip, on top of which red threads of candy were set in due position to form the lettering that could be read through every inch of the rock, indicating its place of origin. All of these operations were carried out in spotless metal trays, yards long, kept at a steady temperature to allow the confectioners to manipulate the candy and roll it into various sizes, thicknesses and shapes.

Wielding wicked-looking shears, the Rock Shop man would lop off bits from the long candy stalk and mould them to his fancy. The finished confections were wrapped in clear paper and stored on display in tempting pigeon-holes, where the various sizes were sorted together to be sold individually. But there was further entertainment as the man began to make up bargain-packs at different prices, incorporating in each big bag a variety of his products.

As he filled the bag he named each item in a sing-song chant and gave its value. In would go a 'stick for the lodger' − for a 'bob' the biggest and fattest of the whole bagful! Invariably he ended his spiel with, 'and a couple of Gracie Fields ducks and ducks and ducks, and a couple of Gracie Fields ducks!' A mint feast that might have totalled three or four shillings (15p or 20p), would be offered for half-a-crown (two shillings and sixpence, or 12½p). What Gracie Fields and ducks had to do with it, I could never fathom, because the 'ducks' were a couple of black-and-white striped humbugs, nearly as big as his fist! There was enough mint candy in one of them to keep our lot sucking happily for the rest of the afternoon!

Further along the Prom, we could look in at the lifeboat shed for a conducted tour of the boat. It was quite similar to the cobles drawn up on the beach below the Prom. Generations of experience have gone into the design of these boats, so that a type has evolved best adapted to the local conditions of sea, surf and beach. The cobles usually sat on a wheeled axle-beam above high water, ready to be hauled down to the sea for trips on the briny or for longer sessions further out when anglers hired them for a spot of sea-fishing, all gear and boatman provided.

One evening, the grown-ups decided to make up a boat-load − Mam and Dad, Joe Mullander and his wife, the Allisons, and one or two more. *We* could lend a hand to shove the boat down to the water, but so far and no further. Our elders were bent on having a bit of peace to themselves, leaving us with 'uncles', 'aunts' and 'cousins', folk who had no blood relationship with us but who were adopted by us and adopted us, in turn, into their clans. We had met regularly on the same stretch of beach (sometimes we 'digged' in the same street) Stockton Race Week after Stockton Race Week.

This time, somehow or other, Eric had squirmed his way aboard and was not discovered till the boat was out past the surf. There was no putting back to let him ashore. He had to stay. The sea was not unduly rough, but there would be enough pitching, tossing and rolling in a boat that was designed for such conditions. Eric (aptly named and of Viking stock!) was in his element. He was having a great time with a line to himself. Poor Mrs Mullander was already turning various shades of green. Every lurch of the boat was a misery, and Eric's excitement, that seemed to affect the trim of the boat, only made matters worse. Dolefully she pleaded, 'Stop rocking the boat, sonny!' What? – a tiddler of six stones against a complement of half a ton, at least! Poor lass! How relieved she was to feel the keel grating on the sand again!

The Thompson family of Thornaby (already mentioned as first-footers at New Year), along with the Whitfields from the same town, were adopted kinsfolk. Such was the nature of the new kinship that we not only looked forward to annual reunions at the seaside, but exchanged visits in between times.

Young Joe Thompson was a fair bit older than ourselves, a youth amongst us bairns. Cricket brought us all together, and cricket held Joe during his sporting life. In later years we looked for his successes on the field, reported in the 'Gazette' or *The Northern Echo*. He was a very handy bowler and a steady batsman. Joe, his dad, was fair proud of the lad. If we met during the season, you can be sure we were well informed of Young Joe's latest success with bat or ball or both.

We learnt a thing or two about bowling from Young Joe, just using a tennis-ball – even if it was only on a sand wicket still hard from the ebbing tide. When weather and tide permitted, we could play for hours – such was the extent of the beach; but, as the tide came on the flood, the stumps were drawn bit by bit up the sands. We could get too close for the comfort of other holiday-makers, who had little pleasure in fielding a tennis-ball off their heads or sunburnt backs!

Then it was time to turn to 'Hot Rice', with more of the 'gentle sex' joining in. Cricketing skills were less called for, though the batsman used a bat to defend his legs from the shies that could bring his innings to an end when they struck home. Then the successful shyer took his place.

On reaching the sands at the beginning of the day, everybody sought a rallying-point. Always popular were the cobles, because of the shelter they gave on the leeward side when a cooling breeze was blowing. Inside them, and across their seats, we found ample storage space for clothing, towels and lunch-packs, which we liked to keep free from sand. It was no joke being dried down with a gritty towel, especially if the torso had been over-exposed to the sun! If the cobles were all occupied, then we the youngsters had to get stuck into some vigorous digging – 'What do you think you've got those buckets and spades for?' – and hollow out a large hole to accommodate our elders and the day's gear.

Similar efforts could reap rewards in the daily sand-castle building competitions. Spectators were really amazed at some of the artistic winning designs, which introduced to the ephemeral architecture shells, seaweed and adaptable bits of jetsam.

Another type of money-spinner money-winner gimmick (though I doubt whether that word was used in those days) was thought up by the newspapers. Their representative would be scheduled to visit the resort on certain days, in particular areas, at specified times. We could only know his itinerary by buying the paper, which also contained a photograph of the 'Mystery Man' (usually taken from behind his left ear, allowing a glimpse of a pipe and a trilby, rakishly worn). On spotting him, we had to challenge him with the passwords, spoken word-perfectly; for example, 'You are Mr Northern Echo, and I claim the Northern Echo prize.' At the same time, we had to proffer the newspaper in question.

Was the prize five bob or a fiver (25p or £5)? Let us be generous and plump for the latter. In any case, neither was to be sniffed at, the one being a tenth of a man's weekly wage and the other − a fortnight's bounty! I am pretty sure that Mam got herself involved in some hilarious challenges with folk who had nothing to do with the stunt. These encounters were related to the assembled kins-folk amid much laughter. Over the holiday years, many a serious hour was spent chasing an elusive gander. Did any of the news-men write their side of the story?

More organized forms of entertainment were available at Coat-ham, where I was born. The local authority had incorporated in one complex a boating-pond, a fine unheated salt-water swim-ming-pool outdoors, and a heated swimming-bath indoors. Cou-sin Ray had learnt to swim. We would have to learn too, since Ray's water-wings were now available for the next student. This was a new line in the system of handing-down articles, so much a feature of working-class life. Usually, clothing that an older child of the extended family had grown out of was passed on to the next-in-line, now big enough to fit the garments.

It was clear that the best time to go to the baths was for the first session at 8.00 a.m. That was no problem for *us*, who could wake with the birds. The burden fell on Dad and Uncle Charlie, who were wanting a break from early-rising.

At eight o'clock the shallow end of the indoor pool was less crowded, but still too populous for my liking. Standing on tiptoe in the 3ft. 6in. (1 metre) end, I had enough trouble keeping my chin above water. Any extra jumping about by other youngsters was likely to cause a minor tidal wave, which sent salty chlorinated water into my mouth and eyes. The water-wings seemed devoid of float. I had no confidence in them. That was the end of *that* experiment. Eric fared no better. Yet all of that changed from the moment at Norburn, when we *knew* we could swim!

The boating-pond hardly registered any better success than our early attempts at swimming. Failure here was due solely to an unwillingness to co-operate. Eric and I had to share a paddle-boat, a squat little tub with a handle on each side which we cranked to turn a paddle-blade. We both felt we could handle a pair ourselves; so we wanted a boat each. However, the parental 'kitty' could not run to two boats.

In the one boat, we were cast off with each turning his own handle. All would have been fine – if we could have struck up a balanced rhythm. But we were not in the mood for seeing eye to eye. The more we paddled against each other, the less progress we made – until we found ourselves, out in the middle of the pond, going round in circles. The boatman in charge came out to our rescue and towed us in.

Far better was the trip we made in Locke Park, in a proper rowing-boat, with Dad at the oars. He manœuvred us through a circuit of channels, criss-crossed by rustic bridges, which lent a somewhat romantic atmosphere to the place, especially in the gloaming when the fairy-lights went on.

Another centre of regular entertainment was presided over by 'Uncle Tom', a special kind of uncle. He was not kin, nor had we adopted him, like the Thompsons. He must have been 'Uncle' to thousands of bairns from Teesside and far beyond, for he was the evangelist who ran the seaside mission of 'Sunshine Corner' on Redcar sands. Three times a day (morning, afternoon and evening) he conducted the mission with his cheery band of faithful helpers.

They worked from a stage, facing the Prom, below which ranged tiers of wooden benches down to the sand, where folk could sit in deck-chairs or just on the sand itself. Singing was at the heart of all the meetings − with lively rhythms, easy-to-learn tunes and verses. Bairns of all ages were encouraged to come forward and sing. Sometimes they sang a new chorus that was being taught − at others, well-known choruses remembered from previous years.

Much of the singing was competitive, with prizes to spur on the songsters. An air of excitement, often of awe, fell upon the spectators when the twin brothers from Thornaby stepped up and sang. Time and time again they were voted prize-winners, after we had listened spellbound to their angelic reverent rendering of a song. There would be laughter too as a tiny tot, piping away, would suddenly stop on recognizing a gran or some other relative in the audience and give them a wave, and perhaps ask 'Uncle Tom' for her prize there and then!

I suppose the gist of the message, put over so ardently by 'Uncle Tom', was, 'God is Love. Jesus loves us and died for us, so we must love Him too.' Perhaps at this point in the proceedings we felt it was time to sidle off back to the cricket; but, at the end of the holiday, the tunes went with us, back home to Billingham. Even now, nearly sixty years on, I can still sing the signature tune − 'Sunshine Corner, oh, it's jolly fine ... ', and other choruses, like 'O, it was Heaven ever ... ', or 'Keep your oil in your lamp, oil in your lamp ... ', so fervently did we sing in those happy days. That fervour and sincerity is carried on today in the Christian

Fellowships springing up in many communities. Is it because folk are feeling disillusioned with the Established Church, which does not seem to have the ability to satisfy the needs of our modern age?

A donkey-ride on a donkey that only walked, when others managed to get their mount to jog along; the sight of a donkey, hooves well dug in because it was being spurred on by an over-weight adult; the smooth coldness of a Pacitto's Gold Medal ice-cream, when we were heading back from the Marske-end of the links — from the paddling-pool where, enviously, we had watched better-off kids sailing their toy yachts, or had respectfully fol-lowed the actions of a pensioner making some adjustment to the trim of the sails of a lofty scale-model of a famous racing-yacht (these were the days of Sir Thomas Lipton and his attempts to wrest the America's Cup from the USA). All are memories of those summer days, so many years ago. Some of this happiness we took back home to the 'Pagoda'.

CHAPTER THIRTY-TWO

The 'Pagoda'

WHAT A NAME! For what? It had arrived one evening after work
on a horse-drawn flat cart, a pile of slabs of wood that had once
been a packing-crate big enough to house an elephant but, more
than likely, used to crate a piece of machinery for one of the
process plants. Anyhow, Dad had 'put his name on it'.

I have just a vague recollection of how the slabs were assembled
and erected to form a summer-house at the top of the garden
where there was a patch of lawn. Window spaces were shaped,
diamond-fashion, with lattice-work in the corners as a decorative
feature. There was no glazing. Protection against the elements
was minimal. It was, after all, a 'summer'-house! To Mam it must
have been something exotic, hence the name that she bestowed
upon it!

The grown-ups could go up and take a breather, sitting on rough planks that formed the seating round the walls. We kids even slept out in it on a fine summer's night, re-living the adventures of Robinson Crusoe or the Swiss Family Robinson. Tea-parties were held in it when, in favourable conditions, we entertained relatives and the 'uncles' and 'aunts' we acquired from our holiday weeks on the sands at Redcar.

It was after these holidays that the 'Pagoda' assumed its important role, as stage and back stage for our re-enaction of Pierrot shows we had seen from the Prom at Redcar. The Pierrots were only better off than we were in that their stage was bigger and back stage more spacious; but the whole was nearly as ramshackle as our 'Pagoda'.

Ours were charity performances, given to other kids in the street who had not been able to go off for a week's holiday to the seaside. With a bevy of uncles and aunts in the district, we fell heirs to many a cast-off garment for dressing-up. Audience and actors could take turns at acting or just parading in dress-up. Plenty of scrap wood was to hand so that swords could be made for heroic duels. However, such scenes tended to be frowned on by anxious parents, as the duellists became so absorbed in the fight that it took on an earnestness that could easily have ended in injury.

Kids did their party pieces, singing or reciting. Under Joyce's leadership, the lasses performed dance routines, tripping themselves up in the folds of over-size garments that had seen better days on the backs of Gran and aunties. We lads were in hysterics.

The 'corny jokes' routine brought a respite to the energetic performances. The jokes are corny now, but they came more or less red-hot from the lips of Pierrots at Redcar − 'I say, I say. I can prove to you that you are not here!' 'I bet you a fiver, you can't.' 'Done!' Make-believe fivers were handed over to a by-stander, who was to hold the stakes. 'Right. Are you in London?' 'No!' 'Are you in Birmingham?' 'No!' 'Are you in West Hartlepool?' 'Of course not!' 'Well, if you are not in London, Birmingham or West Hartlepool, you must be somewhere else. And, if you are somewhere else, you can't be here!' Whereupon, the patter-merchant claimed the fivers!

As likely as not, the mood would change. A session followed based on Sunshine Corner, the seaside mission directed by 'Uncle Tom' and his band of devout evangelists. We had spent happy hours at those outdoor mission meetings on the beach. We knew umpteen choruses by heart. Back at home we wanted to pass on their cheerful melodies and encouraging words to our pals. Nobody ever thought of them as 'cissy'. We were just carried away by the singing.

> Sunshine Corner, oh, it's jolly fine.
> It's for children under ninety-nine.
> All are welcome. Seats are given free.
> Redcar Sunshine Corner is the place for me!

The years moved on, and so did the 'Pagoda'. Eric and I, in our respective post-primary schools, began to learn the rudiments of wood- and metal-working. Oh, the ignominy! To have a name like Smith and, at my first attempt at putting a point on a piece of square-sectioned bar in the school forge at the 'Sec', to present to 'Daddy' Watson the technical master, an object more akin to a corkscrew than a simple spike! The worst of it was that 'Daddy' was known to Mam and Dad (he sang in a Baptist choir), and he lived next door to Uncle Charlie and Aunty May!

At home we began to gather together a kit of sundry tools, most of them old and well-used, borrowing as occasion demanded some of Dad's kit, which was not extensive, consisting of screwdriver, saw, hack-saw, hammers, pliers, pincers, a belly-brace and bits, and a soldering-bolt. So the 'Pagoda' became a workshop. We moved it to the opposite corner of the garden, down nearer the house. There we could mess about to our heart's content − hammering, sawing, drilling holes, and even attempting some of the basic joints we were learning at school. That freedom was something I really enjoyed and appreciated. Other lads were not so lucky. Either they had no workshop, or their dads, if they had sheds, stored garden tools neatly inside. Entry was taboo!

When Mam died in 1970, and we were clearing out No. 11, the 'Pagoda' was a sorry sight. The roof leaked. The worm-eaten boards were coming away from each other. A rusty sheet of corrugated iron was propped against the doorway, now minus a door. Inside was a jumbled heap of scraps of wood and broken off-cuts of plasterboard (the paper backing torn and white shards of gypsum pointing accusingly at the neglect).

On the right-hand bench, its plywood deck gaping, its tall mast broken, lay one of the model sailing-yachts we had lovingly and cautiously hollowed out from a block of yellow pine that Dad had brought home from the pattern-makers' shop in the factory. That wood had been a delight to work, a softness of gouging and a redolence of pine. With a lead ballast screwed to the oaken keel, balancing a two-foot high Bermudian-rigged mast, our home-made yacht, built well below the contract price, had out-sailed the shop-bought tarted-up models, six times as expensive, that indulgent wealthier parents shared with their offspring on Redcar's paddling-pool. And, as if to add insult to injury, Eric and I had one such yacht apiece!

Now the glory of her triumphs only rocked on the waves of memory. Yet her ending was fitting. Like the long ships of our Viking ancestors, she met her end ablaze. The 'Pagoda' went up in flames with her.

Was there a phoenix to rise from the ashes? I suppose the genes of that mythical bird were already astir throughout our post-school days, as we applied the lessons learnt in school workshop to the multifarious jobs we saddled ourselves with as we settled down to married life, home-ownership and ultimate guiding of sons-in-law through the same rigmarole.

Part II

WIDER HORIZONS

CHAPTER ONE

The 'Scholarship' and Entry to the 'Sec'

IN HER WORKROOM in our home, my wife has at hand my birthday present of September 1933 − *Chambers Etymological Dictionary*. Books figured quite often amongst our birthday and Christmas gifts. Just yesterday (26th September 1987), at a car boot sale, I handed over to a little girl *The Bairns' Budget*. I was on the point of selling for 5p my birthday present of 21st September 1927, gifted to me by 'Auntie' Jessie Yellow! As the little girl stretched out her hand I explained that, just over sixty years earlier, I had received the book on my sixth birthday. I watched her walk away, wondering what she would tell her friends when she showed them her bargain.

We ourselves made out the order to Santa for Christmas books like *Tiger Tim's Annual*; birthday books were often the choice of generous relatives. The dictionary was, however, something quite different. It was a 'must'. Stockton-on-Tees Secondary (Boys') School advised parents to provide the book as an essential tool for making good scholastic progress. As the Secondary school year began in mid-September, I may have received my twelfth birthday present a little earlier than usual.

In the Spring of that year, along with my peers in the catchment area of the 'Sec', I had sat the 'Scholarship', a competitive exam. A place in the Secondary School was the reward of the top seventy to eighty successful candidates in the competition. I was one of that number. Vague are the memories now of the three papers we took − arithmetic, composition and grammar.

In the arithmetic paper we had, for 'starters', straightforward calculations in long division, fractions and decimals, and conversions of tons, cwts. (hundredweights), quarters, stones and lbs. (pounds) to ounces; or miles, furlongs, chains, yards and feet to inches! Alternatively, we could face thousands of ounces or inches to be converted back into the bigger components, which made more practical sense, at least! Usually there was a bill, a practical test of dealing with shopping-lists and expenses. As we read this problem, we set it out in the prescribed manner taught to us by our teachers, e.g.:

	£	s	d
1¼ lbs of tea @ 1/8 per quarter		8	4
6 candles @ 1/9 per dozen			10½
3 boxes of matches @ 12/- a gross			3
Total		9	5½

How much change would you get from a £1 note?

Ans:		10	6½

Then came the 'problems' − trains starting from stations 'A' and 'B', running towards each other at different speeds. Where did they meet? The time element, to have the paper completed, exerted too great a pressure on the candidates for any of them to comment inwardly, 'Cor! What a crash!'

Rooms of houses still remained to be papered, with door and window measurements included, and rolls of paper to be costed at 1/11¼d a roll (one shilling and eleven pence farthing − just under 10p today). If that was not sufficient a headache for the aspiring householder, the bath was being filled from taps letting in water at one rate, whilst the plug was missing, allowing it to run out at another! It is a wonder the examiners did not ask, 'How long would it take to bath a family of three, immersing them all at the same time?' I have papered walls since then (at least, I have been on hand at the measuring and pasting, whilst my wife has done the hanging); but I leave the water problems of household affairs to the plumber!

Vaguer still are the elements of the 'English' papers. There was a choice of essay subjects or 'composition' as it was called. The grammar paper included a passage to punctuate. The wireless comedian, Stainless Stephen, would have been in his element here, with his 'semi-consciouses' in place of semi-colons! Meanings of words, parts of speech (noun, adjective etc.), synonyms, collective terms for groups of creatures (aspirations of authors!), all were grist to the examiners' mill.

The 'Sec' was not the only post-primary establishment in Stockton. Up Yarm Road the 'Queen Vic' stood regally in its own grounds as the 'Queen Victoria School for Girls', where well-to-do parents paid handsome fees to have their daughters educated. To us, it was a 'snob' school. Many of us from the rural areas of Redmarshall, Bishopton or Stillington must have appeared to its young ladies as country bumpkins, whilst the 'townies' from run-down depressed areas like Tilery could only have been social outcasts.

At the corner of Garbutt Street and Norton Road stood the gloomy building of the Grammar School, hemmed in by old houses and shops, and subjected to the constant rumble of traffic passing in front of it along the busy main thoroughfare, the A19. This was Ron Davy's school. I think it also took in fee-paying pupils. Another old Billingham school pal, Walter Wright, studied there with distinction.

Entrance to the 'Grammar' and the 'Sec' set the students apart from pals in Billingham, academically but not necessarily socially, at least for a year or two. As lads in the road, we still played football and cricket together; but, at 14, Tom and Ro Arnott, Eric, Les Brown and 'Pluff' Jelley were all to start work, as messenger-boys in the factory attached to the offices, as shop-boys with the Co-op, or helping about the local farms until they could begin an apprenticeship in a trade at the age of sixteen. We at the 'Sec' or the 'Grammar' found ourselves saddled with homework, a burden that grew heavier as we progressed up the school.

Bill Palmer was already at the 'Sec'. He and 'Stiff' Meachen regaled me with terrifying tales of initiation ceremonies performed on new boys in the toilets at the back of the 'Sec'. However, I was to be spared this trauma, as cousin Ray was already two years ahead of me and had two or three sturdy chums (Ken Dodsworth and Alan Ditchburn) to keep an eye on me and warn the 'initiators' off!

Before I stepped into the schoolyard though, Mam had to take me on a shopping trip to kit me out with school uniform. This was made up of a green cap topped with a blue button, a green blazer bearing on the left breast-pocket the school badge (an oak tree with the motto, 'Pas à pas, on va bien loin'), grey trousers (shorts or 'longers') and black footwear. In addition I needed football boots, shorts and a strip (self-coloured blue in my case, as relatives had the privilege of fostering the same House spirit, so I was to be in Blue House like Ray). We, the lesser fry, were also expected to wear the school tie of horizontal grey and green stripes, which was changed for one with diagonal stripes when the wearer became a prefect. That little lot must have knocked a fair hole in Dad's pay-packet. I remember that my football boots, armed with steel toe-caps and strengthened with a steel brace in the sole, cost 7/6d (37½p).

Another preliminary to dispose of was the question of bus travel to Stockton. I was a seasoned traveller in that respect. Discussion concerned the matter of a 'pass'. Our application came to naught, as in New Road we did not live beyond the three-mile limit which warranted a free pass. New Road was about as near to Stockton as one could get in the new township. Scholars from Central Billingham or from 'over the station', from Cowpen Bewley or Haverton Hill, all qualified for the pass, which had to be carried daily and shown to the conductors or conductresses on the Corporation buses. Nevertheless, for lads like Alec Williams and me from New Road, or others in the vicinity of the Green, there was a concessionary fare of 1½d return, valid till 5 p.m. We bought these tickets in advance, say five to do the week. It became a routine matter for us to check that we had our ticket for the day before leaving home in the morning.

Alec and I used to catch the 8.25 workmen's bus, which came from the Portrack – South Gate end of the factory. When the bus drew up, we dashed up the open rear stairway to the top deck to find a seat at the front. The air was thick with tobacco smoke, as the men from the late shift relaxed on their way home. We went up Mill Lane, turned left at the Picture House, headed along the main road to the Top of Billingham Bank, then left the township behind for Stockton.

Of course, as 'regulars' we got to recognize the staff of drivers and conductors and even inspectors, some of whom were Stockton folk like Mam and Dad and known to them. So we had friendly folk about us on our journeys. One driver we called 'Old Slow-coach!' He seemed to crawl along, 'parp-parping' his horn at every lamp-post. When he was driving I was on tenterhooks, fearing I should be late for school. Really, there was no need for my concern, as the excuse to the late-prefect, 'The bus was late,' was accepted without demur.

There were also 'Specials' for 'Sec' pupils, buses which we caught at lunchtime and after school at 4.00 p.m. We enjoyed many a hectic journey on the 'One-o'clock Special', going back to school after lunch, not because of the driving, but because of the battles we fought on the top deck. Armed with rubber-bands as catapults, stretched between index-finger and thumb, we fired paper pellets, folded from scraps of paper. Edna (Ginger) Dickinson and her female acquaintances bore the brunt of our fire. Most ungallant! But, in such ways, even 'Andy Capp Junior' shows his affection or interest in his 'Flo' in our northern part of the world!

CHAPTER TWO

The School Building and Routine

THE 'SEC' was a red-brick building in Nelson Terrace, just off
Dovecote Street. It was not simply a Boys' School. The northern
half of the building housed the Girls' School. The girls did not
share classes with us, though they had to share facilities like the
science labs for chemistry and physics, and the music room and art
department. The movement of girls' classes into our domain was
so timetabled that we rarely saw those attractive creatures!

For the girls, the music room performed a double, perhaps one may even go so far as to say a triple, function. It was their common-room. Situated on the ground floor, there was access to it through a door which opened on to the boys' yard, at the back of the school. This was our entrance when we went along to our music class. For the girls there was no exit from it. However, it had windows which opened onto the boys' yard. Though they were protected by a metal grille, they still allowed scope for the age-old 'Pyramus and Thisbe' act. To a member of another race, that rear section of the building might have appeared, on the face of it, as 'The Wailing Wall'. No doubt pleas and protestations passed across the sills, in many cases successfully as, from among the frequenters of this trysting-place, quite a few couples plighted their troth and later married. Bob Coulson and Joan Jeffs were one such pair among our contemporaries. The third function? A marriage bureau!

My contemporaries and myself, as a first year intake of pupils, were divided into two classes, 2M and 2Sc. The Sc's were obviously science-orientated and took chemistry. 'M' stood for 'Modern' and, much less obviously, M's took Latin! To this day, nobody has explained to me why we began as class 2! I chose M for no other reason than that Ray was also in an M class, 4M. There was one further distinction made especially in our year between the M's and Sc's; we of M were taught Latin by W.H. Munday, and never came into classroom contact with 'Old Nick' Nicholson, the 'chem' master. To us he was 'Old Nick', not because he was the Devil Incarnate, but simply because 'Young Nick' was his son and one of our classmates!

Our classrooms were right at the top of the school. On many an occasion, climbing from the basement, I have counted the ninety-six steps we stormed up in pairs from the 'lines' in the playground. In our room, if we stood on a desk to look through the back windows, we were looking towards the River Tees, which flowed beyond the High Street. From the front of the school the 'stinkers' of 2Sc looked out over the house-tops between Nelson Terrace and the railway-line, westwards towards the Town Moor. The Sixth Form and their teachers had to come through our room to reach their 'Holy of Holies', forbidden territory to us unless we were hauled up in front of one of the prefects there, to explain why our 'punishment-lines' were not to hand!

Our classroom was a pretty bare place — no pictures on the wall that I can recall, a cupboard, the teacher's desk and chair, wall-blackboards and one on an easel, and our six rows of desks, six deep. These desks had hinged lids covering a storage compartment that housed our books, pens and pencils etc. A hasp and a staple, fixed to lid and desk, were provided for a padlock, so that the contents of the desk could be kept secure.

In our reckoning, F.W. Woolworth ('Woollies') in the High Street must have made a fortune from selling padlocks to us pupils. Luckily they were mass-produced, since quite frequently, either from forgetfulness or a hole in a pocket, some luckless fellow found he could not open his desk as he had no key. Bill Palmer, who had had to repeat his first year, was a dab hand at picking locks with the point of a compass, a skill that many more of us acquired out of sheer necessity, without any future criminal intent in mind! To buy a different lock elsewhere, say at Pickersgill's, the ironmonger's, so that a desk might be more secure, could lead to problems, taxing the skill of Bill and Co. and landing the hapless pupil in detention or with a sheaf of 'lines' to write for the next day, handed out by masters who stood for no nonsense.

Unlike our former teachers in Billingham Intermediate, who taught in lounge suits, our masters at the 'Sec' wore gowns. 'Billy' Ball, our ageing maths teacher and deputy head, was seen to wear a mortar-board as well.

Billingham and the 'Sec' had the same system of teachers coming to the class to teach. Masters must have had strong arms, not from the practice of administering corporal punishment, but because they could have three dozen exercise-books to carry up and down stairs from and to the staffroom, as well as any text or reference books they needed for the lesson. Since there was less movement of personnel about the school, a quieter atmosphere prevailed in the building, though a hubbub arose if a master was delayed at the change-over of classes. A 'spy' keeping look-out on the top landing had to be quick off his mark when 'Tot' Munday bounded up the stairs. Though he did not give any impression of athleticism, 'Tot' was tall and could clear four steps at a time. In a couple of bounds he was on the landing below the watcher.

Punishment usually came in 'lines' or detention, which was held in the 'detention room' straight after school for forty-five minutes on Mondays, Wednesdays and Fridays. The masters had a duty roster for supervision of detainees. This was not an occasion to get ahead with the evening's homework. Special tasks were set by the master who had penalized the culprit. If they were not completed in detention, they had to be done in addition to homework that evening!

The detention-book was kept in the staffroom. Many a 'new boy', knowing only the master's nickname, would be sent down by the history teacher, G.G. Armstrong, with orders to fetch the book. A teacher, answering the knock at the staffroom door, might say, 'Well, boy, what is it?' 'Please, sir, may I have the detention-book for Mr Jute?' When a pupil had three detentions 'on the trot', the luckless offender had a date with the 'Boss', Dr J.R. 'Jackie' Kinnes, who administered 'six of the best' on the victim's trouser-seat with a butter-pat!

Prefects had the right to dish out 'lines' for minor misdemeanours in the building and playground − talking or pushing on the stairs, hanging about in the cloakrooms and corridors, cycling through the yard to the bike-shed, or doing a 'Tarzan' act on the long ladder that lay across the bike-shed rafters! Smoking in the lavs incurred severe penalties, awarded by the duty-teacher responsible for playground supervision. The normal injunction for lesser crimes was, 'Write me out 100 lines of the school motto for tomorrow!' Failure to do so led to a doubling of the original figure. I suppose that even those who failed French in the 'Matric' still remember the 'Step by step, one goes very far'. Had Chairman Mao heard of us with his 'The longest journey begins with the first step.'?

CHAPTER THREE

The Teaching Staff

EACH NEW INTAKE was offered a common syllabus comprising English, History, Geography, Maths, Physics, French, Art, Music, Woodwork and Metalwork, and P.T. (Physical Training, which included a weekly games afternoon). The only difference was that the M's did Latin and the Sc's took Chemistry. At the top end of the school, those who stayed on into the Sixth Form were treated to a weekly lesson of Musical Appreciation. The 'Sec' was a 'rugger' school. No provision was made for soccer, which was far and away the most popular winter game in the North-east. No doubt for that very reason, rugger was introduced to broaden our sporting interests. It was played over the Autumn and Winter terms. Those who did not fancy the vigorous body-contact of the game were allowed to take up cross-country running. In the Summer term, cricket was the main game. Athletes came into their own at the annual School Sports Day and as representatives of the School at inter-school athletic meetings.

Some teachers were specialists in their subjects, and were involved in presenting candidates for the Matriculation exam of the Northern Universities Joint Matriculation Board, which led on to the Higher Leaving Certificate, on the favourable results of which County Scholarships were offered. Other members of staff taught a wider range of subjects, but not to the same academic level.

Many teachers gave up hours of their own spare time on our behalf, coaching and umpiring rugger and cricket, adjudicating at inter-house debates held under the aegis of the Literary and Historical Society (the 'Lit & Hist'), or chairing meetings of that body when visiting speakers entertained us with slide-shows of their travels or talks on local history. They accompanied us on school trips to local places of interest. They spent an exhausting day exploring the Scottish capital. Even in my final holiday, when in a sense I was no longer a pupil, two of them supervised a wartime work camp in S.W. Scotland for a fortnight.

At the head of this highly professional staff was Dr J.R. Kinnes, M.A., holding a First Class Honours Degree in Modern Languages (French and German) of Aberdeen University. He was a Boxing 'Blue' of Aberdeen, probably at one of the lighter weights, as he was a smallish chap. He also received a decoration for gallantry in the First World War, in which an enemy gas attack had impaired his health. Typical of clever Scots, he had left his homeland to become head of a foreign institution.

Known as 'Jackie' or 'The Boss', he maintained his interest in French by doing a weekly stint with our class, first period after lunch on Mondays. Within a few weeks, for homework he was setting us the complete tables from 'Heath's Grammar' of the very important auxiliary verbs AVOIR and ETRE. We were just coming to grips with the present tense of each of these verbs in our regular lessons. Jackie insisted on us learning the whole range of tenses − future, imperfect, past historic, conditional, etc. − plus the present and past participles and the imperative mood! Woe betide the unfortunates who could not readily come up with the French for 'He would have had' or 'We shall be', or any other form of these verbs. To coin a phrase, 'They would have had it!' However, 'The Boss' was not always available on Mondays, so we breathed a communal sigh of relief.

I owe him special thanks. In my final year I decided to gain a certificate in German. He became my private tutor, as he was the only member of staff with a degree in the subject. Again, his classes with me were irregular; but my experience with Latin Grammar helped me through the similar intricacies of German as explained in Spanhoofd's grammar book. Success in the certificate exam brought me a 'County Schol' of £80 per annum for 3 years, with which I completed studies in the same languages, graduating as an Hons. B.A. at Manchester.

We had a very rare insight into another of his abilities. Only on two occasions did I see it revealed, and that to an audience of colleagues, parents and us in the Jubilee Hall in Leeds Street. We were gathered for the evening celebration of the annual Speech Day and the award of prizes for academic and sporting achievement. We saw 'Jackie' clutching in his right hand what, at our distance from him, looked like a very fat cigar about fifteen inches long. His left arm was raised, caressing the neck of an enormous double-bass, and the strings attached to it. For that ceremony he was a member of the School Orchestra. If he had not been so short he would have been less noticeable. That sounds rather Irish; but his shortness of stature meant that he had almost to hop about to reach some of the notes at the top of the instrument, whilst the short bow had him prodding to and fro as if he were a piston of *The Flying Scotsman*! To me it was all irreverently hilarious.

'Billy' Ball was his deputy during my first and second year at the 'Sec'. Responsible for general school discipline, he appeared at the end of 'break' at the main door leading from the playground, a frail figure with a shake in his voice. From his pocket he drew a whistle, summoning us to line up for return to classes. On his retirement a lively inspiring maths man, Barraclough, took over. His stay was short. Destined for greater things, he moved out of teaching into administration – with Leeds City, I think. Mr Laverick, another maths teacher, carried on for a while, only to leave teaching to go into business.

William 'Phizzy Bill' Baker was the last incumbent I knew in the deputy's post. His colleague in the Physics lab, Mr Bremner, mystified us with the effects of rubbing ebonite and glass rods with bits of fur, so that our hair stood on end and a sliver of gold rose and fell in the gold leaf electroscope as rods were brought near or taken away. At the end of 3M I said 'Good-bye' to Physics. I have a vivid recollection of refusing to stand on a block of paraffin-wax and join hands with classmates whilst the teacher cranked a handle to make a fat blue spark jump from the fingertip of a pupil across to a revolving metal ball. Electricity of any sort was too mysterious to be trifled with in this way!

As deputy, 'Phizzy Bill' introduced a system of 'reports'. Prefects were armed with notebook and pencil to jot down the names of offenders and the offence. So many 'reports' landed the offender in detention. It all involved a lot of paper-work, cabinet meetings to change policy and sessions to discuss findings. When the War broke out and we were evacuated temporarily to Ragworth Hall on the edge of Norton Green, the system faded quietly into the background.

'Taffy' Rhys was influential in our early years in the 'Sec'. A short thickset Welshman, with a countryman's weather-beaten complexion, he was a keen advocate of fresh air and good posture in class. 'Book, desk, chest, parallel!' was his clarion call in an accent that had a not unpleasing hint of the Welsh lilt about it. He once called me a 'dolt' and told me to 'Sit up straight!' He taught English and History.

Every day − rain, snow, hail, sun or blow − he rode his bicycle in from Eaglescliffe. On the front handle-bars was strapped a wicker basket with a lid, that we said carried a pigeon which bore home to his wife messages relating to Taffy's post-school shopping and time of return. He always wore a stout pair of golden-brown shoes, probably the world-famous 'Veldtschoen'. Legend had it that he had worn them since the day of his 'demob' at the end of the First World War!

'Sid' Dumble, W.H. 'Tot' or 'Bill' Munday, 'Creamy' Manners, Gordon 'Rats' Rattenbury and G.G. 'Jute' Armstrong were other members of the cycle brigade. 'Creamy', doyen of the French department, owned a de luxe Raleigh, enamelled in green, with oil-bath and Sturmey Archer three-speed gear. He once spoke in class of cycling through Normandy, painting a clear picture of those straight up-hill and down-dale 'routes nationales' in that province.

Little did I realize then that I was to follow in his cycle tracks twenty years later; only *I* was more fortunate in my choice of bike. The Lindsay brothers of Victoria Road, Dundee, cycle agents from whom I bought a 'Parkes' with one of my first pay cheques, were to lend me an ordinary roadster fitted with a back-pedalling brake. I added a 'Power-Pak' 49 cc engine-unit that drove the machine through a roller, meshing with the tread of the rear tyre. It relieved a lot of the slog on those seemingly endless hills as I rode from Dieppe to Yvetot (to call on 'le Petit Roi'!), then on westward, via Lisieux, to Bayeux and its Tapestry.

I surmise that Mr Manners was given the nickname of 'Creamy' because he was prone to use the phrase 'crème de la crème' which, surely, one *must* associate with a gentleman of 'manners'. One noticeable feature about him was the size of the shoes which encased his flat feet. They must have been about size 12.

For most of the subjects we stayed in our 'M' and 'Sc' divisions. For French, however, we came together into a 'top' section taught by 'Creamy' and a 'bottom' section which 'Rats' took. In the grammar period, 'Creamy' would start with a question directed at the pupil in the left-hand corner of the back row. He would be checking our ability to manage pronouns in French. 'Translate "I give him some." ' Failure to answer correctly meant that the question passed along the row and beyond, if necessary, until he heard, 'Je lui en donne.' The responder went to the top of the class and everybody shuffled down one place, books, bags and all. This system sounds disruptive and time-wasting; but it kept all of us on our mental toes. In one class period we probably all had a fair proportion of time allotted to us. At the end of term it gave an indication of our progress.

Today, pupils studying French will no doubt be surprised to learn that our basic 'Reader' in the early stages, began with 'Il y avait une fois trois ours' (Once upon a time there were three bears!) Yes, for twelve- and thirteen-year olds, the story of 'Goldilocks' that we had listened to at our mother's knee in infancy! For my part, I should be less surprised to hear today's child ask me, 'Who was Goldilocks?' The present-day text-book in French is probably two thirds pictures and one third words. Ours were mostly words. VOCABULARY and THE NEED TO KNOW IT was writ large in our system!

'Sid' Dumble, our gym-master, was a spare Cumbrian, walking on the balls of his feet, with a spring in his step. Like 'Taffy' and 'The Boss', he was not tall. He put us through our paces in the gym, which ought to have been a swimming-bath! Its unpolished parquet floor was a good six feet below the level of the ground floor. We entered down a short flight of steps from either end, to line up against the walls which were tiled as in a pool. The original plans had, indeed, included a swimming-bath.

'Sid's hallmark in the geography class was his 'thumb-nail' sketch! We learnt to incorporate in these sketches the essential environmental features of a place, on which its importance was based. An area marked 'anhydrite', bounded on the north by the Durham coalfield and the main railway lines, and to the south by the River Tees with Billingham Reach Wharf clearly marked, would appear in our sketch of essential items, from which we could frame our written answer to a question in the 'Matric' on the development of the fertilizer industry at Billingham. Such a tip served to boost our chances of exam success.

'Nobby' Morris took Sid's place for the coaching of senior pupils who chose Geography as a subject for the Higher Leaving Certificate. He was a tall imposing figure, as bald as a bladder of lard. An erudite scholar, he tended to lecture to his students as a university don would have done. Having had the benefit of Sid's succinct direct teaching methods, we took some time to adapt to 'Nobby's style. His gentle sarcasm had us wondering whether he was 'pulling our legs' or being really serious in his criticism. Had we known better, we should have realized his ways were gently introducing us to the liberty of university scholarship, where personal discipline in the organization of study was important.

Reference to the Higher Certificate exams calls for an outline of the strategy involved. Candidates opted for subjects at Principal and Subsidiary level. Principal subjects had a value of 120 marks, subsidiary papers were worth 60. The maximum total for the whole exam was 360. Average candidates like myself were advised to enter for four subjects, three at principal level and one at 'subsid', on the basis that the weakest of the principal subjects might be relegated to subsidiary level the following year. In a way, our first full attempt was a trial run for a subsequent effort that would be rewarded with a County or State Scholarship. A candidate would expect to score high marks in such a relegated subject, as fuller knowledge had been acquired in it, and the subsidiary exam was easier.

At my first attempt I offered French, Latin and Geography at principal level and subsidiary History. In my final year I kept French and Latin as principal subjects, relegated Geography to subsidiary level and replaced History with subsidiary German. The tactics paid off. I was awarded a County 'Schol'.

Roy Stewartson, a sixth-form classmate, had a younger brother who, in his first year in the Sixth, chose a programme in maths and won a State Scholarship worth £240 per annum for 3 years, a fortune in our eyes! That Autumn he went up to Cambridge to read mathematics. Three years later, at the age of 19, he gained First Class Honours in the Cambridge Tripos exams.

Since only M's did Latin, we had 'Tot' Munday to ourselves. Having bounded up the stairs, he would appear suddenly framed in the doorway brandishing a length of rubber gas-tubing, which he wielded unerringly up and down a row of desks, across the shoulders of pupils who failed to respond to his 'passwords', uttered challengingly from the door, 'The verb "to be" ... ' We chorused: 'Has no object!' Another challenge from 'Tot', 'All neuter nouns ... ' Back came the reply, 'Have the accusative like the nominative, and in the plural, both end in "a"!'

I persevered with Latin till the end of my schooldays. I owe a debt of deep gratitude to 'Tot' who, throughout the summer holidays before my final year, tutored me by letter, from his native Hampshire, so that I was able to leave school for university with an exemption from Latin classes in my languages course. Otherwise, I should have had that subject as an extra burden during my first year of university study.

'Rats' was the son of a missionary who had served in China, which may have been his birth-place. He certainly had the cast of features, particularly about the eyes and cheek-bones, that hinted at a Chinese background. He was a tall angular young man, who played alongside us seniors when it was our sports afternoon at 'Field'. He had a position in the scrum, where he helped to strengthen the reserve set of forwards pitted against the First XV men.

At one stage he took over our French section, teaching us one of La Fontaine's fables, which we learnt by heart. We took enormous delight, feeling really bold, when we came to the end of 'Le Corbeau et le Renard' (The Crow and the Fox). The whole class was reciting with expression:

> Le corbeau, honteux et confus,
> JURA, mais un peu tard,
> Qu'on ne l'y prendrait plus!

(The crow, ashamed and embarrassed, SWORE, somewhat late, he wouldn't be caught out like that again!). At the word 'JURA' the whole class bawled it out at the top of their voices, faces laughing, eyes glistening with bold devilry. 'Rats' always enjoyed a chuckle too at that point!

'Jute' was the history master and careers adviser, though that was not an official post. He had his finger on all that pulsed in the areas of Civil Service exams, university courses (whether 'Oxbridge' or 'Red-brick'), the teaching profession both north and south of The Border, and other careers he steered his charges towards, knowing their capabilities. It was possible to know pupils quite well, as we were a school of ideal numbers, about 500 at the most.

I did not discover till years afterwards, at a reunion of Old Daltonians in Manchester (I had been in residence in Dalton Hall), why G.G. Armstrong had acquired the nickname of 'Jute'! It was another member of the clan, Bob Armstrong, taught by 'Jute' in Arbroath in the County of Angus, who related the following apocryphal story of his former history master. It had been the fashion in those days to wear tight-fitting trousers. 'Jute' had been in the body of the class, bending over to look at a pupil's work. Some wag in the class took out a linen hanky and tore it. Thinking that the seam of his pants had burst 'Jute', like a startled rabbit, shot to the front of the class and stood for the rest of the lesson, teaching his students with his back firmly braced against the blackboard.

I had never known of 'Jute's connection with Arbroath. It was only when I began my own teaching career in Dundee (famed for the three 'J's: Jute, Jam and Journalism), that the reason for 'Jute's nickname became obvious. Working only seventeen miles from Dundee, he must have had opportunities to visit the city, 'Jute-opolis'. Arriving in Stockton from that part of Scotland, he would have been readily associated with Dundee, hence his by-name.

I well remember the advice he once passed on to us as senior pupils, looking ahead to our careers. If we were intending to teach in Scotland, we were to make sure that we taught under Chapter V of the Teaching Regulations in Scotland, and not under Chapter III. Teachers qualified under this latter chapter were primary teachers with only an ordinary degree, whilst Chapter V professionals were Honours graduates, who taught in Secondary education on a higher salary scale and with greater prospects of promotion.

In the classroom his blackboard was usually covered with copious notes, or he spent the best part of the time dictating them to us. In this exercise he was engrossed in what he had written, so that he was unaware of the activity of some of his pupils. His dictation was fraught with hesitation. 'At the battle of ... er ... Austerlitz, Napoleon, finding ... er ... that the enemy was about to ... er ... attack ... ' So it went on. Some of the scribes in front of him had abandoned pen for chalk, notebook for slightly raised desk-lid, and proceeded to record the 'ers' as a scorer at cricket might record runs. I have no idea what 'Jute's best innings came to. If, by chance, he noticed something untoward, his reprimand would be preceded by a resonant, 'Now, boy!'

In my last year I deserted him, staking my chances of success on one year of German at 'subsidiary level', supported by a penchant for languages. History, even when it was limited to a specific period and area, still ranged over a wide field of interest. I had already faced the exam, merely gaining pass marks. I no longer had the stomach for a second diet. Now, two generations later, I find myself caught up in some gentle research into social history for the benefit of my grandchildren, so 'Jute's efforts have not been entirely wasted!

C.W. 'Cuthbert' King took over from 'Taffy' and 'Sid' to finish off our education in English and bring some 'culture' into our lives. I seldom drink red wine without the celebrated lines from Keats coming to mind: 'beaded bubbles brinking at the brim and purple-stainèd mouth'! 'Dungeon Ghyll so foully rent' became alive when, some years later, away from 'Cuthbert's room, I was rock-climbing in Langdale with members of the Manchester University Mountaineering Club. In the Old Dungeon Ghyll Hotel, I downed a delicious 'half' of cider, drawn from the wood, after a long day rambling from Langdale to Great Gable and back in perfect summer weather.

However, 'Cuthbert's interests were not limited to English language and literature. He was responsible for carrying his cultural influence into French, opening for us a window on to the world of Louis XIV, 'Le Roi-Soleil', and the literary figures of his reign. To help me, as I was making heavy going of 'literary criticism', he arranged private tutorials with an Old Boy of the school and Oxford graduate, John Gale. I grappled with the art of the literary critic, but I feel that my heart was not really in the work. I have to confess that a 'good read', for me, means a book that is gripping or highly humorous. I am not unduly concerned with the author's style. If I lose interest in what I am reading, I do not begin to analyse the work to find out why. I simply lay the book aside.

Two memories I do have of 'Cuthbert's' classes. He was a keen traveller on the Continent. His tip for avoiding the triple French embrace was, 'In the morning, when they come to greet you, be busy lathering your face for shaving!'

I looked at him questioningly one afternoon. He had been gazing at me for quite a time. 'You know, Donald,' he said, 'I am watching the afternoon sun glint on your incipient whiskers!' I did not have sufficient growth to warrant the expense of shaving-tackle, so there were one or two straggling hairs to be seen.

On my return to school in 1938, 'Cuthbert' found a way of giving me the status of prefect by providing me with a specialized post which was of some use to himself. I was nominated 'Library Prefect' with various responsibilities in the issue of books and the maintenance of records of books 'out' and 'returned'.

In the Sixth we arrived at the 'Holy of Holies', accessible only through the room where all our 'Sec' days had begun. Having only a limited number of subjects to study, we had quite a few 'private study' periods in the week. Space in the school was limited, so we had to sit at the back of whatever class was being conducted in the Sixth Form room.

Only then did I gain some acquaintance of T.B. 'Tibby' Brooke, another English teacher and close colleague of 'Cuthbert'. Unlike him, 'Tibby' was not for going abroad. His interests lay much closer, at home in the local county of Durham and over into North Yorkshire. As someone remarked, 'What "Tibby" does not know about this area, could be written on the back of a halfpenny stamp!' His reading of passages from English literature, or the arguments in which he engaged students like George Watson or George Wing, simply put paid to any private study we were intending to do.

'Tibby' and 'Cuthbert' shared one great interest — music. They took it in turn to play recordings of classical music — Beethoven, Mozart, Schubert, Tchaikovsky, symphonies, sonatas and concertos — pointing out the intricacies of the composition, which were duly dictated as notes for our private reference. I still have that notebook.

Symphony No. 5 in E Flat. Op. 82   Sibelius
1. Jean Sibelius was born in 1865. At the age of 32 the Govt. of Finland gave him a pension so that he could devote himself to composition free from financial anxiety. He lives now in the country outside Helsinki.
2. Critics & music lovers agree in finding his music the characteristics of the natural features of his land – the austerity of a land of hard winter; the charm of a land of short but brilliant summer" as one writer puts it. He

During the War, flush with my sergeant-pilot's pay, I bought the set of 12-inch records of Beethoven's 'Pastoral' Symphony, and listened to the 'ranz des vaches' theme, explained to us by 'Cuthbert' in happier times. 'Tibby' could not only explain the music, he could also play the part on whatever instrument the composer had chosen for his theme. He was a highly-talented man, without any airs and graces, speaking in the flat accent of Teesside and probably, on account of that, the more approachable by those pupils who shared his interests.

Our music teacher proper was Gavin Kaye, a flamboyant figure both in dress and gesture. He wore a bow-tie. The preliminary minutes of the singing-class were devoted to scales and problems on them. Most of us were hopeless at the technical side of music; but the problem was easily solved. We cribbed the day's answers from the class coming out from the music room just as we were about to enter. The rest of the time was spent singing traditional songs from the *National Song-book.* I could amaze my pupils in Dundee with my knowledge of local songs like 'The Piper o' Dundee' or 'Will Ye no back again?' Gavin trained us in the choir which performed at the 'Speech Day' ceremony.

Cultural experiences were carried on across the yard at the back of the school, where K.L.G. Hart ran the art department in a separate building from the main school. He was a handsome man, often surrounded by a bevy of girls pestering him about their art, as his room adjoined their playground. I did not improve on my artistic efforts of the infant class days at Hartburn.

The same building housed 'Daddy' Watson, whose ears waggled when he talked. He taught us the technical skills of working with wood and metal. Despite my failure to make a 'spike' in the forge, I did take home, after many periods of hard slog working with oak, a practical piece of furniture, an umbrella-stand that stood for years at the side of the front door at No. 11 New Road.

As I write this, I realize more and more what teachers of quality we had to set us on the road of life. I should like to think that I did not fail them when I entered the same profession.

CHAPTER FOUR

Pupils and the Part They Played

THE PUPILS too were not lacking in 'characters' or 'heroes'. Parents were middle-class professional folk, farmers, business people and members of the working-class, amongst whom many dads were unemployed.

Rural schools, serving areas like Hartburn, Bishopton, Redmarshall and Stillington, contributed only one or two 'Scholars'. In the town, Trinity School (attached to Trinity Church, Stockton) had a reputation for the scholarship of its protégés who, until the advent of Billingham Intermediate, had formed the bulk of each year's intake of 'Scholarship winners'. Len Turner, Dennis Russell, Alan Metcalfe and the Twiddy brothers Peter and Eric, were Trinity boys.

At the other end of the town-scale were schools like Tilery, which functioned in a 'slum' area. Today its pupils would be classed as 'socially deprived'; but I doubt if any of us looked down on the Sammy Manns or Sid Colliers who were brought up in that area. Our judgement of our peers related not to social status or home background, but to sporting ability first and, perhaps, academic achievement next.

I had some affinity with the Tilery lads, as Uncle Charlie had taught not only most of them, but also their dads and even a grandad. Sammy was usually in trouble – homework not done, books mislaid, lines forgotten, and all accounted for by some ready excuse. He had had to repeat a year, so he was a 'marked man'. Having seen it all before, Sammy was able to pass on useful tips and dodges that saved others from landing in trouble. Bill Palmer, Roy 'Deddy' Dedman and he were a formidable trio, held back from the previous year.

Quite a stir was caused one day, when a pair of 'characters' from further up the school, who were always in each other's company, set fire to some scrap-paper in a waste-paper bin on the top floor. During the lunch break they had been aping 'Tarzan' as they swung from rung to rung of a ladder spanning the rafters of the bike shed. Unfortunately 'Jackie' was crossing the schoolyard on his way back from lunch, caught them in the act, and dealt with them immediately in his office. They had taken exception to his summary punishment, so they had made their way quietly upstairs, where they had attempted arson. Expulsion followed.

Swinburne was appointed prefect by 'Phizzy Bill' when Billy Ball retired from the deputy-headship. Poor Swinburne wished to establish a tradition by wearing *the* prefect cap, distinctive by its red colour. He must never have heard of 'white' blackbirds. On every possible occasion, *that* cap was the object of some attack, knocked off the wearer's head and kicked about the yard. His readiness to 'report' offenders only made matters worse.

If we needed 'heroes' to worship, those of us who were sports-minded were well served, often through our House and School captains. The annual Swimming Gala, held in the old Stockton Baths, was an event where heroes were prominent, each standing alone to represent his House. In a strange atmosphere of silence, we watched George Stirling, Captain of the School, prepare to take the 'plunge'. He was the champion in that event over a long number of years. When he launched himself from the pool side at the 'deep end', the mass of his tall well-muscled frame carried him far beyond his rivals. We wondered when he was going to surface!

Christopher 'Kit' Urwin was our own Blue House swimming champ and also the school's representative in local competitions. A six-footer, he could out-distance all his school rivals in the 'crawl'. But it was as 'last-man-in' in the inter-House relay that Kit did Blue proud. On one occasion, with a gap of half-a-length to make up, Kit threw himself in at the shallow end in a flat racing-dive and, flailing with arms and legs, thrashed his way into the lead to win by a 'touch'. The noise of our cheering was enough to lift the roof!

He was also a great player to have in the rugby scrum. At a sports afternoon at 'Field', where the 1st XV was practising against the 'Seconds', strengthened by two masters playing in the pack, there were some shenanigans going on amongst the scrummaging forwards. Kit was standing no more nonsense. He straightened up, forcing both packs to stand erect. If 'Rats' the junior French master persisted in any more dirty tactics, Kit threatened to 'do' him! 'Rats' himself was as tall as Kit, so it was no mean threat!

'Field' was held on Tuesday afternoons for the Junior School, and on Thursdays for the Seniors. We had to go westwards out of town, a mile beyond Fairfield. Cyclists made their own way there. The rest of us piled noisily into two double-deckers, which made their way by separate routes, one via Oxbridge and Fairfield Back Lane, the other via Newtown. I have a fancy the drivers made a race of it. The key point was the junction just beyond Fairfield. The first bus to reach it was assured of success, since only half a mile of narrow country road lay between it and 'Field'. No driver was going to risk overtaking on such a stretch.

'Field' was in fact two large fields, shared with 'Grammar'. Three or four pitches were equipped with rugby posts. There was also a soccer pitch, but that belonged to 'Grammar'.

In the summer season a cricket square was laid out and maintained by a groundsman, but it was our duty as players of the 'home' side to turn up early and mark out the wicket.

Changing accommodation was really primitive – a couple of wooden huts and an outside cold tap for sluicing off the thickest of the mud from the rugger pitch. With such poor facilities, we felt apologetic towards our guests, especially when we enjoyed hot showers and the warmth of their changing-rooms for the return match.

One Christmas holiday, I was chosen to play in a representative game at Middlesbrough Rugby Club ground. A clear dry day had followed a cold frosty night. The grass was tipped with hoar-frost. Playing at full-back in this game, I was not overtaxed, but I do remember the enormous bath of steaming hot water that we all jumped into at the end of the match.

We were to improve our image. Towards the end of the 'thirties, 'Nobby' Morris took over the running of school cricket. He had a brilliant idea. He arranged for a tiny marquee to be erected up by the square. Primus stoves, kettles and teapots were provided. We were instructed to bring along enough sandwiches, cakes and biscuits to do for ourselves and our opposing numbers. In this way, we were able to have a lunch-break and play the game out as it was meant to be played.

With this hospitality, *we* were one up on our opponents, who usually had us escorted to some local café after the match, where they, of course, footed the bill. As this entertainment had to fit in with the café's routine, 'away' matches were restricted to an agreed number of 'overs' or played to a time limit. 'Nobby's scheme was more economical, but nonetheless enjoyable. We learnt something of the gentle art of entertaining into the bargain. As a teacher responsible for some of the cricket at Morgan Academy, Dundee, I recalled 'Nobby's idea and put it into practice in the school's sports pavilion. We could offer an even more attractive service, as young ladies were on hand to do the honours. Scottish academies are usually 'mixed' schools!

Our First XI boasted some fine batsmen and bowlers. Over the seasons, as the 'Sunday Post' offered cricket bats for outstanding performances in school matches, for high batting scores and excellent bowling figures, quite a few bats came our way. Vic Avery may have won more than one 'S.P.' bat. He could hit a powerful drive, or delicately glance a fast ball down to the leg boundary. His Saturdays were full, as he turned out for Norton in the afternoons, playing in the North Yorkshire and South Durham League. George Wing was our pace bowler who, like Vic, was awarded an 'S.P.' bat for dismissing practically all the opposing side for a meagre tally of runs.

Though I enjoyed cricket, I never made the First XI. I did, however, captain the 'Seconds', a merry band of lads − Kit Urwin, Brian 'Nick' Nicholson, Arthur Trenholme, Sid Collier, Hector Goddard, Geoff Ord, Ken Happer, Jack Enderwick, 'Ginger' Porter and Bob Shields. That was the 1938 team.

In that same year, as I was batting at Guisborough, an 'Autogiro' flew overhead, clattering through the sky like an airborne haymaking-machine! I stood aside from my wicket, not so much because its passage was playing havoc with my concentration, but rather the better to see the modern marvel, forerunner of today's 'choppers'.

Winter sport offered cross-country running. Ray was a keen member of the House team, so he would have me run too. Being already out in the country, we had no difficulty in making up courses through fields around Carlton and Redmarshall. Ray's advice was for me to keep going till I finished the course, as points were awarded on a team basis. 'Gink' Gedling was our ace, a slim, wiry, bespectacled fellow, a 'brainy' type who was also no mean exponent of the moves on a chessboard.

The School Sports Day was held annually in the warmth of July. 'Field' was too remote and rough a terrain for the sprinting and jumping of an athletics meeting; so we had the use of Stockton Cricket Ground, which was also more accessible to parents and friends.

For a week or two in advance of the event, pupils were invited to bring in goods in kind for the teas (sugar, tea, tinned fruit, meat pastes, etc.) and, on the morning of the Sports Day, sandwiches, cakes, biscuits and milk. In the afternoon, these ingredients of a tea-party style meal would be on sale in the cricket pavilion at 1/6d (7½p) per head as spectators and competitors felt the need for refreshment.

The sports events were traditional. Enthusiasts of today may be surprised to know that there was an 80-yards sprint, as well as the 100, 220, 440 and 880-yards. The mile was the last event before the team relays. The gallant plodder who stuck it out was cheered almost as generously as the winner.

To round off the day, 'The Boss' made a speech of thanks to his staff, the competitors, and parents and friends who had contributed in cash or in kind to the success of the day. Prizes were awarded to the winners, useful gifts like fountain-pens and Ingersoll watches, as well as silver cups and medals. The Victor Ludorum bore off his trophy amid cheers from one and all; but the biggest cheer was reserved for the captain of the winning House –

most often, Green.

From the results of this day, athletes were chosen to represent the school in the inter-school sports, which brought together the cream of Teesside senior schools – Coatham Grammar, Middlesbrough High, Darlington Grammar, Barnard Castle, Bishop Auckland, Henry Smith's of West Hartlepool and ourselves. This meeting was held in the evening, each school providing the venue annually in turn.

On one occasion I cycled with a pal to Bishop Auckland to support our team, a round trip of forty miles! I considered the effort was worthwhile, as Eric 'Tich' Tingle won the high jump in face of much taller opposition by clearing 5 feet 1 inch, then to the amusement and amazement of the spectators walked back to the take-off point, erect under the bar. I never saw anybody else clear his own height in the event.

The extramural sporting side of school life was, in some measure, counterbalanced by the indoor intellectual activity of the 'Lit and Hist'. Ray press-ganged me into joining, as he had done over the cross-country business. A keen House-man, he felt that I ought to appear at inter-House debates, a regular feature of the winter programme. I was not a skilled debater. It all boiled down to simple arithmetic. No matter how well or poorly a debater spoke, whether he stood up in the debate and rambled on for his allotted span or just blurted out a heart-felt, one-sentence opinion, a point was gained for the House. A sufficient excess of supporters participating could turn the result to a House's advantage and ultimate success. Furthermore, as all activities scored points towards the final award of the House Cup, those odd gains might in the end just tip the balance, where rugger, cricket and athletics results were fairly even.

'Lit and Hist' meetings were on a Friday night at 7.00 p.m. in the art/technical annexe behind the main building. 'Hat Nights' could be hilarious but traumatic occasions, depending on what subject was drawn from the hat. We also knew we had to stand up and 'ad-lib' for five minutes to expound on it. Frank W. Dobby, a Haverton lad, had the audience in stitches, masters and pupils alike, when he made a highly humorous speech on the all-embracing properties of 'Aspro' in the curing of everything from head-aches to broken limbs. (The tablets could be ground down and mixed with a gluey compound to make the cement of plaster-casts!)

We were also entertained by visiting speakers, lecturing on foreign travel, historic castles, and so on, with sepia slides as illustrations. Colour slides were a rarity.

'Jute', 'Tot' Munday and 'Rats' were regular chairmen of these evenings. In the inter-House debates they would be supported by two judges from the other two non-competing Houses, a system which proved to be fair and acceptable to all concerned. Points were assessed on 'content', 'delivery' and 'pluck' (for standing up and speaking in public). George Watson and George Wing were a formidable pair of debaters for Red House (Watson with his dour Scottish logic and Wing, the more flamboyant, with a waspish wit).

A knock-out chess tournament ran its course, but I cannot tell whether that was organized by the 'Lit and Hist'. However, Blue had its champion in 'Gink' Gedling, whose other forte was long-distance running, cross-country and the mile. Perhaps staying-power underlined his field and board successes.

CHAPTER FIVE

School Travel

In 1931 (or 1932), Ray took a trip to Holland on board the SS *Grangemouth* of the Gibson-Rankine Line. Their boat sailed from Leith in Scotland (the port of the capital, Edinburgh) calling in at the Tees en route for Rotterdam. Ray boarded the *Grangemouth* in Middlesbrough with the rest of the party for the journey across the North Sea. That voyage may have fired him with the desire to follow a career in the Merchant Navy. However, the officials failed him because his eyesight was not up to standard.

In the meantime, after his return from Holland, he spent lunch-breaks and hours at the end of the school day, haunting the Stockton wharfs where, prominent in his school uniform, he was known to quay-side workers, stevedores and crane-men. Crew-men of ships putting regularly into Stockton passed on to him news of their voyages and information about the cargoes they were carrying. Throughout that period, Ray began to keep a register of commercial ships of all nations, records of shipping movements in and out of the Tees as published in the local 'Gazette', and a correspondence with like-minded enthusiasts. This detailed knowledge stood him in good stead when, after the War, he became an officer with the Customs and Excise.

In 1937 the pair of us biked up to Sunderland to meet up with Johnnie May of the *Tory Island*, a tramp steamer that plied up our way in the coastal trade. After the best part of three hours on the bikes, we were dying for a bite to eat. Johnnie and his mate regaled us with 'door-step' slices of bread, liberally coated with black treacle, washed down with a mug of cocoa so thick that the spoon almost stood upright in it. Twenty years later, from my home in Dundee, we made a special pilgrimage to the 'Broch' (Fraserburgh, Johnnie's home port, on the north-east tip of the coast above Aberdeen), spending a happy weekend with him and his family, recalling pleasant memories.

I did not take part in any foreign travel, though 'Creamy' once approached me about an exchange with a Catholic family in Niort, France. I was to be the guest of parents with eight children to their name; but that was not the factor that put me off. It would have cost too much. Instead, I persuaded Dad to buy me a 'Midge' tent from Edgington's, Old Kent Road, London, suppliers to Everest expeditions. Though it cost £5, many a pal has enjoyed a camping holiday in it, and I have pitched it in the Highlands and across in the French Alps. Yet I have never passed through Niort. Fifty years on, the little tent is still serviceable.

Of the official school excursions which took place during my time at the 'Sec', I went on the 1934 trip to Edinburgh. This meant an early start. 'Pompey' Heathcote (he had come up from Portsmouth) met me at the foot of our steps in New Road. Together we walked the whole of the way to Stockton station (about two and a half miles) to meet up with the rest of the party.

Today, memories of that outing focus on the City itself — Princes Street Gardens and the Floral Clock, the Scott Monument, Carlton Hill (where I was 'snapped' sitting astride a cannon-barrel) and Edinburgh Castle (with another snap of me standing alongside a 'Jock' on sentry-duty, resplendent in his kilt). Inside the Castle we paid a visit to a hall of the Scottish regiments, to survey (solemnly but without comprehending) the Roll of Honour of those who had died in the Great War.

Happier recollections take me back to the Chambers Street museum, a boy's paradise, since models of railway locos, steamships and all manner of engineering marvels could be set in motion at the touch of a button. On an upper floor, a roomful of information was displayed about lighthouses with impressive mirror systems that converted the light from bulbs of relatively small power into flashing beams that could be seen for miles.

From there we made our way to the top of the Waverley Steps, to catch a bus out to the Zoo at Corstorphine. The zoo-keeping authorities were in the vanguard of modern techniques, seeking to give the animals in their charge a greater sense of freedom and natural living. This was something for us to note. But it was not *that* philosophy which intrigued *me*. It was a novel idea on the bus journey out to the Zoo that tickled my fancy and made me smile.

'Jute', being in charge of the party, was responsible for the various payments that had to be made, like bus fares. He had about three dozen tickets to buy for the run to the Zoo. Without so much as a second glance, the conductress proceeded to churn out the tickets on a little machine that I had never seen before. She set a couple of levers, cranked a little handle, and out spewed the tickets like a printed runaway roll of 'Izal' toilet-paper. I just gawped. In a matter of seconds she had completed the transaction, whereas 'Slow-coach's mate, on the school bus back in Stockton, would still have been pulling out the tenth ticket from his little ticket-rack, fitting it under the punch and pulling the trigger to 'click' it!

The visit to the Zoo was a strenuous affair as we climbed up the slope of Corstorphine Hill, where the open pens were set out at different levels. There the animals were not constrained to a relentless pad-padding in front of the iron bars of a cage. We, the spectators, were safe, looking down on them over a concrete wall above a wide moat. At least the polar bears and seals were enjoying what was, to the 'big cats' and wolves, a water-barrier below an unscaleable parapet. At the end of a long day trudging about, we were only too glad to head back to Waverley station.

The journey home was in lighted carriages for most of the way, as we did not get back till about midnight. We wandered along the corridors to join our pals in other compartments. At one point I sat in amongst the 'Big Boys', some of the prefects in the 'Sixth', who were earnestly debating future prospects of a job. Some had their sights set on training college in Durham; others pointed to the surplus of teachers and talked of having a crack at the Civil Service exams instead. Their talk did not inspire a 'junior' who had ambitions to be a schoolmaster. In any case, that future lay quite a long way off, and I had enough on my plate with day-to-day living.

'Pompey' was one of my companions on the only other trip I made with the school; the other was Bob Shields, son of a dentist and Dux of the school in his final year. Again our destination was Scotland, a forestry camp in Kirkcudbrightshire. We were members of a working party of twelve senior pupils, supervised by two masters, Mr Stone and 'Nobby' Morris (whose idea it was). It was the summer holiday of 1940, our last at school. The War was almost one year old. 'Nobby' must have thought we ought to do our bit in the national struggle, so he had asked us to work a month's contract.

The other nine pupils, and the teachers, went by train. 'Pompey', Bob and I cycled. The first day we did eighty miles to Rockcliffe Youth Hostel near Carlisle, after a tough slog over Stainmore. Next day we completed the remaining sixty-plus miles, passing through romantic Gretna Green, Annan and Dumfries as we headed towards Castle Douglas and St John's Town of Dalry, with Kendoon Youth Hostel at our journey's end. Just before Dalry we passed through Balmaclellan. I could not resist renaming it 'Bally-mucky-ellen'!

Our first task on arrival at Kendoon, after signing in with the warden, was to pitch our tent. As sleeping-quarters only, the 'Midge' was big enough for three. There was ample storage room in the hostel for our luggage. The rest of our fellow Stocktonians introduced us to other hostellers who were also contracted to work in the forest. They were a small party of Edinburgh University students – Bob Sutherland, a 'medic' who was familiar with the area; Johnnie Paterson; and two overseas students from the sub-continent of India, Ravi Chang and Patamba Dass Saksena.

Next morning we set out to work, crossing one of the barrages of the Blackwater Dam scheme, which provided hydro-power from the river which flowed down the valley into Loch Ken. We found ourselves face to face with a hillside on which young pine trees, barely a foot tall, had been planted but were now almost lost beneath a growth of weeds and tall grass. Each of us was equipped with a sickle and a sharpening-stone, which we had to learn to use to keep the cutting blade sharp.

It was a back-breaking job to begin with, as we bent over the tiny trees and hacked away at the grass, moving slowly up the slope, yard by yard, the spacing set by the foresters to allow the saplings to develop. We worked in all weathers; but the worst of it was during the muggy hours till mid-morning, when the midges took their fill of our rich blood. They came in droves. A fortune awaits the person who can find *the* antidote to the Scottish midges, which plague the scenic Highlands and Islands from June to the end of September. Our only respite from attacks came when a strong wind blew or the air was cold.

A fortnight of this purgatory was enough for the 'train-gang'. With money in their pockets, they decided to cry 'quits'. They packed their bags and, accompanied by the two masters, left 'Pompey', Bob and me to honour the contract.

One morning, at about four o'clock, 'Pompey' was up and away. He did the whole of the return journey of 140-plus miles in the day. Forty-seven years after the event, I met him for the first time since the forestry camp. 'Pompey,' I said, 'I've always wondered why you shot off from the camp so early without explanation. It struck me that you might have had some urgent family news calling you home. What was behind your sudden departure, if the question is not indiscreet?' 'No, it was quite simple. I was due to begin another job on a farm the following day!' I take my hat off to my old pal. He had made an early start to do 140 miles of tough cycling which took in the crossing of the Pennines midway on his journey, and then he was to begin a physically demanding job without a break to recover. That certainly called for a toughness of spirit and stamina.

Though the War was going on, we realized at Kendoon that we were better off than folk back at home. We had our ration books with us, but the local baker was not concerned about our bread coupons or sticking to the official ration. His shop-window displayed a whole range of bread and 'tea-breads' − as the Scots call scones, bannocks, oatcakes and currant-bread. Still, he did not make anything like our good old *Yorkshire* teacake!

On the camp we had to do our own cooking; so it was arranged from the start that one of the squad would stay behind each day, to prepare the meal for the workers on their return to the hostel. When it came to my turn, I decided I should be a little more ambitious and try something slightly different with the ingredients to hand.

Mrs Hutcheson, the hostel's warden, lived in a cottage across the road. Her husband, Will, was one of the charge-hands or gangers of the forest, who kept an eye on our efforts whilst working alongside us. I went across to her house and asked her if she had a cookery book she could let me have.

She went back to her kitchen and returned with the Scottish W.R.I. cookery book, issued by the Women's Rural Institutes. My wife has a copy where, under the section headed 'Oatmeal Dishes', I read the same quotation by Dr Johnson which struck me so forcibly when I first came across it in 1940. His definition of oats was, 'A grain, which in England is generally given to horses, but in Scotland supports the people.' The reply was made, 'Yes, Sir, but where will you find such horses or such people?'

Back in the hostel kitchen, I glanced through the pages. I was tempted to try an apricot dumpling, which would be a filling dessert. We had dried apricots in store. The problem was to find a big enough pot to hold a pudding to satisfy our crowd. After some searching, the only utensil I could find was a large fire-bucket.

All went well until I realized I needed a more presentable container in which to serve up the finished dish. In making the transfer I spilt some of the pud out on to the hostel floor, which I had been responsible for cleaning earlier in the day. Working from the premises that 'What the eye does not see, the heart does not grieve over,' and 'You've got to eat a peck of dirt before you die,' I just scraped the bits up off the floor and added them to the dessert! Nobody was any the wiser when they tucked into it, served up with lashings of custard. In fact, I was complimented on the welcome change to the meal!

Success must have gone to my head. On the following Saturday I tried my hand at a fruit cake, using the temperamental side-oven of the hostel stove. I had a good fire going and the cake in the oven when, about halfway through the baking, a couple of deaf-mute cyclists turned up from Coatbridge. Thankfully, I had studied their sign-language in *Scouting for Boys*, so I was able to convey to them the delicate nature of the situation. The oven must not be tampered with nor the fire allowed to burn low. I simply spelt out on my fingers, C-A-K-E I-N O-V-E-N, pointed to three on the clock, and slapped my wrist to signify, 'Naughty, naughty, no touch!' They joined the rest of us in a tasty bite for tea.

Nevertheless, the seriousness of the War situation was brought sharply home to Bob and me another weekend. As the weather promised to hold, we made up our minds to climb Corserine, the highest point near us in the Rhinns of Kells (a range of the Southern Uplands, bordering our valley on the west). It is a fair climb at 2669 feet above sea level. We could not get away until mid-afternoon on the Saturday, so we took my tent with us, intending to spend a night out on the mountain.

By late afternoon we had reached a suitable point on the mountain-side to call a halt, leaving ourselves a canny climb to the summit and ample time to make the return to base on the Sunday. In the angle of a dry-stane dyke (moorland stone-wall), we pitched the tent out of the wind and slept soundly.

Next morning we had finished our breakfast and struck camp when suddenly, on the other side of the wall, appeared the menacing face of a local shepherd, as we thought. He was not. He was serving as a 'bobby' in the Glasgow force and had come home for the weekend to the shieling higher up the glen. He had seen the white cloth of our tent and had come to investigate. What made matters worse was that the little tent had a fly-sheet, so that we had two white packs neatly folded at our feet!

'Let me see your identity cards!' he ordered. We had not thought to bring them with us for this remote part of the country. We went through the motions of searching in our pockets. 'Sorry,' we stammered 'We've left them back in the camp at the Kendoon Youth Hostel.' He was far from satisfied.

Just then I remembered that one of the last things I had done before we came away had been to pick up my mail. Mam had sent me a letter from home. I had read it in the peace of the evening, in the tent. I handed it to him with an explanation. That folded sheet of paper in Mam's round hand was all that stood between us and arrest as 'German parachutists'. The 'Bobby' told us that Lord Haw-haw, the English traitor who broadcast Hitler's propaganda from Germany, had hinted at the probability of German paratroopers landing in our country.

We parted amicably. I shall never forget the six-foot frame of that hill-man, topped with ginger hair!

When our contract was completed, Bob and I pedalled southeast, making towards the Lake District, where we parted company. He had planned to spend the rest of his holiday there touring. I pushed further south to Kendal and its hostel.

I signed in as a 'self-cooker', making my own meals in what was the traditional manner of hostelling north of the Border. In the English hostel I had the distinct impression that 'self-cookers' were an inferior species, for we were pointed towards a separate wooden shed to perform our culinary art, while the superior English-style members dined according to the warden's menu, having booked their meals in advance. On that occasion I missed the camaraderie of the Scottish hostels that I was to enjoy once again five years later.

Further south, from Skipton, the last part of my ride took me back east over the Pennines. At Blubberhouses on the Skipton – Harrogate road, in what I recall was a lone house-cum-shop on the moor, I bought *The Northern Echo*. I had never had to buy the local paper before, as it was delivered to our house from Mr Burns' shop in South View. This was a most important moment. The inside pages were just one mass of names, publishing the results of the N.U.J.M.B. Higher Certificate exams. Along with other classmates, 'Pompey', Bob and I had passed. That moment marked the end of boyhood and the entry into another stage of life – University, the armed forces and manhood.

CHAPTER SIX

The Cleveland and North Yorkshire Exploration Society

'POMPEY'S LONG RIDE back from the forestry camp to Teesside certainly was an achievement. My own return, done at a more leisurely pace over three stages, with a detour via The Lakes, Kendal and Ripon, covered a good two hundred and twenty miles. I had had the experience of distance cycling under tough conditions with the Cleveland and North Yorkshire Exploration Society.

Who had founded the Society, and who were its members? Having thought up a title like that, the founder had to be someone from the area, an enthusiast with a sense of the importance of his aims. It had to have the cachet of 'society'; a mere 'club' would not do. Exploration conjured up visions of Scott and his brave companions, pitting their strength against the harshness of the Antarctic. The Society's first expedition was to subject its members unexpectedly to somewhat similar conditions. The founder, then? Why, cousin Ray, of course! And the membership? Joe Soap! And for one expedition only, brother Eric!

I still have the exercise book issued to Ray by the school authorities. On the line marked 'NAME .... ' I can make out the faint 'Counter R.' he had written before deciding to appropriate the book as a journal of our activities. He may have tried to erase his name with an ink-rubber. Inside, he wrote the title of each expedition and its log. My task was to write up an account of the event. In 1937, between Easter Saturday (27th March) and Bank Holiday Monday (2nd August), six expeditions

EXPEDITION No 3

TRIP to BURTON'S HEAD (1489')

ROUTE:

	MILES	HOURS	TOTAL MILEAGE	TOTAL TIME	TOTAL CYCLING TIME	CYCLING AVERAGE m.p.h	DAY'S AVERAGE m.p.h
			4.3 43½	6	5½	7.6 7 9	7.? 7 25
STOCKTON (HOME)		dep 2·30 p.m					
BILLINGHAM (HOME)		dep 2·30 p.m					
MBRO (ACROSS)	4.6 4½	ar 3·10 p.m					
STOKESLEY	7½	ar 3·40 p.m					
EASBY	3¾	ar 4·5 p.m					
INGLEBY GREENHOW	1½	ar 4·12 p.m					
BANK FOOT	¾	ar 4·20 p.m					
INCLINE TOP	3	arr ?·?0 p.m					
		dep ?·50 p.m					
BROUGHTON CROSS	1	ar 5·25 p.m					
BURTON'S HEAD	2½	arr 6·15 p.m					
		dep ?·45 p.m					
CLAY BANK	2	arr 7·15 p.m					
GT. BROUGHTON	2½	arr 7·30 p.m					
STOKESLEY	2?	arr 7·50 p.m					
YARM (ACROSS)	1½	arr 8·? p.m					
STOCKTON (HOME)	4½	arr 8·30 p.m					
BILLINGHAM (HOME)	4½	arr 9·0 p.m					

DETAILS OF RUN

Ray and I met at Acklam and set off along the familiar route to Stokesley. In accordance with our usual custom we were cycling into a day which was rather unpromising. The wind from N.W–N.E was in a favourite quarter, but leaving an quite ... it was of very little use to us. From Stokesley we followed the road to Easby and then on to Ingleby Greenhow.

The village appeared to us in a different light on this second visit. Some previously at ... it had been more anxious on inches of snow, we now the snow was gone and the old trees in the village registered the effect of ... brought on by this passing ... Once a strenuous pull out of the village we were all set for Bank Foot.

As before Bank Foot witnessed the ...ing of our adventures. A discussion took place as to whether we should proceed by the road or not, being hindered ... and go by the railway. After weighing up the ... and cons we set out in the usual way, ... going by the railway, leaving me to go by the ... some little ... way in taking the latter route. I was to ... out as it was called when the road, and so the ... arose ... into a race to decide the winner of the two ... and not over two miles to the ... of the road led to the increased wind velocity at a higher altitude. The rain according to ..., so were carried out.

They were: No. 1, 27th March (Easter Saturday), The Exploration of the Rosedale Railway; No. 2, 30th March, Intended Trip to Rosedale, diverted to Doubting Castle and Freeborough Hill, owing to adverse weather conditions; No. 3, 15th May (Whit Saturday), Trip to Burton's Head (1489 feet). Burton's Head is not a pub situated at that altitude, but the highest point on the North Yorkshire Moors! In any case, if we had been visiting a hostelry, we should have been under-age drinkers!; No. 4, May 17th (Whit Monday, and Mam's 42nd birthday!), Trip to Falling Foss; No. 5, 17th July (Saturday), Trip to Aerial Ropeway at Great Ayton, an evening run; and, finally, No. 6, August Bank Holiday Monday, Trip to Scugdale. On this outing, we ran no risk of being caught up in the annual traffic jams of some holiday-makers. We were hauling our bikes up sheer moor-sides and wading with them through bracken four feet high!

Ray was meticulous in his part of the recording of events. On the left-hand page, in the first column, he wrote the stages of the journey. In the next column were recorded the miles between each stage, even down to furlongs ($\frac{1}{8}$ of a mile for the generations not brought up on the Table of Length – inches, feet, yards, etc.) This precise measuring was done with reference to the '1 in. to the mile' Ordnance Survey maps, of which we owned the local sheets. I ordered sheets 14 (Darlington) and 15 (Middlesbrough and Hartlepool) when I gained class prizes in sessions 1935-36 and 1936-37. I bought No. 16 (Whitby and Saltburn) and 22 (Pickering and Thirsk) so that we had the whole area of our Exploration Society mapped out for ready reference.

In the third and last column, Ray marked down the time of departure from home, the moment we passed through a stage-point, arrival at and departure from a destination, and the time of our return to base. Using all of this information, he finished with a summary of the total mileage, total time and total cycling time, from which he calculated our cycling average speed in m.p.h., and the day's average.

Hours spent together over Christmas holidays playing with Ray's Hornby train set, and outdoor hours passed as we sat perched on the top of the Ninety-Nine Steps, train-spotting, were all indicative of an interest in railways. It was only natural, therefore, that we should choose as objectives for our expeditions the old iron-stone lines, which linked the mines of the area to the iron- and steel-works on Teesside. These routes were clearly marked on the O.S. maps as mineral- or tram-ways.

The Rosedale line was particularly appealing, as it penetrated into the heart of the moors and incorporated a singular engineering feature at Incline Top. This had been a winding-station above a steep gradient of roughly one-in-four or one-in-five, where the loaded wagons, going downhill, hauled up the empties returning to the mine, through a system of endless ropeway.

To explore this feature, we took the Ingleby Greenhow – Farndale road which, like the Incline, had to climb the steep escarpment of the moors. I quote from my account: 'Here the road wound tortuously to the summit through deep snow, rendering our progress difficult.' Looking back today, I recall a surface that was more like the bed of a moorland beck, a mosaic of yellow sandstone rocks held in place by yellow clay.

If it had been a different season of the year I might have said, 'Like the page following Wenceslas, I dragged myself and my bike up the hill and along to Incline Top for a good hour, to cover only three miles!' This was in spite of the fact that 'once at the top, we were able to cycle with great trepidation.'

We had our dinner in a hut amongst the ruins of the derelict hauling-station. For some reason, I neglected to mention in my account that I had the strange experience in the hut of seeing everything through a purplish haze. Was it the first signs of snow-blindness? We had been travelling over a snowy landscape and were seated in dark surroundings whilst we ate lunch.

The next stage of the journey was along the old railway-line itself. It crossed the undulating moortop through a series of cuttings and above embankments. Our first encounter was with a cutting. We sank knee-deep into the snow that filled it. That should have deterred us from going on; but we just gritted our teeth and hauled ourselves and bikes ahead. The next five miles took an hour and a half.

I noted: 'At last, we reached civilization. We had arrived at Little Blakey on the main Castleton — Farndale road.' A snow-plough had cleared this, so that all we had to do was to keep going. We did, heartened by quite a bit of downhill to Castleton village. At Urlay Nook, D.F.'s cottage on the other side of the valley, tea and cheerful company restored our spirits. We did the final thirty miles from Little Blakey in just over three hours.

What if the mist had come down on the moortop? What if one of us had sprained an ankle in the deep snow, out in the wilderness? We had no compass. The nearest farms were a couple of miles away, over craggy hill-sides, down in the dales. My reference in the preamble to Scott and the Antarctic was, perhaps, not so far-fetched, given that we were mere youths and not experienced men who had trained hard and long for their expedition!

In comparison to the Rosedale outing, the trip to the Aerial Ropeway at Great Ayton was idyllic. It was a summer's evening jaunt of thirty miles, amid 'green meadows, hedges and yellowing cornfields.' On the return journey, 'peace and serenity reigned over the whole panorama before us,' in what for the want of a better term might be called the Stokesley Basin.

The search for the tarn above Scugdale, which took a summer afternoon and evening, combined elements of both the above-mentioned trips. We had to negotiate steep moor-sides. Head-high bracken had taken the place of knee-deep snow. Both are serious obstacles to weighty bikes. Clear of Scarth Nick, 'the only pass in the hills worthy of the name,' we had an extensive view of civilization, the wide expanse of the lower Tees Basin, rich farmland and fume-laden industrial belt. In fact, with ultra-powerful binoculars, I might have been able to see our Mam sunning herself in our front garden.

The 'daddy' of all our explorations, in which Eric was involved, was the longest, seventy-eight and three-quarter miles according to the log. My kid brother was not quite fourteen, and had never done anything like that distance on a bike before. He only had an ordinary roadster, without a three-speed gear, which was another disadvantage. Before we left home, I may have been told, 'Look after your brother and don't be doing anything daft!'

'Two's company ... ' Ray was riding behind, having stopped to clear the road of some bricks that a lorry passing earlier had shed. Further along, over the top of a sharp rise, he hit a half-brick. There was no justice. His tyre was punctured and the front wheel buckled. That should have been enough for us to call the trip off there and then; but Ray is a determined character. Though we had no compass, we did have a repair outfit. He mended the puncture and on we went.

At Falling Foss, our objective, we were forty miles from home. Eric had never done so many miles on a bike in one go, had never climbed such hills or followed such hairy tracks. Like most of us, he was used to having fun on a bike, riving about the street or going to the village for messages. Now, in mid-afternoon, he was faced with the prospect not only of another forty miles, but also of starting off on them along a rising, stony moorland path, where cycling was out of the question. Falling Foss! A moorland cascade, shimmering in a sylvan bower, its name harking back to our Norse ancestry. I bet no such poetic thoughts were passing through *his* mind then. I suspect they were not passing through mine either.

Ahead, we were to encounter some more unpleasantness. We ran into a thunder-storm, which was particularly frightening out on the open moor. As we made our way up out of Egton towards the Whitby — Middlesbrough road, we were afflicted by thirst. The only solution to bring us relief was for us to lap up the rainwater caught in the hollows of our cycle-capes. It had a sooty taste. Little wonder that Eric did not insist on being included in any more of our mad ramblings.

He did take part in another trip, but not with the 'Society'. Along with some more lads from New Road and me, he went up to Durham for a session at the ice-rink there. This was a summer jaunt, as I recall that the rink-owners had difficulty in keeping the cooling-system working efficiently. There was a film of water on the surface of the ice, which added to any discomfort one naturally felt in falling.

Eric's moan this time was that he was hungry. It was not surprising. The twenty miles to Durham had taken a couple of hours on the bikes. For another hour we had hurtled round the rink, as we could all skate. We really needed something inside us for the run home, but nobody had any spare cash to buy anything. He just had to grin and bear it. My appetite was such that Mam used to say, 'Donald, your stomach will be the end of you!' Yet, like a camel, I could and still can go on long enough without food. Is it surprising that Eric soon became disenchanted with our style of cycling?

Now, when I look back to the beginning of my cycling experiences and calculate the miles I have done, I should not mind 5p for every mile biked. Furthermore, in those days there was relative freedom even on main roads, so that each pleasing aspect of a run could be appreciated to the full.

CHAPTER SEVEN

The Kayak

THOUGH ERIC Eric did not share our interest in cycling (quite probably because he did not own a new bike), there was one mode of transport that did interest all three of us — boating. The seasonal flooding of Billingham Bottoms, and the availability of scrap wood and empty oil drums on the coke dump, were an encouragement to aquatic sports. Some of the lads made a few attempts at floating rafts on the flooded fields, and Cowpen Pond, with tragic results. We were under strict orders to keep out of such risky ploys. Fields could lie under three feet of water and, at the edges, much deeper drainage ditches were no longer distinguishable.

Eric and I had made our own model sailing-boats. Ray and I read books from the public library about various single-handed voyages round the world. Two of our heroes in this sphere were Joshua Slocum and the Breton, Alain Gerbault. Later, I was to read his account, written in French, and wax almost lyrical to a senior French class when we came across an extract from 'In Quest of the Sun' (*A la Recherche du Soleil*), which had to be translated into English. I have owned a sailing sharpie, and Eric has not only *owned* a catamaran and a cabin cruiser, but designed and built them both inside the confines of his own backyard!

What set us on the track of our first craft may easily have been the account of canoeing through Europe in *Canoe Errant* by Major Raven-Hart. Canoeing, especially in Germany, was all the rage, in 'folboots' with collapsible frames which allowed them to be readily dismantled, transported in back-packs and re-assembled at 'portages'. Perhaps the use of D.F.'s flat-bottomed punt, during camping holidays at Castleton, had had an influence too.

Eric reminded me that the kayak appeared in *The Scouter* as the 'Blyth Scout Kayak', with plans for building it and adapting it for sail. On its completion we reckoned that it had cost us about £2.50. A wooden framework of ribs was covered with crash linen, made waterproof with liberal coats of a black tarry paint. Ray knew of a timber-yard down by the Victoria Bridge, on the Stockton side of the river; but it was Mam's advice we needed about the purchase of the linen.

All the materials were to hand by teatime one Saturday afternoon in the summer of 1938. We did not waste much time over the meal, eager to make a start on the construction. Three pairs of hands made short work of setting up the stem- and stern-posts at each end of the keel. Paper patterns simplified the shaping of the cross-sections which, with ribs attached, gave shape to the kayak. When the sections were assembled at the appropriate intervals along the keel-plate, we were ready to fix the gunwales (strips of wood fifteen feet long, three inches wide and three eighths of an inch thick.)

At this point we hit a snag. Perhaps we had ordered the wrong thickness of wood and were trying to bend lengths that were a quarter of an inch thicker than the plans demanded. We just could not get the strips to bend easily to the contour of the boat. It was too risky to use brute force. Then a bright idea struck us. What if we could steam the all-important stern end of the wood, where the bend was most pronounced?

It now became obvious that the designers of the houses in New Road had had amateur boat-builders in mind from the start! The kitchen (today's living-room) had a window that opened out onto the back garden where we were working. A fifteen-foot length of timber could protrude from the garden into the kitchen and come abreast of the hearth. All we then needed was a long wooden sheath to house the end to be steamed, and a steadily replenished kettle puffing steam up into the well-lagged sheath so that the steam could have its maximum effect and soften the fibres of the recalcitrant wood. I do not know of another mam in New Road

who would have allowed such goings-on. Mam did not keep an untidy house, but a comfortable home where folk felt at ease. That was our Mam's way.

The waiting fairly tried our patience; but we held out. Finally we removed the wood, which bent as smoothly into the desired contour as we could have wished. We only had time to screw it into place, as it was already growing dark. The second piece would have to wait for treatment later.

The fitting of the second gunwale was child's play, as was the fixing into place of the ribs, over which the linen was to be stretched. We could not help but admire our handiwork. Then, for some inexplicable reason, we felt that this framework had to be protected from the elements. Yet for all its working life it was to be immersed in water! So where on earth could we store it till the tarred skin was in place? The 'Pagoda' was not big enough, neither was Dad's greenhouse. In any case, he was the least likely of persons to acquiesce to any request like that.

There was only one answer − up the stairway. What far-sighted men those architects were! We carried the kayak round to the front-door, where the stairs led straight up from the open door-way. The kayak was as broad in the beam as the stairs themselves. There was only one way for it. We turned it on its side, leaning it against the port-hand wall of the stairway.

Until we came to covering our craft in linen, everybody had to go upstairs to bed sideways. The more portly members of the family had quite a job to squeeze past. To make matters worse, if we faced the kayak the hand-rail which was fixed to the starboard wall of the stairway poked us in the back. Normal progress upstairs was impossible, as we had not enough clearance from the frame to be able to take one leg past the other to walk up normally. We had to assume a crab-wise gait. Somehow I have a fancy that, during this period, Dad was working away from home down in Bedfordshire.

Getting the kayak into shelter was one thing; getting it out again, for the final process of stretching on the linen, was quite another. Somehow the cumbersome nature of the frame prevented us from taking it out backwards through the front doorway.

Wonderful chaps, those architects! They had designed an opening window on the top landing directly in line with the stairway. And that is the way she went — up, out, and gently down to waiting hands below in the back garden.

Six-yard lengths of fifty-four inch wide linen are not the easiest of materials to fasten into place on a contoured surface like a boat's frame. But we managed to end up with the skin beautifully taut and unpuckered, ready for the waterproof paint. That presented no problems, except that the drying taxed our patience.

The finished surface looked marvellous, but vulnerable. I could almost feel the rough stones of a shallow stream or the protective masonry of the river-bank scraping that delicate surface. We decided to add a false keel, a rubbing-strip, as a protection. It was simply a matter of screwing a length of wood onto the keel-plate. We spaced out the screws and each took a hand at driving them home. In my efforts to screw the first one in firmly, the screwdriver slipped. Oh, no! Our kayak was holed before she had even entered the water. However, the patch we fitted never leaked.

The launch took place in front of the house, down at the beck. We carried the kayak across the field and gently lowered her into her element. I cannot remember who had the honour of the first paddle; but I do recall that whoever it was commented on the tendency the kayak had to ease to starboard as she drifted after a couple of strokes.

Where had we gone wrong? After much thought and head-

scratching, it dawned on us. We had had only enough time on the Saturday night to fit one gunwale. No work had been done on the Sunday, so naturally, over thirty-six hours at least, the wood had tried to straighten itself and, in so doing, had given the keel a twist. Mind, unknowingly we had solved a problem encountered by canoeists who use a single-bladed paddle solely on the starboard side. Their push naturally sends the canoe to port, so that they have to use a slight twist of the blade to keep a straight course. This manœuvre has a minimal braking effect. Our kayak went straight of its own accord at full momentum!

Initially we had plenty of scope for our paddling on the main beck and along our branch stream. Two of us could be accommodated in the cockpit. Mick, our springer spaniel, enjoyed excursions with us. Of course, he was a water-dog.

But puddling about in the beck, once we had acquired the knack of using the double-bladed paddle, soon began to pall. Though the instructions hinted that the craft had a degree of seaworthiness, we were too well acquainted with the breakers which could come crashing up onto the sands along our coast to want to go to sea.

The river was the magnet that drew us, but not as water to paddle on, particularly in the reaches that were close at hand. Who wanted to risk capsizing into the stinking oily filth which flowed between the river-banks? From the back of South Site, ICI could paint the beck in rainbow colours with the effluent it discharged from the chemical works. Worst of all, as we looked at our fragile cloth-skinned craft, were the sharp chunks of slimy millstone grit, forming the river embankment which could easily rip that skin into shreds. Sitting only a foot or so above the water, we would see little round about us, hemmed in as the Tees was by all those wharfs and miles of levees.

Up to Victoria Bridge, the Tees was a highly industrial river, an artery of international commerce. We had watched the big bulk iron-ore carriers unloading on the far side of the river, near Portrack. It was even more exciting to follow the fussy movements of the little tugs as they nudged their towering charges into a berth. Tramp steamers, coasters, boats of lesser draught, would head up to Stockton, tying up at the quaysides within a couple of hundred yards of the High Street. There were lightermen in small craft and once, a real beauty, a German 'tall ship', the training-vessel 'Passat', moored at Billingham Reach Wharf. In her passage up-river a chunk had had to be lopped off her mainmast to let her sail under the Transporter. It was long years after, when the word cropped up in a German text, that I found how appropriate the ship's name was. 'Passat' is German for 'Trade-wind'.

If only there was some tributary stream, some quiet backwater where we could laze beneath arched branches, gaze upon the rural scene and explore. I suppose we were looking for a more local version of the Cleveland Esk, where we punted in D.F.'s craft. A camp-site too, as on the banks of the Esk, would be an attractive prospect.

We knew Norburn Beck and its lower course. It flowed into the Tees close to the estuary, through a swamp of brackish water and brine-wells, between banks of sheer mud. On the south side of the Tees, more or less opposite to us, was the Old River, an arm that had either been cut off naturally or left to wither when a new, more direct channel, had been dug to Stockton. Anyhow, it lay in 'The Wilderness', as that area was known to local folk, bounding the Stockton Racecourse and the newfangled dirt-track. The name 'Wilderness' was, in itself, far from inspiring.

On that same southern side, only further upstream near the head of the tidal reach, flowed the answer, the River Leven. It was cousin to the Esk, as the watershed near Kildale separates the two streams. The Esk flows east to Whitby. The Leven meanders westward to Crathorne and, almost as tortuously, north to the main river just below Yarm. We had scraped the rubber-sheathed bottom of the punt on Esk pebbles, so we were not going to subject our kayak to such maltreatment on the upper Leven.

If we had had thoughts about the Tees above Yarm, our enthusiasm had been cooled by the spectacle that the river presented. From Yarm Bridge we had viewed its wide sweep and black depths. As we crossed Yarm viaduct in the train, we had glanced at pebbly shoals and strong eddies, and noted that the banks were pretty steep too. So we took our bikes and made a recce along by Leven Bank.

There we fell in with Joe Goldsborough (in the land-lubberly sense of that expression). Joe, a town lad from Stockton, was working on Ingleby Hill Farm, just above the Leven and close to its confluence with the Tees. He fixed it with the farmer for us to camp in a field by the tributary.

The plans for the trip were simple. The three of us would each take a turn at paddling his own stretch of the voyage. I was to do

the first section, taking the kayak down the beck into the river.
Ray would take over from me and Eric would do the last stage.
Once I had finished paddling I was to walk back home, load up my
bike with the camping gear, head off to the camp-site and set up
the tent.

We knew the area like the backs of our hands. Oh, aye! But
that was as cyclists. We had never been down below the level of
the land on a river like the Tees, with next to no reference points
to guide or inspire us. What did it matter, anyhow? The Leven
was the first turn-off on the left, just short of Yarm, and if we did
not see the town we were bound to see the viaduct, high above.
We had no need of a map. There was no question of charts. The
waterway just lay ahead, so what problems could there be?

It was not the stink, the slime, the stony banks or the width of
the river that might have put us off the idea. The factor we had
not taken into account was ... the TIDE! We knew the river was
tidal. Our awareness of this phenomenon was limited to the sight
of the river water being almost atop the bank at high tide and, at
low water, the same filthy flow ebbing between sloping, deep
expanses of embankment, falling away below us. What the current was doing was just a mystery, but not for long.

It must have been close after high water when I set out, otherwise the beck would not have been navigable down to the river.
So my bit was easy. Ray had come down on his bike, and had had
the forethought to bring a length of rope. Eric was to try towing
Ray in the kayak, taking some of the strain that the current might
be exerting on the craft. This operation became progressively
more difficult as the water sank away on the ebb-tide and the
kayak went further down the embankment with it. By this time
the current was ebbing quite strongly. Finally, a fence sloping
down the embankment put an end to his efforts.

Meanwhile I was back at No. 11 New Road, where I tucked
into a good Saturday dinner of Yorkshire pud and sirloin, with
potatoes, cabbage and gravy. A good filling sweet followed. The
meal was enjoyed in the company of Aunts Kek (Ethel) and Lil,
two of Dad's sisters, who had come up from Leeds to visit us. As I
set out for the camp-site, replete with all that good fare, my

parting words to my aunts were, 'Don't forget to give us a wave, when you go over Yarm Viaduct!'

I had ten miles to do on the bike through Stockton and Yarm, no great hassle in those days, even with Stockton High Street crammed with shoppers in the market. A canny hour would see me to my destination.

That is how it worked out. I must have had the tent up in nice time to settle down to making tea. Once that was over, I took a stroll down the field to the edge of the Leven. What disenchantment! Gone were all the images of an idyllic rural scene. Tree roots, blackened with river mud, seemed to writhe like water-snakes across the empty channel. The Leven was not much more than a trickle. Yet that shock-wave did not carry me on to the Tees, just a few hundred yards away, and make me wonder what the prospect was like in the main river itself.

Time passed. No sign of Eric. A mist began to creep up the bank. The summer evening air was turning chill by the water. Nine o'clock. Where could he be? I was about three-quarters of a mile from the Tees. The banks were steep and wooded at one point. I simply did not know what to do. If I went back home to tell Mam and Dad, they would be in bed by the time I arrived. Then they would be calling out the police. I had visions of them dragging the river. There was nothing else for it but to go back to the tent and wait. In the end I curled up in my sleeping-bag and slept fitfully.

It must have been about six o'clock on the Sunday morning when I poked my head out of the tent. Everything was shrouded in river-mist. I sensed an eeriness in the air. Suddenly, out of the damp greyness a figure emerged, but not from the right direction. I was expecting Eric to come up the slope from the Leven. This ghostly apparition was walking along the bank-top. Was it a ghost in that early light? I heard a voice say, 'Have you got any grub?' It was Eric! I dived back into the tent and handed him an orange and a banana. He did not say another word. He just took the fruit and ate peel, skin and all. He was ravenous.

Then the story came tumbling out. It had taken a lot longer on Ray's section than we had calculated. The annual Tees Swim

was taking place over a five-mile course from the Victoria Bridge, Thornaby, to the Transporter. Eric paced back and forth on the bridge, looking out for Ray and concerned for his safety, in case he had been swamped by the contestants. The tide had caused the delay and was soon to show its power. Close to the change-over point Ray raised his arm to wave to Eric; in a trice, he was swept across to the other side of the river! After a struggle he reached the change-over point and handed the paddles to Eric, who now realized the nature of the task ahead, yet not wholly, as, of the three of us, he had the least idea of his whereabouts. He did learn one useful lesson from observation and paddling: in the curve of an inside bend, the current tended to swirl with him, but he still had to fight his way out of the main flow.

For my stint, I must have paddled about four miles at the very most, with the tide helping me. Ray, who was the strongest of the three of us, had struggled another four against the tide. Eric, the youngest, had found himself at the beginning of an eight-mile haul, which must have seemed like eighty. One glance at the map would have shown the inequality of the task. We had reckoned in land miles, but the Tees is no respecter of foot-sloggers or wheelers! It and Billingham Beck meander their murky way for the best part of nearly twice the land mileage!

Inside the tent, Eric and I did not waste any more time on such ponderings. We left for New Road. He sat bunched in front of me on the cross-bar of my bike as I pedalled him back home. No explanations to Mam. We helped him into a hot bath, where he fell sound asleep.

Later on that Sunday morning, when he came to, we heard the full tale. Though the kayak only drew three or four inches of water, Eric found that he was gradually running out of that element as the tide ebbed. At last he could make no more headway. He was down in the bed of the river, midway between slimy banks. He had struggled ashore, pulling the kayak over the slime. He had tied it to a tree with the mooring-rope.

His last real meal had been breakfast on Saturday morning. We had all expected to be sharing a meal in mid-afternoon, round the camp-fire. Ashore in the late evening, he had found in his pocket a match and a scrap of paper where he had written the numbers of the fag-cards he wanted for a set of 'The Laughing Cavalier'. (W.D. & H.O. Wills, the cigarette firm, was offering classical prints in exchange for the mosaic of picture cards found in cigarette packets. Once the set was complete it was sent off to the firm. Back came the print. Titles on offer were *The Boyhood of Raleigh*, *Mother and Son*, *When did you last see your Father?* and *The Laughing Cavalier*.)

Eric had taken the match, lit the paper and managed to get a fire going to keep himself warm for a while. He had nothing in his pockets to eat; but he was on the edge of a cornfield, so he had plucked a few heads of green corn and munched at them to try and stay the pangs of hunger.

We spent a month by the Leven, being joined by pals in ones and twos, who either brought their own tents and stayed a while with us, or came for the day on their bikes to share in the fun of the kayak if the tide was favourable. That was a limiting factor which we had not taken into our calculations when setting about this camping trip. However, all in all, a good time was enjoyed by each and every one.

We felt much more competent and river-wise when it came to the time to strike camp and return home. I had no part in that voyage. I was simply the sumpter-beast, carrying home on my bike all the camping gear. Eric was to do the whole run himself, knowing that the ebb-tide would be a boon this time.

He made an early start whilst I tidied up the site, packed the gear and leisurely cycled home. Our calculations were about right. So it was with some surprise that we did not find Eric joining us at the dinner table on the final Saturday afternoon. We waited a while, then began to grow edgy. The thought ran through my head, 'Oh, no! Eric doesn't know the river well enough. Perhaps he has missed the turn-off into Billingham Beck (again, first left) just below the New Tees Bridge. He'll be carried out to sea!'

'Look,' Dad said. 'I think we'd better have a walk along the beck and find out what has happened.' So, off we went, Dad and I. There was no path along the back of South Site. We struggled through breast-high grass and nettles. That works' property was just a wilderness.

We climbed up to the Portrack road at the bridge over the beck, about a mile from the New Tees Bridge and the river. A voice hailed us on the other side of the road, a body-less voice, rising from the depths. Looking down from the bridge, we spotted Eric. He had made good time down river with the tide; but that same tide was emptying the beck. He had run out of water again!

However, that was not his only problem. Some local urchins were hanging about. He feared for the safety of the kayak. It did not do in those days in that area to own anything out of the ordinary. The likelihood was that, if the gang could not have had some fun with the kayak, in their annoyance they would have wreaked their vengeance on it. Dad stayed on guard with him, whilst I went back home to fetch a pair of wheels on an axle which we used as a trailer. In this less dignified way we wheeled the kayak home.

The summer was virtually over. Further adventures would need to wait for another season, or so we thought. Browsing through the sailing section in the library, we came across an article on adapting a canoe for sailing. Further research led us back to the Scouts, who had a separate pamphlet for the conversion of the kayak to sail.

We studied the details illustrating modifications which would involve opening up the deck. We came to the conclusion that this might jeopardize the watertightness of the little craft. We should have to see if we could not do things our own way, especially since we had plenty of scraps of timber in the 'Pagoda', now relegated to a workshop.

Just as we had done for the 'steaming process', we made a smaller sheath, which we mounted on the deck just in front of the cockpit. This would house the mast. The sail was made from a largish piece of plain material, which was laid out on the kitchen floor to allow us space to cut out the square shape. I fancy we had to sew up the edges by hand. One warm September evening, we were ready for trials.

I paddled up our beck, under the Stockton road and into the main beck above the 'Waterfall'. Our beck was much too narrow for sailing, and flowed well below the level of the coke dump for our sail to catch any wind. The main beck flowed in open country, where any wind that blew would fill the sail.

On this occasion there was hardly any breeze at all. I hoisted the sail. Next to nothing! I was almost on the point of blowing into the sail myself. What airiness there *was*, however, was sufficient to get the kayak inching along *against* the current. A disbelieving youngster, walking along the bank beside me, shouted disparagingly, 'What do you think you're doing, Mister?' I looked disdainfully at the soulless philistine. We were making way upstream, however slowly. We were sailing!

A few days later, conditions were just the reverse. It may have been the tail-end of an equinoctial gale that blew. Ray had come up from Stockton to enjoy a trial run. This time we set sail from the Chapel Lane bridge, at the big pool where the lads swam on hot summer days. The wind was northerly, astern. After the big pool, the beck took a slight bend to port. We were going to have to gybe. We had read about gybing, but had never actually experienced the manœuvre.

We headed the kayak downstream and downwind, then hoisted the sail. Whoosh! The wind just about tore the sheet out of my grasp. (For the uninitiated, the 'sheet' is the length of rope tied to the boom, which controls the movement of the sail.) From the bows came a lovely rippling sound as we scudded along before the wind, literally at a rate of knots. To negotiate the bend, the sail had to be hauled over on to the other 'tack' (side).

We may have had only about fifteen square feet of sail, but in that bellying cloth was quite a press of wind. We ducked as the sail whipped over our heads − then, swoosh! The wind had caught it on the other tack. For one awful moment we thought the kayak was going to capsize. Water rushed along the deck, now tilted below the surface. Then the pressure eased, and away we scudded on down the beck. To stop, we had to drop the sail and back-paddle. 'Let's have another go at that!' chortled Ray. 'By, she wasn't half going some!'

Back we paddled to the starting-point, a couple of hundred yards or so, and off we went again. It really was thrilling. A boat under sail is a living thing. You can feel it. Like many living things, it can also be unpredictable. The second time we were just as elated as at the first. We had to give it a third go.

In the excitement of re-living the incident, I have forgotten to mention how we were accommodated aboard the kayak. Normally, the cockpit could take two passengers. This time the complement included our dog, Mick. I was in the stern, Mick in front of me, and Ray, sitting between my feet, had his own feet up on the deck, wrapped around the mast-sheath.

'Right, let her go!' shouted Ray. Maybe the breeze had stiffened slightly. At the bend we gybed all right; but that extra wee bit of pressure was just enough to tip the balance. Over we went. Ray, who was already half out of the boat in any case, took a header into the beck. Mick, in his element, was paddling his way to the bank. I went half over and managed to get my feet down on the bottom. The water was barely waist-deep, so my left side was quite dry. There I stood, laughing my head off − and Ray, who came up spitting out beck-water and the odd tiddler, joined in the laughter, too. Shades of the Esk episode!

'Look,' he said, 'there's no use both of us staying wet. You get home and get changed. I'll paddle the kayak back down the beck.' By the time I had trotted home and changed, Ray was below the house with the kayak. In her waterlogged state, we had quite a job to haul her out of the beck and turn her upside-down to empty her.

Ray was just oozing water. There was no sense his coming into the back kitchen to drip water all over the place whilst he changed. He would be just as well stripping off in the back garden, leaving the dampness outside. He was almost done when he heard the tap-tap of shoes coming up the passage between the houses at Nos. 12 and 13. It was obviously the tread of a lady. Standing now in only his left sock, Ray was not for waiting to see who was coming. He took an almighty leap from the garden, cleared the narrow back yard and landed in the back kitchen. Just in time! It was Marjorie Allison, a rather fetching teenager, coming home!

That was my last recollection of fun with the kayak. In September 1939 the sirens went. We were at war. Fearing for the safety of the kayak, which now lay upside-down on the back lawn, we decided to evacuate her. A target like ICI on our doorstep might draw bombs whistling down or, even worse, shrapnel from

our own guns might damage the fragile craft. (An ack-ack squad
was sited in the 'Rec'.) I think Joe Goldsborough found a home
for her on the farm by the Leven. I have no idea of her fate.

But we had been bitten by the bug. After the War, we went a-
sailing again in something more substantial. I battled against the
tides of the Tay in a sharpie. On a visit to Dundee, Ray came
aboard for an outing on the river at Inchyra, where he held our
eldest daughter at the prow so that she could let the ripples tickle
her toes. Eric had sport in the estuary of the Tees aboard his own
craft. In these last years he has sailed our coastal seas off Yorkshire and ventured across the Channel.

Epilogue

IN ALBERTA, CANADA, our grandchildren are passing through childhood. This book has been written for them. It has also been written for great-nephews, great-nieces, cousins 'unto the third and fourth generation', all members of our 'extended' family, and for the 'extended' families of pals whose childhood enters these pages.

This is very much a personal account which mirrors in flashes, from time to time, experiences of childhood of others of our generation. In his letter to me dated 27th February 1988, 'Pluff' writes: 'There is no-one anywhere, who's had happier schooldays than we had, that's for sure, and we all had strong family ties, as did the majority of working families in Billingham.'

Nostalgia may tint our view of things. Is it not human to recall, more readily, joyful events and happy experiences? I have hinted that it was not *all* joy and happiness; but the strong family ties gave a certain stability to life, to tide us over the bad times.

I look back on the childhood of our own children, recorded in snapshot, film, and tape-recordings of their parties, birthdays, Hallowe'ens and Christmases; their play and ploys ·at home and on holiday with grandparents, parents, aunts, cousins and friends. Through it all, I believe they had the security of knowing they were loved, and were given a sense of values. My wife and I were only passing on to them what we had been privileged to receive.

Note to readers

The publishers of this book hope that you have enjoyed reading it. They are always interested in considering good manuscripts, on any subject, with a view to possible publication. An approach should be made in the first instance by means of a letter addressed to: The Editor, Bridge Publications (Ref. 243), 2 Bridge Street, Penistone, Sheffield S30 6AJ.

Also from Bridge Publications:

Brownhill, R.N., **THE PENISTONE SCENE: captured in photographs over the years**. [ISBN 0 947934 15 4 (pbk) £5.95]

Cooper, Stephen, **A HOUSE DIVIDED: the life and death of John Billam of Thorpe Hesley**. [ISBN 0 947934 11 1 (pbk) £4.50; 0 947934 12 X (hbk) £8.95]

Crossland, Phyllis, **ECHOING HILLS**. This is a down-to-earth story of human existence and experience in all its richness and harsh reality. [ISBN 0 947934 20 0 (hbk) £12.95]

Daniels, L.T., **FRONTIER CHALLENGE: being the story of the Revd W.J. Ringer and the Afghan Border Crusade 1904 to 1985**. [ISBN 0 947934 13 8 (pbk) £4.95; 0 947934 14 6 (hbk) £9.95]

Dunlop, Ian G., **THINKING IT OUT: Christianity in thin slices**. [ISBN 0 947934 06 5 (pbk) £3.50; 0 947934 07 3 (hbk) £6.50]

Lawrence-Smith, Kathleen, **GOD HATH MADE ME TO LAUGH: a Worcester childhood**. [ISBN 0 947934 00 6 (pbk) £3.95]

Lawrence-Smith, Kathleen, **LAUGH WITH ME: from the Severn to the Golden Horn**. *Foreword by George Thomas, former Speaker of the House of Commons*. Sequel to *God Hath Made Me to Laugh*. [ISBN 0 947934 08 1 (pbk) £4.95]

Ottley, Sheila Margaret, **WHILE MARTHA TOLD THE HOURS: a South Yorkshire tapestry**. *Foreword by W.R. Mitchell, former Editor of* **The Dalesman**. Hoyland in the 'twenties and 'thirties. [ISBN 0 947934 17 0 (pbk) £10.95; 0 947934 18 9 (hbk) £15.95]

Shaberman, R.B., **EGYPTIAN NIGHTS: tales of fantasy**. A beautifully polished assortment of stories, with themes which explore the mysteries and ambiguities of space, time and existence. [ISBN 0 947934 21 9 (pbk) £8.95 est.; 0 947934 22 7 (hbk) £10.95 est.] Publication due Autumn 1989.

Wallace, E.M., **THE CHRISTMAS TREE: a new look at the Nativity story**. [ISBN 0 947934 05 7 (pbk) £1.50; 0 947934 05 7 (illustrated pbk) £2.00]

Wilkinson, John F., **FARMSTEAD OF THE BRITONS: the story of a West Riding village**. The book traces the history of the village of West Bretton, Yorkshire. [ISBN 0 947934 25 1 (pbk) £4.95 est.; 0 947934 26 X (hbk) £9.95 est.] Publication due Autumn 1989

Wootton, Alan W., **BETWEEN THE LINES**. This is a tale of survival against the odds in foreign lands and at home. An imaginative and original blend of vaguely-apparent reality in which what could pass for the truth often seems stranger than fiction. [ISBN 0 947934 27 8 (pbk) £9.95 est.; 0 947934 28 6 (hbk) £12.95 est.] Publication due Autumn 1989

The above books are available from stock or to order from all good booksellers or, in case of difficulty, by post from the publishers. In the case of orders by post, please add postage and packing fee of 10% of total cost. Three books or more, post free.